DATE DUE

Concepts and Fuzzy Logic

Concepts and Fuzzy Logic

edited by Radim Belohlavek and George J. Klir

The MIT Press
Cambridge, Massachusetts
London, England

For information about special quantity discounts, please email special_sales@mitpress .mit.edu

This book was set in Stone Sans and Stone Serif by Graphic Composition, Inc., Bogart, Georgia.

Printed and bound in the United States of America.

Library of Congress Cataloging-in-Publication Data

Concepts and fuzzy logic / edited by Radim Belohlavek and George J. Klir.
    p.   cm.
Includes bibliographical references and index.
ISBN 978-0-262-01647-6 (hardcover : alk. paper)
1. Fuzzy logic. 2. Concepts. I. Bělohlávek, Radim, 1971–. II. Klir, George J., 1932–.
QA9.64.C66   2011
511.3'13—dc22
2011010038

10 9 8 7 6 5 4 3 2 1

Contents

Preface

Our decision to organize this book was not based, as it might seem, on a suddenly emerging feeling that such a book was needed. Instead, it was a rather natural consequence of a series of events that began some ten years ago, at the very beginning of the twenty-first century. The following is a chronology of these events.

In early 2000, it was pointed out to us (at a discussion following a seminar on the fuzzification of formal concept analysis at Binghamton University) that fuzzy logic had apparently been found useless within the field of the psychology of concepts and had been totally abandoned. This casual information stimulated our curiosity. We knew that fuzzy logic was well developed at that time and its usefulness established in many areas of human affairs. We were wondering what the arguments were for its rejection in the psychology of concepts.

After searching through the relevant literature in the psychology of concepts, we found that the arguments had been advanced in a single paper published in 1981. By examining these arguments in detail, we found, to our surprise, that all were fallacious. We also discovered that, by and large, they had been accepted uncritically as valid within the literature on concepts. The very nature of science required that these discovered errors be corrected. We decided, together with two of our colleagues at Binghamton University (Harold Lewis and Eileen Way), to write two articles on these disturbing discoveries.

In our first article, which was published in 2002, we focused solely on analyzing in detail the various erroneous claims. In the second paper, our aim was to describe how these claims adversely influenced attitudes toward fuzzy logic in the psychology of concepts. Writing this paper took much longer since it required us to delve deeper into the literature on concepts. The article was eventually published in 2009.

Two reviews we received for our second article were very thorough and positive. Both reviewers considered it very important that we exposed the errors and showed how they had led to the virtual renouncement of fuzzy logic in the psychology of concepts. However, they argued that this alone would not likely change the unfavorable situation. Therefore, they both recommended to us, in slightly different ways, to go one step further and demonstrate that fuzzy logic is actually a useful mathematical tool for dealing with some problems in the psychology of concepts. This recommendation created an interesting dilemma for us. On one hand, we wholeheartedly agreed with it. On the other hand, we realized that it was beyond our capabilities. We felt that cooperation between psychologists of concepts and mathematicians working in the area of fuzzy logic was requisite for accomplishing the recommended additional step. After considering how to stimulate such cooperation, the idea of organizing this book emerged as the winner.

We thus consider the primary purpose of this book to stimulate cooperation between psychologists of concepts and mathematicians working in the area of fuzzy logic. We are fortunate that the MIT Press, one of the leading publishers in the psychology of concepts, expressed a strong interest in publishing the book. We are also fortunate that our contributors are outstanding psychologists who are genuinely interested in supporting the purpose of this book.

The material for this book was carefully selected with the intent to stimulate cooperation between the two communities of researchers. Invited contributors were asked to write chapters on specific topics pertaining to the purpose of the book. Once the writing of all chapters had been completed, efforts were made to eliminate duplications between chapters and, more importantly, to achieve consistency and completeness of the covered material with respect to the purpose of the book. The work on the book has been, at least to some degree, a team effort of the editors and invited contributors alike.

The primary audience for this book consists of researchers in the two academic communities we directly address—psychologists of concepts and mathematicians pursuing research on fuzzy logic. The secondary audience is likely to be quite broad and may include researchers in linguistics, cognitive science, artificial intelligence, and history and philosophy of science. This book may also be useful as supplementary reading in graduate courses in any of these areas.

Radim Belohlavek and George J. Klir

Acknowledgments

We would gratefully like to acknowledge a few people who contributed to this book in certain specific ways: Dr. Eduard Bartl (Computer Science Department of Palacký University, Czech Republic), who prepared some of the book's figures; Professor Gregory Murphy (Psychology Department of New York University, United States), who provided us with useful advice at some critical stages of this project; and Ellen Tilden (Thomas J. Watson School of Engineering and Applied Science, Binghamton University, United States), who scrutinized the language of several parts of the manuscript and made some of the book's figures.

In addition, Radim Belohlavek would like to acknowledge support from two grants for research on formal concept analysis and fuzzy logic, including partially his work on this book: Grant No. 103/10/1056 of the Czech Science Foundation and Grant No. MSM 6198959214 of the Czech Government.

1 Introduction

Radim Belohlavek and George J. Klir

1.1 Concepts and Fuzzy Logic

To avoid any confusion about the terms *concepts* and *fuzzy logic* in the title of this book, let us explain at the very outset what we mean by these terms and how we use them throughout the whole book. We use the term *concepts* as it is commonly used in the literature on the psychology of concepts. Other aspects of concepts, such as philosophical or logical aspects, are not of primary interest in this book. The principal issues involved in the psychology of concepts are presented in chapter 2. We use the term *fuzzy logic* to refer to all aspects of representing and manipulating knowledge that employ intermediary truth-values. This general, commonsense meaning of the term *fuzzy logic* encompasses, in particular, fuzzy sets, fuzzy relations, and formal deductive systems that admit intermediary truth-values, as well as the various methods based on them. An overview of basic ideas of fuzzy logic is presented in the form of a tutorial in chapter 3.

1.2 From Classical Logic to Fuzzy Logic

As is well known, classical logic is based on the assumptions that there are exactly two truth-values, *false* and *true*, and that the truth-value of any logical formula is uniquely defined by the truth-values of its components. These assumptions are usually called *bivalence* and *truth functionality*, respectively. The various many-valued logics, which have been of interest and under investigation since the beginning of the twentieth century (Rescher 1969; Gottwald 2000), abandon bivalence while adhering to truth functionality. This means that additional truth-values are recognized in each many-valued logic. Even though it is not obvious how to interpret these additional truth-values, they are usually viewed as intermediary truth-values between *false* and *true* and interpreted as degrees of truth. Many-valued logics differ from one another in the sets of truth-values they employ and in the definitions they use for basic logical operations, that is, negation, conjunction, disjunction, implication, and equivalence.

Classical logic is closely connected with classical set theory. Each predicate is uniquely associated with a classical set. In other words, for any given object, a proposition formed by the predicate is true for this object if and only if the object is a member of the associated set. The associated set plays the role of the extension of the predicate. For example, the predicate *prime(x)* is true for a particular number *n* if and only if *n* is a member of the set of all prime numbers, that is, the set associated in this case with the predicate. Therefore, the set of prime numbers represents the extension of the predicate *prime(x)*. Moreover, each logical operation on predicates has a unique counterpart—an operation on the associated classical sets. For example, the counterparts of negation, conjunction, and disjunction on predicates are the operations of complement, intersection, and union on the associated sets, respectively.

When the assumption of bivalence was abandoned in the various proposed many-valued logics, the connection between predicates and sets was lost. Classical sets were simply not able to play the role of extensions of many-valued predicates, that is, predicates that apply to objects to intermediary degrees. The connection was eventually renewed when Lotfi Zadeh introduced the concept of a fuzzy set in his seminal paper (Zadeh 1965).

The connection of fuzzy sets with many-valued logics was recognized by Zadeh in his seminal paper only in a one-sentence remark in a footnote. However, it is worth noting that, independently of Zadeh, set theory for many-valued logics was also investigated in the 1960s by Klaua (1966), as documented by Gottwald (2000).

Zadeh returned to the connection between fuzzy sets and many-valued logics ten years later after his seminal paper, and began to use the term *fuzzy logic* (introduced first by Goguen [1968–69]) in the following sense (Zadeh 1975, 409): "A fuzzy logic, FL, may be viewed, in part, as a fuzzy extension of a multi-valued logic which constitutes a *base* logic for FL." However, he also attempted to expand the notion of fuzzy logics in this sense (usually referred to as fuzzy logics in the narrow sense) with the aim of developing approximate reasoning that would ultimately be able to emulate commonsense human reasoning in natural language. To this end, he introduced appropriate fuzzy sets for representing certain types of linguistic terms employed in human reasoning. For example, fuzzy truth-values are fuzzy sets defined on the set of recognized truth-values (usually the interval [0,1]) that represent linguistic terms such as *true, false, very true, more or less true, very false,* and the like; fuzzy probabilities are fuzzy sets defined on [0,1] that represent linguistic terms such as *likely, unlikely, very likely, highly unlikely,* and so on; and fuzzy quantifiers are fuzzy sets defined on appropriate sets of numbers that represent linguistic terms such as *many, most, almost all, very few,* and so forth. This expanded notion of any of the fuzzy logics in the narrow sense is usually called a fuzzy logic in the broad sense.

It is interesting that Zadeh recognized the need for fuzzy logic a few years before he published his seminal paper on fuzzy sets. In a paper discussing developments in the area of system theory (Zadeh 1962, 858), he writes:

[T]here is a wide gap between what might be regarded as "animate" system theorists and "inanimate" system theorists at the present time, and it is not at all certain that this gap will be narrowed, much less closed, in the near future. There are some who feel this gap reflects the fundamental inadequacy of the conventional mathematics—the mathematics of precisely-defined points, functions, sets, probability measures, etc.—for coping with the analysis of biological systems, and that to deal effectively with such systems, which are generally orders of magnitude more complex than man-made systems, we need a radically different kind of mathematics, the mathematics of fuzzy or cloudy quantities.

Then, he begins his seminal paper as follows:

More often than not, the classes of objects encountered in the real physical world do not have precisely defined criteria of membership. For example, the class of animals clearly includes dogs, horses, birds, etc. as its members, and clearly excludes objects as rocks, fluids, plants, etc. However, such objects as starfish, bacteria, etc. have an ambiguous status with respect to the class of animals. The same kind of ambiguity arises in the case of a number such as 10 in relation to the "class" of all real numbers which are much greater than 1.

Clearly, the "class of all real numbers that are much greater than 1," or "the class of beautiful women," or "the class of tall men" do not constitute classes or sets in the usual mathematical sense of these terms. Yet, the fact remains that such imprecisely defined "classes" play an important role in human thinking. . . . The purpose of this note is to explore in a preliminary way some of the basic properties and implications of a concept which may be of use in dealing with "classes" of the type cited above. The concept in question is that of a *fuzzy set*, that is a "class" with a continuum of grades of membership. (Zadeh 1965, 338)

To represent and deal with classes of objects that are not precisely defined was thus the principal motivation for introducing fuzzy sets. Since such classes are pervasive in all human activities involving natural language, fuzzy sets opened new and potentially useful ways of looking at human cognition, reasoning, communication, decision making, and the like. Perhaps the most important of these was a new way of looking at knowledge expressed by statements in natural language. Such knowledge assumed a new significance owing to the possibility of representing it and dealing with it in a mathematically rigorous way. Its utility in science, engineering, and other areas of human affairs has been increasingly recognized, especially since the early 1990s, as is briefly surveyed in section 3.8 of chapter 3. In the next section, we examine how this utility has been viewed in the psychology of concepts.

1.3   Fuzzy Logic in the Psychology of Concepts

Shortly after Zadeh introduced fuzzy sets, Joseph Goguen, a mathematician and computer scientist, published an important paper entitled "The Logic of Inexact Concepts," where he writes:

The "hard" sciences, such as physics and chemistry, construct exact mathematical models of empirical phenomena, and then use these models to make predictions. Certain aspects of reality always escape such models, and we look hopefully to future refinements. But sometimes there is an elusive fuzziness, a readjustment to context, or an effect of observer upon observed. These phenomena are particularly indigenous to natural language, and are common in the "soft" sciences, such as biology and psychology. . . . "Exact concepts" are the sort envisaged in pure mathematics, while "inexact concepts" are rampant in everyday life. . . . Ordinary logic is much used in mathematics, but applications to everyday life have been criticized because our normal language habits seem so different. Various modifications of orthodox logic have been suggested as remedies. . . . Without a semantic representation for inexact concepts it is hard to see that one modification of traditional logic really provides a more satisfactory syntactic theory of inexact concepts than another. However, such a representation is now available (Zadeh 1965). (Goguen 1968–69, 325)

It is interesting that Goguen refers in this quote specifically to biology and psychology as areas of science in which fuzziness is common. However, these two areas of science have been, paradoxically and for different reasons, the slowest ones to harness the capabilities of fuzzy logic. In the following, we focus on the psychology of concepts and show how positive attitudes toward fuzzy logic in the 1970s in this area, revealed by occasional remarks in the literature, changed abruptly to strongly negative attitudes in the 1980s.

Prior to the 1970s, it had been taken for granted in the psychology of concepts that concept categories are classical sets. This generally accepted view of concepts, referred to as the *classical view* (see chapter 2), was seriously challenged in the 1970s, primarily as a result of experimental work by Eleanor Rosch (see chapter 4). Rosch designed and performed a series of psychological experiments that consistently demonstrated (among other things) that concept categories are graded and, as a consequence, that they cannot be adequately represented by classical sets. This led to a virtual deposition of the classical view in the psychology of concepts.

Recognizing Rosch (1973) for her experimental demonstration that concept categories are graded, Lakoff (1972)[1] argued that this was also the case for statements in natural language:

Logicians have, by and large, engaged in the convenient fiction that sentences of natural languages (at least declarative sentences) are either true or false or, at worst, lack a truth value, or have a third value often interpreted as "nonsense," . . . Yet students of language, especially psychologists and linguistic philosophers, have long been attuned to the fact that natural language concepts have vague boundaries and fuzzy edges and that, consequently, natural language sentences will very often be neither true, nor false, nor nonsensical, but rather *true to a certain extent and false to a certain extent, true in certain respects and false in other respects.* (Lakoff 1972, 458, italics added)

Lakoff further argued that fuzzy set theory, as suggested by Zadeh (1965), was potentially capable of dealing with degrees of membership, and hence, with categories that do not have sharp boundaries:

Fuzzy concepts have had a bad press among logicians, especially in this century when the formal analysis of axiomatic and semantic systems reached a high degree of sophistication. It has been generally assumed that such concepts were not amenable to serious formal study. I believe that the development of fuzzy set theory ... makes such serious study possible. (Ibid., 491)

The potential role of fuzzy set theory in dealing formally with vagueness in natural language was also recognized by Hersh and Caramazza (1976):

Recently, there has been considerable interest on the part of linguists in such problems as the role of vagueness in language and the quantification of meaning. Much of this interest has been the result of the development of fuzzy set theory, a *generalization of the traditional theory of sets*. (255; italics added)

Another author who recognized a potentially fruitful connection between fuzzy sets and concepts was Gregg C. Oden. He addressed this connection in two papers, both published in 1977. In his first paper (Oden 1977a), he builds on previous psychological studies, which "have shown that many subjective categories are fuzzy sets," by studying how proper rules (or operations) of conjunction and disjunction of statements that are true to some degree can be determined experimentally within each given context. His overall conclusion is that "it is not unreasonable for different rules to be used under various situations" (Oden 1977a, 572). This, of course, is well known in fuzzy set theory, where classes of conjunctions, disjunctions, and other types of operations on fuzzy propositions are well delimited and have been extensively researched (see chapter 3 of this volume).

In his second paper (Oden 1977b), he addresses the issue of the capability of human beings to make consistent judgments regarding degrees of membership (or degrees of truth). His conclusion, based on experiments he performed, is positive:

Recent research indicates that class membership may subjectively be a continuous type of relationship. The processing of information about the degree to which items belong to a particular class was investigated in an experiment in which subjects compared two statements describing class membership relationships. The results strongly supported a simple model which describes the judgment process as directly involving subjective degree-of-truthfulness values. The success of the model indicates that the subjects were able to process this kind of fuzzy information in a consistent and systematic manner. (Oden 1977b, 198)

Needless to say, experiments of this kind are considerably more attuned to the spirit of fuzzy logic than the more traditional experiments. Moreover, they also seem to be more meaningful from the psychological point of view. A subject is not required to make a choice between two extremes, neither of which he or she may consider appropriate, but is explicitly allowed to respond in a continuous manner.

The two types of experiments were compared by an experimental study performed by McCloskey and Glucksberg (1978). The study demonstrated that results of experiments that allowed subjects to judge category memberships in terms of degrees showed a significantly higher consistency, especially for intermediate-typicality items, than those in which membership degrees were not allowed.

By and large, these positive attitudes toward fuzzy logic by some psychologists and linguists drastically changed in the psychology of concepts in the early 1980s, and fuzzy logic started to be portrayed as useless for representing and dealing with concepts. It was virtually abandoned in the psychology of concepts as a viable generalization of classical logic. This situation contrasts sharply with numerous other areas, where the expressive power of fuzzy logic has been increasingly recognized and utilized, sometimes in quite profound ways (see chapter 3, sec. 3.8, of this volume).

It is certainly possible that fuzzy logic is completely useless in the psychology of concepts. However, such a conclusion would have to be supported by convincing arguments. As a matter of fact, no such convincing arguments have ever been presented in the literature on the psychology of concepts. As is shown in detail in chapter 5, all the arguments that have actually been presented are, for various reasons, fallacious.

It is clear that this undesirable situation in the psychology of concepts can be resolved in one of two possible ways. One is to find a sufficiently convincing argument that fuzzy logic is not applicable, at least in its current state of development, to the issues of concern in the psychology of concepts. The other way is to demonstrate that fuzzy logic is essential or at least better than classical logic for dealing with at least some of the issues. We believe that neither of these ways of revising the situation can be successful without the cooperation of the two communities involved—psychologists specializing in concepts and mathematicians specializing in fuzzy logic.

In this cooperation, psychologists should explain to the mathematicians those problems regarding concepts for which no mathematical treatment is currently available and challenge them to find the solutions. In a narrower sense, they should also challenge mathematicians to scrutinize any possible new arguments against the use of fuzzy logic they want to pursue. On the other hand, mathematicians should suggest to psychologists some applications of fuzzy logic in the psychology of concepts and challenge them to critically examine their psychological significance.

We are convinced that the time is ripe for such a mutually beneficial cooperation between the two communities, and the main purpose of this book is to stimulate such cooperation.

Cooperation between researchers working in different areas is always difficult, but it is usually very fruitful. The challenges and benefits involved in such cooperation are well captured by Norbert Wiener in his famous book on cybernetics (Wiener 1948). The following quote from the book is based on Wiener's own experience. Wiener, a mathematician, collaborated with a Mexican physiologist, Arthuro Rosenblueth, at the end of World War II, and this collaboration led to profound results in physiology. We took the liberty to add a few words to the quote (all bracketed and in italics) to make the quote more explicitly related to the purpose of this book:

For many years Dr. Rosenblueth and I had shared the conviction that the most fruitful areas for the growth of the sciences were those which have been neglected as a no-man's land between the various established fields. . . . It is these boundary regions of science which offer the richest opportunities to the qualified investigator. They are at the same time the most refractory to the accepted techniques of mass attack and the division of labor. If the difficulty of a physiological [*or psychological*] problem is mathematical in essence, ten physiologists [*or psychologists*] ignorant of mathematics will get precisely as far as one physiologist [*or psychologist*] ignorant of mathematics. If a physiologist [*or psychologist*], who knows no mathematics, works with a mathematician who knows no physiology [*or psychology*], the one will be unable to state his problem in terms that the other can manipulate and the second will be unable to put the answers in any form that the first can understand. . . . The mathematician need not have the skill to conduct a physiological [*or psychological*] experiment, but he must have the skill to understand one, to criticize one, and to suggest one. The physiologist [*or psychologist*] need not be able to prove a certain mathematical theorem, but he must be able to grasp its physiological [*or psychological*] significance and to tell the mathematician for what he should look. (Wiener 1948, 8–9)

1.4 Summary of the Book

To stimulate cooperation between psychologists of concepts and mathematicians devoted to fuzzy logic, the book contains two tutorials, one on concepts (chapter 2, by Edouard Machery) and one on fuzzy logic (chapter

3, by Radim Belohlavek and George J. Klir). The aim of these tutorials is to help readers who are not psychologists to understand, at least to some degree, experimental and theoretical issues that are relevant to the psychology of concepts, and also to help psychologists to understand the current capabilities of fuzzy logic.

In chapter 4, Eleanor H. Rosch describes her experiments that led to the rejection of the classical view of concepts in the 1970s (as mentioned above in section 1.3). She also describes some peculiar events associated with these experiments. Although she was not aware of fuzzy logic when she designed and performed these experiments and was solely interested at that time in understanding the structure of concept categories from the psychological point of view and not in the issue of how to formalize this structure, she reflects now in chapter 4 on the prospective role of fuzzy logic in the psychology of concepts and makes some valuable suggestions in this regard.

Chapter 5 (again by Belohlavek and Klir) is devoted to a careful analysis of arguments against the use of fuzzy logic in the psychology of concepts that were presented in the early 1980s. First, it is shown that these arguments were actually advanced in a single paper by Osherson and Smith (1981) and that this paper has tremendously influenced attitudes toward fuzzy logic in the psychology of concepts ever since. Second, it is shown in detail that all the arguments presented in this paper are fallacious and that, in spite of this, they were by and large uncritically accepted as sound by those in the field of the psychology of concepts.

The problem of constructing fuzzy sets for representing concepts is discussed in detail in chapter 6, by Jay Verkuilen, Rogier Kievit, and Annemarie Zand Scholten. The authors argue that it is important to look at the various issues involved from the point of view of measurement theory. They show how measurement theory applies to these issues, and they present basic methods for constructing fuzzy sets. They illustrate the general principles by describing two examples in specific detail.

Chapter 7, by Belohlavek, deals with a particular data analysis method in which concepts play a crucial role. This method, called *formal concept analysis*, is based on a rigorous theory of concepts that is inspired by traditional logic. The chapter provides the reader with an overview of basic notions of classical formal concept analysis, its extension to data with fuzzy attributes, and appropriate illustrative examples. Belohlavek also discusses the relationship between formal concept analysis and the psychology of concepts, as well as possible interactive research in these two areas.

Chapter 8 deals with an important issue in the psychology of concepts—the issue of conceptual combinations. It is written by one of the leading psychologists pursuing experimental research on conceptual combinations, James A. Hampton. He describes the outcomes of psychological experiments (many of them performed by himself) that pertain to this issue and discusses the possibilities, as well as difficulties, in using fuzzy logic for formalizing conceptual combinations. The difficulties described here are genuine and can be viewed as challenges to the relevance of fuzzy logic to concepts.

In chapter 9, Hampton examines a particularly important type of concept, namely concepts in natural language—or *lexical concepts*. Special attention is given to the issue of vagueness in meaning and the capability of fuzzy logic to represent and deal with vagueness in natural language.

Chapter 10, the title of which is "Epilogue," is a kind of overall reflection by the editors on the purpose of this book. After examining important distinctions between theories of concepts and mathematical theories, which have often been blurred in the psychology of concepts (as discussed in chapter 5), we outline some challenges for fuzzy logic and some challenges for the psychology of concepts that emerged from this book. Finally, we discuss the conditions for effective cooperation between psychologists working on concepts and mathematicians working on fuzzy logic in the future.

Note

1. Lakoff actually refers to a preliminary version of the cited paper, which was released by the Psychology Department of University of California at Berkeley in 1971 under Rosch's former name of Heider.

References

Goguen, J. A. 1968–69. The logic of inexact concepts. *Synthese* 19:325–373.

Gottwald, S. 2000. *A Treatise on Many-valued Logics*. Baldock, UK: Research Studies Press.

Hersh, H. M., and A. Caramazza. 1976. A fuzzy set approach to modifiers and vagueness in natural language. *Journal of Experimental Psychology: General* 103:254–276.

Klaua, D. 1966. Grundbegriffe einer mehrwertigen Mengenlehre. [Basic concepts of a many-valued set theory.] *Monatsberichte Deutsche Akademie der Wissenschaften Berlin* 8:781–802.

Lakoff, G. 1972. Hedges: A study in meaning criteria and the logic of fuzzy concepts. *Journal of Philosophical Logic* 2:458–508.

McCloskey, M. E., and S. Glucksberg. 1978. Natural categories: Well defined or fuzzy sets? *Memory & Cognition* 6:462–472.

Oden, G. C. 1977a. Integration of fuzzy logical information. *Human Perception and Performance* 3:565–575.

Oden, G. C. 1977b. Fuzziness in semantic memory: Choosing exemplars of subjective categories. *Memory & Cognition* 5:198–204.

Osherson, D. N., and E. E. Smith. 1981. On the adequacy of prototype theory as a theory of concepts. *Cognition* 9:35–58.

Rescher, N. 1969. *Many-Valued Logic*. New York: McGraw-Hill.

Rosch, E. 1973. On the internal structure of perceptual and semantic categories. In *Cognitive Development and Acquisition of Language*, ed. T. Moore, 111–144. New York: Academic Press.

Wiener, N. 1948. *Cybernetics*. New York: John Wiley.

Zadeh, L. A. 1962. From circuit theory to systems theory. *IRE Proceedings* 50:856–865.

Zadeh, L. A. 1965. Fuzzy sets. *Information and Control* 8:338–353.

Zadeh, L. A. 1975. Fuzzy logic and approximate reasoning. *Synthese* 30:407–428.

2 Concepts: A Tutorial

Edouard Machery

2.1   Chapter Preview

The goal of this chapter is to review, in the form of a tutorial, the current state of the research on concepts in psychology (for more extensive discussion, see Murphy 2002, Machery 2009). I describe the four principal theories of concepts, highlighting how each of them explains some important characteristics of our capacities to categorize objects and draw inductions.[1] In section 2.2, I clarify the notion of concept, and I spell out the goals of a theory of concepts. In section 2.3, I describe the so-called classical theory of concepts before presenting the prototype theories of concepts in section 2.4. In section 2.5, I turn to the exemplar theories of concepts before describing the theory theories of concepts (also called "the knowledge view") in section 2.6. Finally, in section 2.7, I examine the relations between the existing theories of concepts.

2.2   What Are Concepts?

2.2.1   The Notion of Concept

It is often unclear what psychologists and other researchers interested in concepts—including philosophers, computer scientists, and scientists working in artificial intelligence (AI)—mean by "concept." It is then difficult to assess whether researchers who put forward different views about concepts genuinely disagree or are merely talking past each other, and it is also difficult to identify the criteria that are relevant for assessing any given theory of concepts. To remedy these unfortunate outcomes, it is important to clarify what most psychologists mean by "concept" and to regiment the use of this term to the extent that this is possible. In most fields of psychology and in related disciplines (e.g., cognitive neuroscience, AI), a concept of x (e.g., a concept of dog) is usually taken to be a body of knowledge about x (e.g., dogs) that is used by default in the cognitive processes that underwrite most higher cognitive competences when we make a judgment about x (e.g., a judgment about dogs). Thus, a concept of x is a subset of the knowledge about x we store in long-term memory; or, to put it differently, only part of our knowledge about x constitutes our concept of x. Which part? The part that is used by default when we categorize, when we draw an induction, when we make an analogy, when we understand sentences containing a lexeme expressing the concept of *x*—in brief, when we rely on what are commonly called our higher cognitive competences or capacities (categorization, induction, analogy-making, speech production, and understanding, etc.). This body of knowledge is used by default because it is used in a context-insensitive manner: It is retrieved from memory in every context. It springs to mind, so to speak, whenever we are thinking about its referent. An example might be useful to clarify these ideas. The concept of dog is a subset of our knowledge about dogs. It is retrieved from long-term memory in a context-insensitive manner, and it is used in the processes underwriting our higher cognitive competences. We use it to decide whether to classify something as a dog, to make inductions about dogs, to understand sentences containing the word "dog," and so forth.

2.2.2 Theories of Concepts

A theory of concepts in psychology attempts primarily to identify the properties that are common to all concepts. As psychologist Gregory Murphy (2002, 2) nicely puts it:

> The psychology of concepts cannot by itself provide a full explanation of the concepts of all the different domains that psychologists are interested in. This book will not explore the psychology of concepts of persons, musical forms, numbers, physical motions, and political systems. The details of each of these must be discovered by the specific disciplines that study them. . . . Nonetheless, the general processes of concept learning and representation may well be found in each of these domains. For example, I would be quite surprised if concepts of musical forms did not follow a prototype structure, did not have a preferred level of categorization, and did not show differences depending on expertise or knowledge.

Psychologists have been particularly interested in the following five properties of concepts. First, they have tried to determine the nature of the information that is constitutive of concepts. For instance, as we will see at greater length in sections 2.4 and 2.6, some psychologists—prototype theorists—hold that concepts consist of some statistical information about the properties that are typical and/or diagnostic of a class or of a substance (e.g., Hampton 2006; Smith 2002), while others—theory theorists—insist that concepts consist of causal and/or generic information (e.g., Tenenbaum, Griffiths, and Niyogi 2007). Second, psychologists want to determine the nature of the processes that use concepts. For instance, some psychologists have argued that these processes are based on some similarity computation (e.g., Hampton 1993), while others disagree (e.g., Rips 1989). Third, cognitive scientists develop hypotheses about the nature of the vehicles of concepts. To illustrate, neo-empiricists such as psychologist Lawrence Barsalou and philosopher Jesse Prinz contend that the vehicles of concepts are similar to the vehicles of perceptual representations (e.g., Barsalou 1999, 2008; Prinz 2002). Fourth, for about a decade, cognitive scientists have attempted to identify the brain areas that are involved in possessing concepts (for recent reviews, see Martin 2007; Mahon and Caramazza 2009). Finally, cognitive scientists have developed hypotheses about the processes of concept acquisition.

As we have seen, concepts are used in the processes that underwrite our higher cognitive competences, such as induction, categorization, language production and understanding, and analogy making. By developing a theory of concepts—by explaining what kind of knowledge constitutes concepts, what kind of processes use concepts, and so on—psychologists hope to be able to explain, at least in part, how we classify objects into classes (events into event types, or samples as belonging to substances), how we draw inductions, how we make analogies, and so forth.

2.3   The Classical Theory of Concepts

2.3.1   Definitions
Until the 1970s, most psychologists held a simple view about the knowledge that constitutes a concept (e.g., Bruner, Goodnow, and Austin 1956; Conant and Trabasso 1964): Concepts were thought to be definitions (also called "rules"). According to the most common versions of this so-called classical theory of concepts, a concept of x represents some properties as being separately necessary and jointly sufficient to be an x. The concept *grandmother* is perhaps the best illustration of this approach to concepts: If people have a classical concept of grandmother, they hold that to be a grandmother it is necessary and sufficient to be the mother of a parent. Although proponents of the classical theory of concepts have done little work on the processes using concepts, it is natural to associate a simple model of categorization with this theory: When one decides whether

an object is an *x* (or whether an event is an instance of an event-type or whether a sample is a sample of a given substance), one determines whether this object (event or sample) possesses the properties that one holds to be necessary and sufficient to be an *x*. The classical theory of concepts has not been used to explain how we draw inductions or how we make analogies.

Some psychologists have developed more complex versions of the classical theory of concepts. Instead of representing each property as necessary to be an *x*, a concept of *x* can consist of a representation of any Boolean combination of properties provided that this combination states a necessary and sufficient condition for being an *x*. In the following, (a) illustrates the simple versions of the classical theory of concepts, while (b) illustrates the more complex versions:

(a) Someone is a bachelor if and only if he is male, married, and adult.

(b) In baseball, a batted ball is a fair ball if and only if it settles on fair ground between home and first base or between home and third base, or is on or over fair territory when bounding to the outfield past first and third base, or touches first, second, or third base, or first falls on fair territory on or beyond first base or third base, or, while on or over fair territory, touches the person of an umpire or player.

The properties of being male, being unmarried, and being adult are each taken to be necessary, and together they are taken to be sufficient for being a bachelor. By contrast, the property of being a batted ball that settles on fair ground between home and first base or between home and third base is not necessary to be a fair ball. It is, however, necessary and sufficient that one of the disjuncts of (b) be satisfied for a ball to be a fair ball.

2.3.2 Research on Classical Concepts

Extensive research has examined how people learn classical concepts in experimental tasks. In these experiments (usually called "category learning experiments"; for a historical perspective, see Machery 2007a), participants are typically presented with artificial stimuli that constitute a category satisfying a classical concept, and they have to identify the rule that determines membership in this category. The researcher varies the presentation conditions (e.g., presence or absence of feedback; sequential vs. simultaneous presentation; presentation of noninstances in addition to instances) and nature of the rule (conjunction vs. disjunction, etc.), while measuring subjects' speed and accuracy of learning—which operationalize the difficulty of learning a category defined by a particular kind of definition.

Early work compared the learning of various types of definitions or rules. A robust result is that people more easily acquire conjunctive (*red and square*) than disjunctive (*red or square*) concepts (Bruner et al. 1956; Conant and Trabasso 1964). In addition, researchers showed that a concept is more easily learned from its instances than from its noninstances (Hovland and Weiss 1953). Finally, some researchers tried to determine a measure of conceptual complexity that would predict people's difficulty in learning more or less complex definitions or rules (Shepard, Hovland, and Jenkins 1961; Neisser and Weene 1962). Of particular importance for this latter project was a sequence of six concepts that are increasingly difficult to learn (Shepard, Hovland, and Jenkins 1961). Research on measures of conceptual complexity has in large part focused on explaining why learning these concepts is increasingly difficult.

Much of the recent work on definitions or rules has focused on finding a measure of conceptual complexity. Feldman's (2000, 2003) measure—minimal description length—has attracted much attention. He proposes that "the subjective difficulty of a concept is directly proportional to its minimal Boolean description length (the length of the shortest logically equivalent propositional formula)—that is, to its logical incompressibility" (Feldman 2000, 630). Minimal description length and another principle, called "parity" (viz., when two concepts have the same minimal description length, the concept with a smaller number of positive instances is easier to learn), explain the increasing difficulty of Shepard et al.'s sequence of concepts; it also explains half of the variance in the learning difficulty of 76 concepts developed by Feldman. From a psychological point of view, Feldman (2003, 227) interprets this result as follows:

The chief finding is that subjects' ability to learn concepts depends heavily on the concepts' intrinsic complexity; more complex concepts are more difficult to learn. This pervasive effect suggests, contrary to exemplar theories, that concept learning critically involves the extraction of a simplified or abstracted generalization from examples.

Recent work, however, has cast serious doubts on this proposal (e.g., Vigo 2006), and more complex hypotheses about conceptual complexity have been put forward (e.g., Feldman 2006). The problem with these hypotheses, however, is that their psychological significance is very unclear.

2.3.3   The Rejection of the Classical Theory of Concepts

Most psychologists have abandoned the classical theory of concepts since the 1970s (for some exceptions, see Nosofsky, Palmeri, and McKinley 1994; Ashby et al. 1998; Pinker and Prince 1999; Feldman 2000, 2003, 2006). Three main arguments have been put forward to justify this rejection (for a more extensive review, see Murphy 2002, chapter 2). First, some psychologists have argued that the classical theory of concepts cannot account for the vagueness of categorization—that is, for the fact that it is sometimes indeterminate whether an object is or is not a member of a class (e.g., Hampton 1993). For instance, it might be indeterminate whether some people, who have some but not much hair left on their head, are bald. However, albeit widespread, this argument is unconvincing: A conjunction of predicates might result in vague categorization judgments if the predicates are themselves vague. For instance, because "blue" is a vague predicate, it will sometimes be indeterminate whether something is a blue square, although the concept of a blue square is a classical concept.[2]

Second, suppose that a concept is defined by means of another. For example, people could represent the action of murdering as the action of killing intentionally that also meets some other conditions. Prima facie, this predicts that processing the concept of murdering would take longer than processing the concept of killing. However, Fodor et al. (1980) have shown that this is not the case: These two concepts are processed at the same speed.

Third, psychologists discovered in the 1970s several properties of our categorization decisions that are not explained by any version of the classical theory of concepts—particularly the so-called typicality and exemplar effects (see below).

2.4   Prototype Theories of Concepts

Prototype theories of concepts reject the idea that concepts represent some properties (or Boolean combination of properties) as being necessary and sufficient. They typically propose that concepts are prototypes, and that

Table 2.1
The prototype concept of vehicle (Hampton 1979, 459).

Vehicle
1. Carries people or things
2. Can move
3. Moves along
4. Has wheels
5. Is powered, has an engine, uses fuel
6. Is self-propelled, has some means of propulsion
7. Is used for transport
8. Is steered, has a driver controlling direction
9. Has a space for passengers or goods
10. Moves faster than a person on his own
11. Is human-made

a concept of x represents either the properties that are typical of category members, the properties that are diagnostic of them, or the properties that best weigh typicality and diagnosticity. A property is typical if the probability that a particular possesses this property if it belongs to the category is high, whereas a property is diagnostic if the probability that a particular belongs to the category if it possesses this property is high. So, for instance, a prototype of dogs could represent dogs as being furry, as barking, and so on.

There are various prototype theories (Hampton 2006). The simplest theories (e.g., Hampton 1979; see table 2.1) assimilate prototypes to lists of typical properties. More complex theories (e.g., Smith et al. 1988; see table 2.2) are related to frame theories (Barsalou 1992) in that they distinguish attributes from values. Attributes (e.g., colors, shapes) are kinds of properties: They determine that the members of a category possess a property of a particular kind. For instance, apples are represented as having a color. Values (e.g., red, green, brown) are the properties possessed by the category members. The weight of an attribute represents the importance of this attribute for deciding whether an object is a category member, whereas the weight of a value represents the subjectively evaluated frequency of this particular value among members.

The two theories of prototypes briefly described represent prototypes by means of schemas, whereas other prototype theories represent prototypes

Table 2.2
The prototype concept of apple (Smith et al. 1988, 490).

Apple			
Attributes		Values	
Color	1	Red	27
		Green	3
		Brown	—
Shape	0.5	Round	25
		Cylindrical	5
		Square	—
Texture	0.25	Smooth	24
		Rough	4
		Bumpy	2

as points in multidimensional spaces (Gärdenfors 2000). These two ways of characterizing prototypes differ in how similarities between prototypes and other representations (e.g., the representations of the objects to be categorized) are computed (for discussion, see Storms 2004).

2.4.1 Categorization and Category Learning

In contrast to the classical theory of concepts, prototype theories of concepts are associated with relatively precise models of the processes underlying various cognitive competences, including categorization (Hampton 1993; Smith 2002), induction (Osherson et al. 1990; Sloman 1993), and concept combination (Smith et al. 1988). As an illustration, I review Hampton's (1993) model of categorization before reviewing some of the phenomena that prototype theories are taken to explain (see also Murphy 2002, chapter 2; Hampton 2006; Machery 2009, chapters 4–7).

Hampton's model consists of a prototype model of concepts, a similarity measure, and a decision rule. This prototype model of concepts is similar to the one by Smith et al. (1988) described above. Following Hampton (1993, 73–74), the similarity measure, $S(x,C)$, of an instance x to a category C is defined in terms of valuations $w(x,i)$, each of which is the weight of the value (e.g., red) possessed by x for attribute i of the prototype (e.g., color). A particular similarity measure is defined by some specific way of aggregating the weights $w(x,i)$ for all relevant attributes. For example,

$$S(x,C) = \sum_i w(x,i). \tag{2.1}$$

This means that prototype models typically assume that categorization judgments are influenced by the properties taken independently from one another. Their configuration does not matter. Or, to put the point differently, in these models, categorization cues are independent.

Hampton's decision rule for categorization is a simple deterministic rule,

$$S(x,C) > t \Rightarrow x \in C, \tag{2.2}$$

where t is a criterion (or threshold) on the similarity scale. Nondeterministic decision rules can also be used, and this rule can be modified to explain how people decide whether to categorize an object in one of two categories.

Thus, Hampton's model of the categorization process involves a matching process between representations—namely, the prototype and the representation of the object to be categorized—as well as a linear measure of the similarity between the prototype and other representations. These are trademark characteristics of prototype models of cognitive processes. Hampton's model also assumes that the same process of similarity evaluation underlies both typicality judgments (how typical an object is of its category) and categorization judgments. Typicality ratings are supposed to be monotonically related to similarity.

This type of model accounts for the typicality effects identified at the end of the 1960s and in the 1970s (Posner and Keele 1968, 1970; Rips, Shoben, and Smith 1973; Rosch and Mervis 1975; Hampton 1979). Typicality—the extent to which an object possesses the properties that are typical of a category—has repeatedly been shown to have an extensive influence on people's performances in a range of cognitive tasks. Typicality can be measured objectively for artificial categories (e.g., Posner and Keele 1968, 1970; Rosch and Mervis 1975, experiments 5 and 6); it can be measured by asking people to list the properties of instances of the relevant categories (Rosch and Mervis 1975, experiments 1–4; Storms 2004); or it can be estimated by asking people to judge how good an example a particular object is ("typicality judgments") (e.g., Rosch and Mervis 1975, experiments 1–4; Hampton 1979, 1981).

Rips, Shoben, and Smith (1973) found that typical category members are classified more quickly and more accurately than atypical category members (see also Hampton 1979; for review, see Murphy 2002, chapter 2):

Participants respond more quickly to "a robin is a bird" than to "an ostrich is a bird." Similar results are obtained when the stimuli are presented visually, for instance, when participants are shown a picture or a drawing of the object to be categorized, such as a drawing of a robin (Murphy and Brownell 1985). Similar findings are also found with artificial categories (Rosch and Mervis 1975, experiments 5 and 6).

Typicality with respect to a category predicts the likelihood of being considered a member of this category (Hampton 1979). A similar result has been found in linguistics. Labov (1973) has shown that, in American English, artifacts are called "mug" or "bowl" to the extent that they are similar to a prototypical shape.

Typicality also affects concept learning. Using artificial stimuli, Posner and Keele (1968, 1970) have shown that, following the acquisition of a concept, the most typical member of the category is sometimes more likely to be classified as a category member than the category members seen during training, although this most typical member has not been seen during training. In experiments with artificial categories, participants learn the category membership of typical items faster than the category membership of atypical items (Rosch and Mervis 1975). Participants also more easily learn to classify items in a category if they are trained with typical items than if they are trained with atypical items.

The findings reviewed so far are consistent with the prototype theories of concepts.[3] Since the representation of a target is supposed to be matched with a prototype during categorization, theories of prototype-based categorization expect typicality to affect categorization. Because concept learning consists in forming a prototype, prototype theories also expect typicality to affect concept learning.

The idea that typicality effects support prototype models of concepts has been challenged from several directions. First, Armstrong, Gleitman, and Gleitman (1983) have argued that typicality effects do not show anything about conceptual structure because they are also found with concepts that satisfy the classical theory of concepts (for critical discussion, see Machery 2009, chapter 6).

Second, Barsalou (1985) has shown that typicality judgments ("how good a bird is this robin?") are not merely influenced by typicality (robins are typical birds), but also by how frequently a category member is encountered as a category member (e.g., how frequently robins are encountered and viewed as birds) and by how similar a category member is to an ideal member of a category (how similar a robin is to an ideal bird). These findings raise a problem for prototype theorists because these theorists support prototype theories by appealing in part to the fact that typicality, as measured by typicality judgments, predicts performance in experimental tasks (for critical discussion, see Hampton 1997; Machery 2009, chapter 6).

Third, exemplar theories (see section 2.5) can account for many typicality effects (Medin and Schaffer 1978). It is thus unclear whether the typicality effects found in the 1960s and 1970s support prototype theories over exemplar theories. More recent research suggests that whether a prototype or an exemplar is learned in category learning experiments depends on the category structure (number of category members presented during training, similarities between category members, dissimilarities between various categories) and on the stage of category learning (Smith and Minda 1998, 2000; Minda and Smith 2001; Nosofsky 2000; Nosofsky and Zaki 2002; Smith 2002; Zaki and Nosofsky 2007).

2.4.2 Induction

In addition to the tasks related to categorization and category learning, typicality effects are also found in categorical induction tasks (Murphy 2002, chapter 8; Sloman and Lagnado 2005; Machery 2009, chapter 7). In such tasks, people have to infer whether the members of a category (the target category) possess a property on the basis of being told that the members of another category or of other categories (the source category or categories) have this property. For instance, participants might be asked whether sparrows have sesamoid bones given that robins have sesamoid bones, or, equivalently, how good the following inference is:

(a)   Robins have sesamoid bones.

Hence, sparrows have sesamoid bones.

Several findings show that typicality influences people's inductions. Consider first "the similarity effect." A conclusion that is inferred from a single premise is judged to be stronger to the extent that the source category is judged to be more similar to the target category (Rips 1975; Osherson et al. 1990). Thus (a) is a better inference than the following one:

(b)   Robins have sesamoid bones.

Hence, penguins have sesamoid bones.

Consider also "the typicality effect" (Rips 1975). A conclusion that is inferred from a single premise is judged to be stronger to the extent that the source category is typical of the target category (if the target category includes the source category) or of the category that includes both the target category and the source category (if the target category does not include the source category). Consider, for instance, the following inferences:

(c)   Robins have sesamoid bones.
       Hence, birds have sesamoid bones.

(d)   Penguins have sesamoid bones.
       Hence, birds have sesamoid bones.

Inference (c) is judged to be stronger than inference (d) because robins are a more typical kind of bird than penguins.

Two well-known models of the processes involved in induction explain the similarity and typicality effects (as well as other effects) by assuming that we retrieve from memory the prototypes of the source categories and of the target category (Osherson et al. 1990; Sloman 1993). For the sake of space, I review only Osherson et al.'s (1990) similarity-coverage model. In this model, the strength of the induction is a function of the average similarity between the source categories and the target category and of the coverage of the source categories, defined as the average similarity between the source categories and either the typical subclasses of the target category—when the target category includes the source categories—or the typical subclasses of the lowest-level category that includes both the source and target categories—when the target category does not include the source categories. Similarity is determined by matching the relevant prototypes. The similarity effect falls out from the similarity component in the model. The typicality effect is a consequence of the coverage component of the model because the typicality of a category x, such as robins, with respect to a more inclusive category y, such as birds, is correlated with the similarity between the prototype of x and the prototypes of the typical subclasses of y.

2.5   Exemplar Theories of Concepts

Exemplar theories (Brooks 1978; Medin and Schaffer 1978; Nosofsky 1992) reject the idea that, when people acquire a concept, they abstract some statistical information about the represented class (e.g., information about typical or diagnostic properties). Rather, they propose that people store representations of particular category members (a representation of this kind is called "an exemplar"), and that they use these representations to make categorization judgments, to draw inductions, and so on. So, for these theories, a concept of dogs consists in a set of representations of particular dogs (say, a representation of Fido, a representation of Rover, etc.), which are used in the cognitive processes underlying our higher cognitive competences. Medin and Schaffer (1978, 209–210) have well captured the gist of the exemplar theories:

The general idea of the context model [the name of their model] is that classification judgments are based on the retrieval of stored exemplar information. . . . This mechanism is, in a sense, a device for reasoning by analogy inasmuch as classification of new stimuli is based on stored information concerning old exemplars. . . . Although we shall propose that classifications derive from exemplar information, we do not assume that the storage and retrievability of this exemplar information is veridical. If subjects are using strategies and hypotheses during learning, the exemplar information may be incomplete and the salience of information from alternative dimensions may differ considerably.

Because concept acquisition does not require abstraction (or, at any rate, requires less abstraction) according to exemplar theories of concepts, learning turns out to be simpler on these views. On the other hand, because cognizing involves retrieving from long-term memory numerous singular representations (exemplars) and using them in cognitive processes (e.g., in the process underlying categorization), whereas prototype theories propose that cognizing involves retrieving and using a single representation, cognitive processing is more computationally intensive according to exemplar theories. Another difference between prototype and exemplar theories is that prototype theories assume that categorization judgments—judgments to the effect that something is an x, for instance a dog or a table—and recognition judgments—judgments identifying an individual as an individual, e.g., the judgment expressed by "This is John"—involve two distinct kinds of representation (respectively, prototypes and representations of particulars), whereas exemplar theories propose that both types of judgments involve a single kind of representation (i.e., exemplars).

Most exemplar theories have been developed in a spatial framework (e.g., Nosofsky 1992; but see Storms 2004). Exemplars are represented as points in a multidimensional space, whose dimensions represent the continuous properties of the individuals represented by the exemplars (e.g., color, height). A particular coordinate along one of these dimensions corresponds to a quantity or intensity of the continuous property (e.g., a particular height).

2.5.1 Categorization and Category Learning

Exemplar models of concepts have been mostly developed to account for the findings in category learning experiments, and they account well for most experimental results (but see the last paragraph of section 2.4.1 above). I now present the most well-known exemplar model, Nosofsky's Generalized Context Model (e.g., Nosofsky 1988, 1992), before reviewing the most important findings that support the exemplar theories of concepts.

The Generalized Context Model is an extension of Medin and Schaffer's (1978) Context Model. It consists of a spatial exemplar model of concepts, a similarity measure, and a decision rule. According to this exemplar model, each exemplar represents its referent as a point in a multidimensional space.

In the Generalized Context Model, each target is compared to all the exemplars that constitute a concept. For instance, a dog, Fido, may be compared to all the exemplars of dogs that constitute someone's concept of dog, as well as to all exemplars of wolves that constitute someone's concept of wolf. The similarity between Fido and an exemplar, for instance, an exemplar of a dog, is a function of the psychological distance between Fido and this exemplar. This psychological distance depends on the extent to which Fido and the exemplar match on each of the relevant dimensions for categorizing Fido: The more different Fido and the exemplar are on a given dimension, say k, the further apart they are on this dimension. Formally, for a given dimension, the distance between the target Fido and the exemplar is $|x_{t_k} - x_{E_k}|$, where x_{t_k} is the value of the target, Fido, on dimension k and x_{E_k} is the value of the exemplar on this dimension. Each psychological dimension is weighted: The weight of dimension k, w_k, measures the attention paid to k. Greater values of this weight capture the idea that mismatch along dimension k increases the dissimilarity between the exemplar of a dog and Fido, thus decreasing the likelihood that Fido will be classified as a dog. This parameter is assumed by Nosofsky to be context dependent. Dimension weights sum to one: This captures the idea that decreasing the attention to one dimension entails increasing the attention to other dimensions. The psychological distance between Fido and the exemplar of a dog depends on whether the relevant dimensions are analyzable. Analyzable (or separable) dimensions can be attended independently of one another. Size and weight are analyzable dimensions of objects: We can attend to the size of an object, independently of its weight. By contrast, nonanalyzable (or integral) dimensions cannot be attended independently of one another. For example, hue, brightness, and saturation are nonanalyzable dimensions. When dimensions are nonanalyzable, the psychological distance is computed with a Euclidean metric:

$$d_{tE} = \sqrt{\sum_{k=1}^{n} w_k (x_{t_k} - x_{E_k})^2}. \tag{2.3}$$

When the dimensions are analyzable, the psychological distance is computed with a city-block metric:

$$d_{tE} = \sum_{k=1}^{n} w_k |x_{t_k} - x_{E_k}|. \tag{2.4}$$

More generally, the distance between the target and the exemplar for n dimensions is calculated as

$$d_{tE} = c \left(\sum_{k=1}^{n} w_k |x_{t_k} - x_{E_k}|^r \right)^{\frac{1}{r}}, \tag{2.5}$$

where r depends on whether the dimensions are analyzable and c is a sensitivity parameter, which measures how much the overall psychological distance between a target and an exemplar affects their similarity. The similarity between t and E is an exponential function of the psychological distance between the target and the exemplar (another parameter is sometimes introduced to determine various functions from psychological distance to similarity):

$$S_{tE} = e^{-d_{tE}}. \tag{2.6}$$

Thus, the greater the psychological distance between the target, Fido, and the exemplar of dog, the smaller their similarity. The overall similarity of the target, Fido, to the concept of dog, that is, to the set of exemplars of dogs, is the sum of its similarities to each exemplar of a dog. Formally,

$$S_{tC} = \sum_{E \in C} S_{tE}. \tag{2.7}$$

The decision rule is nondeterministic. If two concepts, say, *dog* and *wolf*, have been retrieved from long-term memory, the probability of classifying Fido as a dog is a function of the overall similarity of Fido to the concept of dog divided by the sum of the overall similarities to the concepts of dog and of wolf. Formally,

$$P(t \in A) = \frac{S_{tA}}{S_{tA} + S_{tB}}, \tag{2.8}$$

where A and B are the two relevant concepts. Some versions of the Generalized Context model multiply S_{tA} by a parameter (β) corresponding to a response bias toward category A. Other decision rules can be formalized by an additional parameter (α) that raises S_{tA} and S_{tB} to an exponent:

$$P(t \in A) = \frac{\beta S_{tA}^{\alpha}}{\beta A_{tA}^{\alpha} + (1-\beta) S_{tB}^{\alpha}}. \tag{2.9}$$

When $\alpha = 1$, people categorize by probability matching; when α is larger than 1, people categorize in a more deterministic manner.

Nosofsky's Generalized Context Model of categorization illustrates the core ideas of exemplar-based models of cognitive processes: The process of categorization involves matching the representations of targets with exemplars and computing, in a nonlinear manner, their similarity. That similarity is typically computed in a nonlinear manner in exemplar models of categorization means that exemplar models assume that the configuration of properties, rather than the properties taken independently from one another, is what matters for categorization.

As noted above, this type of model fits participants' performances in category learning experiments very well (for recent discussion of the quality of fit, see Nosofsky 1992; Smith and Minda 1998, 2000; Minda and Smith 2001; Nosofsky 2000; Nosofsky and Zaki 2002; Smith 2002; Storms 2004; Zaki and Nosofsky 2004, 2007). From a qualitative point of view, exemplar models of categorization are well designed to account for the exemplar effects. First, let's consider the old-items advantage. Participants are asked to learn the category membership of the artificial stimuli that compose two categories. They are then asked to categorize new stimuli, as well as the stimuli seen during training. The finding is that the stimuli seen during training are usually more easily categorized than new items that are equally typical (Nosofsky 1992; Smith and Minda 2000). To give a toy example, it is easier to classify my old pet Fido as a dog than an unknown dog that is an equally typical dog. This effect is not predicted by prototype theories of concepts, since these assume that people abstract a prototype from the stimuli they are presented with in the learning phase and categorize stimuli, old as well as new, by comparing them to the prototype. What matters for categorization is the similarity of the items to the prototype, not whether they have already been seen. By contrast, the old item's advantage falls out from the exemplar theories of concepts and categorization. The similarity of an old item that belongs to a given category A to the set of exemplars of members of A is greater than the similarity of a new item to this same set because the set of exemplars includes a representation of the old item, but no representation of the new item.

The second exemplar effect is the following. A less typical category member can be categorized more quickly and more accurately than a more typical category member, and its category membership can be learned more quickly than the category membership of a less typical category member, if this category member is similar to previously encountered category members (Medin and Schaffer 1978). Again to give a toy example, it may be easier for me to categorize a three-legged dog as a dog than a four-legged dog if my own pet dog lost a leg. Medin and Schaffer (1978) establish this finding as follows. They single out two items among the training items, A_1 and A_2. These two items belong to the same category, A. The critical point is that A_1 is more similar than A_2 to the prototype that participants would plausibly abstract if prototype theories were correct. Thus, prototype theories predict that participants will learn more quickly the category membership of A_1 than the membership of A_2. Because A_2 is highly similar to two other members of A and to no member of the alternative category, B, while A_1 is highly similar to only one member of A, but to two members of B, Medin and Schaffer's Context Model makes the opposite prediction. Medin and Schaffer found evidence that supports their prediction.

2.5.2 Exemplar Models and Natural Language Concepts

Exemplar theories suffer from two major problems. First, almost all the empirical research on this family of theories has focused on participants' performances in category learning experiments. These experiments typically involve artificial stimuli (geometrical figures, dot patterns, etc.) that have little to do with the real objects represented by concepts outside the lab, particularly by concepts lexicalized in natural languages (e.g., *dog* or *water*);

and the learning conditions in these experiments have little to do with the circumstances in which concepts are learned outside the lab. Second, exemplar theories of concepts have not been applied to many higher cognitive competences, a concern already expressed by Murphy (2002). There is, to my knowledge, no research on induction, on concept combination, and so on, inspired by exemplar theories of concepts.

Research by Brooks and colleagues (for review, see Norman, Young, and Brooks 2007) and by Storms and colleagues (for review, see Storms 2004) mitigates the first issue just pointed to. Brooks and colleagues have highlighted the role of exemplars in expert cognition in medicine. They have shown that medical diagnosis by medical experts is influenced by the most recent cases they have considered (Brooks, Norman, and Allen 1991), suggesting that categorization judgments in disease categories are influenced by representations of particular cases (i.e., by exemplars of particular instances of diseases). They have also provided evidence that expertise consists in part in acquiring exemplars of particular cases (e.g., Norman et al. 1989).

Storms and colleagues have turned their attention to the concepts lexicalized in natural languages. Ruts, Storms, and Hampton (2004) have shown that the properties represented by concepts of artifact superordinate categories (in contrast to concepts of natural kind superordinate categories) function as configurational rather than independent cues. This suggests that concepts of superordinate categories of artifacts (vehicles, furniture, etc.) are not prototypes. They might thus be sets of exemplars or perhaps sets of prototypes of basic-level categories (e.g., the concept of furniture would thus be a set consisting of a prototype of chairs, a prototype of tables, etc.). Storms, De Boeck, and Ruts (2001) have also shown that for some concepts expressed by natural language terms ("fruits," "birds," "vehicles," "sports") similarity to the concepts of the categories that are subordinate to the categories expressed by these concepts (e.g., the categories of apples, bananas, peaches, etc., for the category of fruits) tend to predict a range of measures—including typicality judgments and latency in a speeded categorization task—better than the similarity to prototypes.[4] That is, when one evaluates whether a particular fruit is a good instance of the category of fruits, its similarity to the concepts of apples, bananas, peaches, and so on, is more important than its similarity to a supposed prototype of fruits.

2.6 Theory Theories of Concepts

2.6.1 Causal and Generic Knowledge

Theory theories of concepts were originally developed in the 1980s by psychologists working on categorization (Murphy and Medin 1985; Rips 1989) and by developmental psychologists (Carey 1985; Keil 1989).[5] Their core tenets are in part defined negatively: Theory theorists reject the idea that concepts store statistical information about categories, substances, events, and the like, or information about particular category members, samples, events; they also reject the idea that cognitive processes are driven by similarity (Rips 1989). In addition, theory theorists assert that concepts are in some respects like scientific theories (the extent to which this analogy is taken seriously varies from one theory theorist to the other). Like scientific theories, concepts consist of knowledge that can be used to explain events, phenomena, or states of affairs. Theory theorists hold that causal knowledge, nomological knowledge, functional knowledge, and generic knowledge are all used in explanation, and, thus, that concepts consist of these types of knowledge. Finally, concepts are assumed to be used in processes that are in some way similar to the reasoning strategies used in science. Theory theorists often allude to inferences to the best explanation (Rips 1989) or to causal inferences to illustrate the types of processes that are defined over concepts.

To illustrate, a theory of dogs could be a body of causal—for instance, that dogs wave their tails because they are happy—and functional—for instance, that dogs bark to defend themselves—knowledge about dogs. Such knowledge could be used to explain the behavior of dogs or to predict causally how a particular dog would behave in specific circumstances.

Theory theories have been specified in much less detail than the competing theories of concepts reviewed above, in part because until recently they have not been formalized. Recently, however, researchers interested in causal reasoning (see, e.g., Gopnik et al. 2004; Sloman 2005) and in Bayesian reasoning (Tenenbaum, Griffiths, and Niyogi 2007) have characterized the commitments of theory theories in greater detail. Psychologists working on causal reasoning propose that theories are (or are very similar to) causal Bayes nets (e.g., Gopnik et al. 2004). A causal Bayes net is a particular representation of the causal relations among variables (Spirtes, Glymour, and Scheines 2000). Without going into detail here, a causal Bayes net for a set of variables specifies that some constraints hold on the probability distributions for these variables. Particularly, if the variable V is causally related to the variable W, then, once the values for all the variables other than W have been fixed (thereby fixing the probability distribution of W), there is a modification of the value of V (an "intervention") that modifies the probability distribution of W. Bayes nets are associated with algorithms that determine the effects of interventions and with learning algorithms that can infer causal relations from correlations. So, the proposal is that our concepts represent causal relations as causal Bayes nets and that they are involved in cognitive processes that are similar to the algorithms defined over causal Bayes nets.

Psychologists influenced by Bayesianism have criticized this approach (Tenenbaum, Griffiths, and Niyogi 2007). Tenenbaum and colleagues have argued that, although causal Bayes nets might be an appropriate way of characterizing the content of concepts such as *dog*, *table*, and *water*, they are insufficient to characterize the role of theories in cognition entirely. In particular, the causal-Bayes-net approach to theory theories does not explain why in a particular domain theories are defined over similar variables and why causal relations are all similar. For instance, concepts of diseases tend to distinguish symptoms from pathogenic factors and assume that the latter cause the former—not the other way around. Tenenbaum and colleagues propose that theories form a hierarchy and that each theory at a given level of the hierarchy is constrained by a theory at the level immediately above it. Furthermore, at any given level of this hierarchy, the theories that belong to a conceptual system are those that have the highest posterior probability among those that are possible in light of the theory at the higher level. Tenenbaum and colleagues also argued that the psychological processes using theories are unlikely to be similar to the algorithms associated with causal Bayes nets. Instead, they propose that cognitive processes are better represented as Bayesian inferences.

In addition to specifying theories in greater detail by appealing to recent work on causal inferences or on Bayesian inferences, theory theorists have also recently insisted on the importance of generic knowledge in our conceptual representations of categories, substances, events, and the like (e.g., Prasada and Dillingham 2006).

2.6.2 Categorization

The theory theory has been much bolstered by work on psychological essentialism (Keil 1989; Medin and Ortony 1989). Psychological essentialism is the hypothesis that people believe that membership in some kinds is determined by the possession of an essence (even when people are unable to specify the nature of this essence). In addition, it is hypothesized that people believe that this essence causes category members to have the properties that are characteristic of the category to which they belong. For instance, Keil's (1989) classic work suggests that even young children assume that category membership in natural kinds is not determined by superficial, observable properties, but by unobservable, immutable properties. Thus, children judge that a skunk whose appearance is surgically modified to look like a raccoon is still a skunk.

Theory theorists have also highlighted "the causal effects" in categorization—namely, the phenomena found in experimental tasks that are best explained if one supposes that participants bring some causal knowledge to bear on these tasks (Rehder 2003; for review, see Murphy 2002, chapter 6; Gopnik and Schulz 2007; Machery 2009, chapter 6). Ahn has put forward "the causal status hypothesis," according to which "people regard cause features as more important and essential than effect features in their conceptual representation" (Ahn and Luhmann 2005, 278). Ahn and colleagues' findings suggest that people's decisions to classify an object in a linguistically described artificial category are influenced by the causal centrality of the properties that are characteristic of the category. A property is more causally central than another to the extent that it causes a greater number of properties that are characteristic of the category. So, if two objects possess the same number of characteristic properties, but if the properties possessed by one of them are more causally central than the properties possessed by the other one, the former is more likely to be categorized as a category member than the latter. Rehder's (2003) approach is in tension with Ahn's causal status hypothesis. For Rehder, our beliefs about the causal relations among the properties that characterize a category determine which properties we expect to be associated among category members. When an object does not possess the properties we expect to be associated, we judge it less likely to belong to the relevant category. On this view, causally central properties are not necessarily more important in categorization than causally less central properties (to see this, consider common effect causal structures).

2.6.3 Induction

Research on induction also suggests that causal information is sometimes used to assess the strength of an inductive conclusion or to decide how to make an induction (for review, see Murphy 2002, chapter 8; Feeney and Heit 2007; Machery 2009, chapter 7). Proffitt, Coley, and Medin (2000) investigated the judgments made by tree experts (landscapers, taxonomists, and parks maintenance personnel) about the strength of inductive conclusions about trees. In the first experiment, tree experts were told that disease A affects a species of tree, x, while disease B affects another species, y. They were then asked: "Which disease do you think would affect more of the other kinds of trees found around here?" Experts were also asked to justify their judgments.

Proffitt and colleagues found that typicality often did not affect experts' judgments about whether other trees would be affected by the disease. Rather than relying on the typicality of the two species of trees, x and y (as predicted, for instance, by Osherson and colleagues' similarity-coverage model), the pattern of answers and the justifications provided suggest that experts often based their judgments on hypothetical causal mechanisms that could explain the spread of the disease. Particularly, they judged that a disease would likely be present in many trees if the species under consideration were ecologically related to many trees. Proffitt, Coley, and Medin (2000, 818) reported that a participant explained her answer as follows: "For example, one expert mentioned that oaks are likely to spread disease through their roots and that their extensive root system made oaks a stronger base for induction."

The use of causal knowledge is not restricted to experts as can be shown, for example, by the causal asymmetry effect (Medin et al. 2003; Sloman and Lagnado 2005). The causal asymmetry effect is the following: When there is an intuitive causal explanation of why the target category would have a property if the source category had it, switching the premise and the conclusion weakens the strength of the induction. Thus, the induction

> Gazelles contain retinum
> _____
> Lions contain retinum

is stronger than the induction

$$\frac{\text{Lions contain retinum}}{\text{Gazelles contain retinum}}$$

(Sloman and Lagnado 2005, 219).

2.7   Relation between the Theories of Concepts

2.7.1   The Heterogeneity Hypothesis

What is the relation between the theories of concepts reviewed in the previous sections? For a long time, the received view has been that these theories were competing. That is, it was assumed that one and only one of these theories could be correct: Concepts were either definitions, or prototypes, or sets of exemplars, or theories. Thus, psychologists committed to different theories of concepts (say, a particular prototype theory and a particular exemplar theory) focused on discovering properties of our higher cognitive competences (e.g., the exemplar effects reported in Medin and Schaffer 1978) that were easily explained by the theory they endorsed (e.g., the exemplar theory), but that were not easily explicable by the competing theory (prototype theories do not naturally explain the exemplar effects). On this basis, they used to conclude that their own theory, but not the competing theory, was probably correct.

Recently, however, psychologists and philosophers of psychology have proposed to look at these apparently competing theories differently. In recent work (Machery 2005, 2009; for extensive discussion, see the commentaries in Machery 2010), I have argued that each category (e.g., dogs), each substance (e.g., water), each type of event (e.g., going to the dentist), and so on, is represented by several concepts—for instance, by a prototype, by a set of exemplars, and by a theory (a hypothesis known as "the heterogeneity hypothesis"). Thus, I hypothesize, we have a prototype of dogs, a set of exemplars of particular dogs, and a theory of dogs. If this is correct, then some of the actual theories of concepts are not competing with one another, but are simply describing different kinds of concepts—namely, prototypes, exemplars, and theories. Because these three kinds of concepts have little in common, it is also a mistake to assume that there are many general properties of concepts, and that a theory of concepts should attempt to describe these. In addition, the heterogeneity hypothesis contends that prototypes, exemplars, and theories are typically used in distinct processes. For example, we have several categorization processes: a proto-type-based categorization process, an exemplar-based categorization process, and a theory-based categorization process.

What is the evidence for the claim that our long-term memory stores prototypes, exemplars, and theories (Machery 2009, chapters 6–7)? First, when one examines thirty years of research on categorization and induction, one finds that in both areas of research some phenomena are well explained if the concepts elicited by some experimental tasks are prototypes, some phenomena are well explained if the concepts elicited by other experimental tasks are exemplars, and yet other phenomena are well explained if the concepts elicited by yet other experimental tasks are theories. If one hypothesizes that experimental conditions prime the reliance on one type of concepts (e.g., prototypes) instead of other types (e.g., exemplars and theories), this provides evidence for the heterogeneity hypothesis.

Second, more direct evidence suggests that different types of concepts are sometimes competing for controlling behavior. Using visually presented artificial categories, Allen and Brooks (1991) have shown that people can simultaneously acquire and also simultaneously use two distinct concepts—a set of exemplars and something like a definition. In an experiment that used words as stimuli, Malt's (1989) protocol analysis has shown that many participants use both prototypes and exemplars. Looking at lexicalized concepts, Storms, De Boeck, and Ruts (2001) found that prototype models explained an additional proportion of variance in addition to the proportion of variance explained by exemplar models. Studying the bodies of knowledge used by expert physicians to categorize diseases and to reason about them, Brooks and colleagues have argued that expert physicians simultaneously have distinct bodies of knowledge about diseases: a theory, a prototype, and exemplars (for review, see Norman et al. 2006). This latter body of findings is particularly important because it examines people's concepts in the real world, not the concepts they acquire in the highly artificial conditions of concept learning experiments.

2.7.2 Other Approaches

The heterogeneity hypothesis is not the only way to combine the theories of concepts reviewed in the previous sections. I briefly mention two other alternatives. Some psychologists propose that whether a given category is represented by a prototype or by a set of exemplars depends on various properties of this category—including how different from one another the category members are, how different from the members of other categories they are—and on various characteristics of the process of concept acquisition (Smith and Minda 1998; Minda and Smith 2001). In contrast to the heterogeneity hypothesis, this hypothesis proposes that a given category is represented by a single concept, but it concurs with the heterogeneity hypothesis in holding that there are different kinds of concepts.

Others have highlighted the similarities between the kinds of concepts postulated by the theories discussed in this chapter. Particularly, Danks (2007) has shown that the models of categorization put forward by prototype, exemplar, and theory theories can in fact be represented as graphical models. On his view, then, a more general theory of concepts is thus called for, one that could unite prototypes, exemplars, and causal theories (for discussion, see Machery 2010).

Notes

1. For the sake of space, less influential theories of concepts are not reviewed in this tutorial. In particular, I do not examine the view that concepts are ideals (Barsalou 1983, 1985; Lynch, Coley, and Medin 2000; Bailenson et al. 2002), the decision-bound theory of categorization (Ashby and Maddox 1993), the theory of concepts based on mental models (Goodwin and Johnson-Laird 2010), or the view that concepts are similar to perceptual representations (Barsalou 1999, 2008; Prinz 2002). (For critical discussion, see Machery 2007b; Mahon and Caramazza 2008.)

2. On the other hand, theoretical alternatives to the classical theory of concepts, such as the prototype theories discussed in the next section, might provide better accounts of vagueness (Hampton 2006, 2007).

3. Some particular assumptions about the processes of categorization and concept learning must be made to account for some of these findings.

4. Note, however, that these results do not determine whether people rely on genuine exemplars or on prototypes of subordinate categories.

5. For more recent developments, see Carey 2009; Sloman 2005; Gopnik et al. 2004; Tenenbaum et al. 2007.

References

Ahn, W., and C. C. Luhmann. 2005. Demystifying theory-based categorization. In *Building Object Categories in Developmental Time*, ed. L. Gershkoff-Stowe and D. Rakison, 277–300. Mahwah, NJ: Lawrence Erlbaum.

Allen, S. W., and L. R. Brooks. 1991. Specializing the operation of an explicit rule. *Journal of Experimental Psychology: General* 120:3–19.

Armstrong, S. L., L. R. Gleitman, and H. Gleitman. 1983. What some concepts might not be. *Cognition* 13:263–308.

Ashby, F. G., L. A. Alfonso-Reese, A. U. Turken, and E. M. Waldron. 1998. A neuropsychological theory of multiple systems in category learning. *Psychological Review* 105:442–481.

Ashby, F. G., and W. T. Maddox. 1993. Relation between exemplar, prototype, and decision bound models of categorization. *Journal of Mathematical Psychology* 37:372–400.

Bailenson, J. B., M. S. Shum, S. Atran, D. Medin, and J. D. Coley. 2002. A bird's eye view: Biological categorization and reasoning within and across cultures. *Cognition* 84:1–53.

Barsalou, L. W. 1983. Ad hoc categories. *Memory & Cognition* 10:82–93.

Barsalou, L. W. 1985. Ideals, central tendency, and frequency of instantiation as determinants of graded structure in categories. *Journal of Experimental Psychology: Learning, Memory, and Cognition* 11:629–654.

Barsalou, L. W. 1992. Frames, concepts, and conceptual fields. In *Frames, Fields, and Contrasts*, ed. A. Lehrer and E. F. Kittay, 21–74. Hillsdale, NJ: Lawrence Erlbaum.

Barsalou, L. W. 1999. Perceptual symbol systems. *Behavioral and Brain Sciences* 22:577–660.

Barsalou, L. W. 2008. Cognitive and neural contributions to understanding the conceptual system. *Current Directions in Psychological Science* 17:91–95.

Brooks, L. R. 1978. Nonanalytic concept formation and memory for instances. In *Cognition and Concepts*, ed. E. Rosch and B. B. Lloyd, 169–211. Hillsdale, NJ: Lawrence Erlbaum.

Brooks, L. R., G. R. Norman, and S. W. Allen. 1991. The role of specific similarity in a medical diagnostic task. *Journal of Experimental Psychology: General* 120:278–287.

Bruner, J. S., J.-J. Goodnow, and G. A. Austin. 1956. *A Study of Thinking*. New York: John Wiley.

Carey, S. 1985. *Conceptual Change in Childhood*. Cambridge, MA: MIT Press.

Carey, S. 2009. *The Origin of Concepts*. New York: Oxford University Press.

Conant, M. B., and T. Trabasso. 1964. Conjunctive and disjunctive concept formation under equal-information conditions. *Journal of Experimental Psychology* 67:250–255.

Danks, D. 2007. Theory unification and graphical models in human categorization. In *Causal Learning: Psychology, Philosophy, and Computation*, ed. A. Gopnik and L. Schulz, 173–189. New York: Oxford University Press.

Feeney, A., and E. Heit, eds. 2007. *Inductive Reasoning: Experimental, Developmental, and Computational Approaches*. Cambridge: Cambridge University Press.

Feldman, J. 2000. Minimization of Boolean complexity in human concept learning. *Science* 407:630–633.

Feldman, J. 2003. The simplicity principle in human concept learning. *Current Directions in Psychological Science* 12:227–232.

Feldman, J. 2006. An algebra of human concept learning. *Journal of Mathematical Psychology* 50:339–368.

Fodor, J. A., M. F. Garret, E. C. T. Walker, and C. H. Parkes. 1980. Against definitions. *Cognition* 8:263–367.

Gärdenfors, P. 2000. *Conceptual Spaces*. Cambridge, MA: MIT Press.

Goodwin, G. P., and P. N. Johnson-Laird. 2010. Conceptual illusions. *Cognition* 114:253–265.

Gopnik, A., C. Glymour, D. Sobel, L. Schulz, T. Kushnir, and D. Danks. 2004. A theory of causal learning in children: Causal maps and Bayes nets. *Psychological Review* 111:1–31.

Gopnik, A., and L. Schulz, eds. 2007. *Causal Learning: Psychology, Philosophy, and Computation*. New York: Oxford University Press.

Hampton, J. A. 1979. Polymorphous concepts in semantic memory. *Journal of Verbal Learning and Verbal Behavior* 18:441–461.

Hampton, J. A. 1981. An investigation of the nature of abstract concepts. *Memory & Cognition* 9:149–156.

Hampton, J. A. 1993. Prototype models of concept representation. In *Categories and Concepts: Theoretical Views and Inductive Data Analysis*, ed. I. Van Mechelen, J. A. Hampton, R. S. Michalski, and P. Theuns, 67–95. London: Academic Press.

Hampton, J. A. 1997. Associative and similarity-based processes in categorization decisions. *Memory & Cognition* 25:625–640.

Hampton, J. A. 2006. Concepts as prototypes. *Psychology of Learning and Motivation* 46:79–113.

Hampton, J. A. 2007. Typicality, graded membership, and vagueness. *Cognitive Science* 31:355–384.

Hovland, C. I., and W. Weiss. 1953. Transmission of information concerning concepts through positive and negative instances. *Journal of Experimental Psychology* 45:175–182.

Keil, F. C. 1989. *Concepts, Kinds, and Cognitive Development*. Cambridge, MA: MIT Press.

Labov, W. 1973. The boundaries of words and their meanings. In *New Ways of Analyzing Variation in English*, ed. C. J. Baily and R. Shuy, 340–373. Washington: Georgetown University Press.

Lynch, E. B., J. D. Coley, and D. L. Medin. 2000. Tall is typical: Central tendency, ideal dimensions and graded category structure among tree experts and novices. *Memory & Cognition* 28:41–50.

Machery, E. 2005. Concepts are not a natural kind. *Philosophy of Science* 72:444–467.

Machery, E. 2007a. 100 years of psychology of concepts: The theoretical notion of concept and its operationalization. *Studies in History and Philosophy of Biological and Biomedical Sciences* 38:63–84.

Machery, E. 2007b. Concept empiricism: A methodological critique. *Cognition* 104:19–46.

Machery, E. 2009. *Doing without Concepts*. New York: Oxford University Press.

Machery, E. 2010. Précis of *Doing without Concepts*. *Behavioral and Brain Sciences* 33: 195–205; 206–244 (discussion).

Mahon, B. Z., and A. Caramazza. 2008. A critical look at the embodied cognition hypothesis and a new proposal for grounding conceptual content. *Journal of Physiology* 102:59–70.

Mahon, B. Z., and A. Caramazza. 2009. Concepts and categories: A cognitive neuropsychological perspective. *Annual Review of Psychology* 60:27–51.

Malt, B. C. 1989. An on-line investigation of prototype and exemplar strategies in classification. *Journal of Experimental Psychology: Learning, Memory, and Cognition* 15:539–555.

Martin, A. 2007. The representation of object concepts in the brain. *Annual Review of Psychology* 58:25–45.

Medin, D. L., J. D. Coley, G. Storms, and B. Hayes. 2003. A relevance theory of induction. *Psychonomic Bulletin & Review* 3:517–532.

Medin, D. L., and A. Ortony. 1989. Psychological essentialism. In *Similarity and Analogical Reasoning*, ed. S. Vosniadou and A. Ortony, 179–195. Cambridge: Cambridge University Press.

Medin, D. L., and M. M. Schaffer. 1978. Context theory of classification learning. *Psychological Review* 85:207–238.

Minda, J. P., and J. D. Smith. 2001. Prototypes in category learning: The effects of category size, category structure, and stimulus complexity. *Journal of Experimental Psychology: Learning, Memory, and Cognition* 27:775–799.

Murphy, G. L. 2002. *The Big Book of Concepts*. Cambridge, MA: MIT Press.

Murphy, G. L., and H. H. Brownell. 1985. Category differentiation in object recognition: Typicality constraints on the basic category advantage. *Journal of Experimental Psychology: Learning, Memory, and Cognition* 11:70–84.

Murphy, G. L., and D. L. Medin. 1985. The role of theories in conceptual coherence. *Psychological Review* 92:289–316.

Neisser, U., and P. Weene. 1962. Hierarchies in concept attainment. *Journal of Experimental Psychology* 64:640–645.

Norman, G., K. Eva, L. Brooks, and S. Hamstra. 2006. Expertise in medicine and surgery. In *The Cambridge Handbook of Expertise and Expert Performance*, ed. K. A. Ericsson, N. Charness, P. J. Feltovich, and R. R. Hoffman, 339–353. Cambridge: Cambridge University Press.

Norman, G. R., Rosenthal, D., Brooks, L. R., Allen, S. W. and Muzzin, L. J. 1989. The development of expertise in dermatology. *Archives of Dermatology* 125:1063–1068.

Norman, G., M. Young, and L. Brooks. 2007. Non-analytical models of clinical reasoning: The role of experience. *Medical Education* 41:1140–1145.

Nosofsky, R. M. 1988. Exemplar-based accounts of relations between classification, recognition, and typicality. *Journal of Experimental Psychology: Learning, Memory, and Cognition* 14:700–708.

Nosofsky, R. M. 1992. Exemplar-based approach to relating categorization, identification, and recognition. In *Multidimensional Models of Perception and Cognition*, ed. F. G. Ashby, 363–393. Hillsdale, NJ: Lawrence Erlbaum.

Nosofsky, R. M. 2000. Exemplar representation without generalization? Comment on Smith and Minda's (2000) "Thirty categorization results in search of a model." *Journal of Experimental Psychology: Learning, Memory, and Cognition* 26:1735–1743.

Nosofsky, R. M., T. J. Palmeri, and S. C. McKinley. 1994. Rule-plus-exception model of classification learning. *Psychological Review* 101:266–300.

Nosofsky, R. M., and S. R. Zaki. 2002. Exemplar and prototype models revisited: Response strategies, selective attention, and stimulus generalization. *Journal of Experimental Psychology: Learning, Memory, and Cognition* 285:924–940.

Osherson, D. N., E. E. Smith, O. Wilkie, A. Lopez, and E. Shafir. 1990. Category-based induction. *Psychological Review* 97:185–200.

Pinker, S., and A. Prince. 1999. The nature of human concepts: Evidence from an unusual source. In *Language, Logic, and Concepts*, ed. R. Jackendoff, P. Bloom, and K. Wynn, 221–261. Cambridge, MA: MIT Press.

Posner, M. I., and S. W. Keele. 1968. On the genesis of abstract ideas. *Journal of Experimental Psychology* 77:353–363.

Posner, M. I., and S. W. Keele. 1970. Retention of abstract ideas. *Journal of Experimental Psychology* 83:304–308.

Prasada, S., and E. M. Dillingham. 2006. Principled and statistical connections in common sense conception. *Cognition* 99:73–112.

Prinz, J. J. 2002. *Furnishing the Mind: Concepts and Their Perceptual Basis*. Cambridge, MA: MIT Press.

Proffitt, J. B., J. D. Coley, and D. L. Medin. 2000. Expertise and category-based induction. *Journal of Experimental Psychology: Learning, Memory, and Cognition* 26:811–828.

Rehder, B. 2003. Categorization as causal reasoning. *Cognitive Science* 27:709–748.

Rips, L. J. 1975. Inductive judgments about natural categories. *Journal of Verbal Learning and Verbal Behavior* 14:665–681.

Rips, L. J. 1989. Similarity, typicality, and categorization. In *Similarity and Analogical Reasoning*, ed. S. Vosniadou and A. Ortony, 21–59. Cambridge: Cambridge University Press.

Rips, L. J., E. J. Shoben, and E. E. Smith. 1973. Semantic distance and the verification of semantic relations. *Journal of Verbal Learning and Verbal Behavior* 12:1–20.

Rosch, E., and C. Mervis. 1975. Family resemblances: Studies in the internal structure of categories. *Cognitive Psychology* 7:573–604.

Ruts, W., G. Storms, and J. Hampton. 2004. Linear separability in superordinate natural language concepts. *Memory & Cognition* 32:83–95.

Shepard, R. N., C. I. Hovland, and H. M. Jenkins. 1961. Learning and memorization of classifications. *Psychological Monographs* 75:1–42.

Sloman, S. A. 1993. Feature-based induction. *Cognitive Psychology* 25:231–280.

Sloman, S. A. 2005. *Causal Models: How People Think about the World and Its Alternatives*. New York: Oxford University Press.

Sloman, S. A., and D. Lagnado. 2005. The problem of induction. In *The Cambridge Handbook of Thinking and Reasoning*, ed. K. Holyoak and R. Morrison, 95–116. New York: Cambridge University Press.

Smith, E. E., D. Osherson, L. Rips, and M. T. Keane. 1988. Combining prototypes: A selective modification model. *Cognitive Science* 12:485–527.

Smith, J. D. 2002. Exemplar theory's predicted typicality gradient can be tested and disconfirmed. *Psychological Science* 13:437–442.

Smith, J. D., and J. P. Minda. 1998. Prototypes in the mist: The early epochs of category learning. *Journal of Experimental Psychology: Learning, Memory, and Cognition* 24:1411–1436.

Smith, J. D., and J. P. Minda. 2000. Thirty categorization results in search of a model. *Journal of Experimental Psychology: Learning, Memory, and Cognition* 26:3–27.

Storms, G. 2004. Exemplar models in the study of natural language concepts. *Psychology of Learning and Motivation* 42:1–40.

Storms, G., P. De Boeck, and W. Ruts. 2001. Categorization of novel stimuli in well-known natural concepts: A case study. *Psychonomic Bulletin & Review* 8:377–384.

Spirtes, P., C. Glymour, and R. Scheines. 2000. *Causation, Prediction, and Search*, 2nd ed. Cambridge, MA: MIT Press.

Tenenbaum, J. B., T. L. Griffiths, and S. Niyogi. 2007. Intuitive theories as grammars of causal inference. In *Causal Learning: Psychology, Philosophy, and Computation*, ed. A. Gopnik and L. Schulz, 301–322. New York: Oxford University Press.

Vigo, R. 2006. A note on the complexity of Boolean concepts. *Journal of Mathematical Psychology* 50:501–510.

Zaki, S. R., and R. M. Nosofsky. 2004. False prototype enhancement effects in dot pattern categorization. *Memory & Cognition* 32:390–398.

Zaki, S. R., and R. M. Nosofsky. 2007. A high-distortion enhancement effect in the prototype-learning paradigm: Dramatic effects of category learning during test. *Memory & Cognition* 35:2088–2096.

3 Fuzzy Logic: A Tutorial

Radim Belohlavek and George J. Klir

3.1   What Is Fuzzy Logic and Why Is It Useful?

Fuzzy logic is a subject that is too extensive to be adequately covered in one chapter. Moreover, there is no need to cover the subject exhaustively for prospective readers of this book. Hence, we cover in this tutorial only those aspects of fuzzy logic that are needed for understanding the various discussions involving fuzzy logic throughout this book. The reader should thus be on guard against the wrong perception that there is nothing more to fuzzy logic than what is covered here. Some resources in which additional aspects of fuzzy logic are covered are given in section 3.9.

As mentioned in chapter 1, we use the term *fuzzy logic* in its general, commonsense meaning to refer to the principles and methods of representation and manipulation of knowledge that employ intermediary truth-values. To understand fuzzy logic, it is essential to recall the basic motivation that led to its emergence. This motivation, articulated in various forms in early papers on fuzzy logic by Lotfi Zadeh, can be described briefly as follows. Classical logic is appropriate for a formalization of reasoning that involves bivalent propositions such as "5 is a prime number" or "if x is a positive integer and $y = x + 1$ then y is á positive integer," that is, propositions that may in principle be only true or false. In a similar way, classical sets are appropriate for representing collections (of objects) that have sharp, clear-cut boundaries, such as "the collection of all prime numbers less than 100" or "the collection of all U.S. Senators as of January 1, 2010." For any such collection, an arbitrary given object either is or is not a member of it.

Most propositions that people use to communicate information about the world are not bivalent. The truth of such propositions is a matter of degree, rather than being only true or false. As an example, "the humidity outside is moderate" is a proposition whose truth depends on the actual outside humidity. Since humidity values range from 0% to 100%, the term "moderate" refers to values in some vague sense close to 50%. According to our intuition, the farther the actual outside humidity is from 50% (on both sides), the less true is the proposition "the outside humidity is moderate."

In a comparable bivalent proposition, the linguistic term "moderate" would have to be replaced either by a particular real number, h, referring to h% of humidity, or by a pair of real numbers, h_1 and h_2, referring to a range of humidity values between h_1% and h_2%. Specific examples of such bivalent propositions are: " the outside humidity is 50%" or "the outside humidity is somewhere between 30% and 70%." Observe that an arbitrarily small change in the outside humidity can change the truth-value of any bivalent proposition from false to true and vice versa. For example, the truth of the proposition " the outside humidity is 50%" changes abruptly from *true* to *false* when the outside humidity changes from 50% to (50 ± ε)%, where ε is an arbitrarily small real number. Similarly, the truth of the proposition "the outside humidity is somewhere between 30% and 70%" changes abruptly from *true* to *false* whenever the actual outside humidity changes either from 70% to (70 + ε)% or from 30% to (30 − ε)%, where, again, ε is an arbitrarily small real number. Needless to say, this contradicts our intuition and our commonsense way of using the linguistic term "moderate."

Likewise, most collections of objects to which people refer when communicating information do not have sharp, clear-cut boundaries. The membership of objects in such collections is a matter of degree, rather than a matter of membership versus nonmembership. Similar arguments as those given above may be used to argue that the collection of all *moderate humidity values*, the collection of all *tall men* living in New York City, and the like, do not have sharp boundaries.

Since most propositions about the real world employed in human communication and cognition are not bivalent, classical logic is utterly inadequate to formalize reasoning that involves such propositions. Likewise, since most collections referred to in human communication do not have sharp boundaries, classical sets are grossly inadequate to represent such collections. The main aim of fuzzy logic is to overcome the above-described inadequacies of classical logic and classical sets.

The principal idea employed by fuzzy logic is to allow for a partially ordered scale of truth-values, called also truth degrees, which contains the values representing *false* and *true*, but also some additional, intermediary truth degrees. That is, the set {0,1} of truth-values of classical logic, where 0 and 1 represent *false* and *true*, respectively, is replaced in fuzzy logic by a partially ordered scale of truth degrees with the smallest degree being 0 and the largest one being 1. An important example of such scale is the interval

[0,1] of real numbers. A degree from a given scale (e.g., the number 0.9 from [0,1]) that is assigned to a proposition is interpreted as the degree to which the proposition is considered true.

In a similar spirit, scales of truth degrees are used in fuzzy sets to represent degrees to which a given object is a member of a collection with a nonsharp boundary. For example, if 0.8 and 0.9 represent degrees to which two men, say John and Paul, are members of the collection of *tall men*, respectively, it indicates that both are considered relatively tall and that Paul is a little bit taller than John.

Fuzzy logic thus uses scales of truth-values to capture the meaning of propositions and collections that involve linguistic terms such as *warm*, *tall*, *moderate*, and the like. To capture the meaning of such terms, referred to as *vague terms*, in an appropriate way is quite an intricate issue. This brings up an important question of whether the approach of fuzzy logic, based on scales of truth-values, is appropriate. Such a complex question has many facets, ranging from philosophy and mathematics to psychology and cognitive science. Thus far, this question has not been decisively answered. Nevertheless, the use of fuzzy logic is supported by at least the following three arguments. First, fuzzy logic is rooted in the intuitively appealing idea that the truths of propositions used by humans are a matter of degree. An important consequence is that the basic principles and concepts of fuzzy logic are easily understood. Second, fuzzy logic has led to many successful applications, including many commercial products, in which the crucial part relies on representing and dealing with statements in natural language that involve vague terms. Third, fuzzy logic is a proper generalization of classical logic, follows an agenda similar to that of classical logic, and has already been highly developed. An important consequence is that fuzzy logic extends the rich realm of applications of classical logic to applications in which the bivalent character of classical logic is a limiting factor.

The shift brought about by replacing the truth-values, *false* and *true*, of classical logic with a scale of truth degrees has far-reaching consequences. While going from two truth-values to a scale of truth degrees seems an obvious choice, the development of appropriate formal methods generalizing those of classical logic, which is the principal aim of fuzzy logic, is quite challenging.

As mentioned earlier, we use the term *fuzzy logic* in its commonsense meaning. Two other meanings, referred to as *fuzzy logic in the narrow sense* and *fuzzy logic in the broad sense,* are the subjects of sections 3.6 and 3.7, respectively.

3.2   Classical Sets versus Fuzzy Sets

The concept of a classical set is fundamental to virtually all branches of mathematics, pure as well as applied. Intuitively, a set is any collection of definite and distinct objects that is conceived as a whole. Objects that are included in a set are usually called its *members.*

Classical sets satisfy two basic requirements. First, members of each set are distinguishable from one another, and second, for any given object it is specified whether the object is, or is not, a member of the set. Fuzzy sets, which were introduced by Zadeh (1965), differ from classical sets by rejecting the second requirement. Contrary to classical sets, fuzzy sets do not require sharp boundaries that separate their members from other objects. The membership of any object in a given fuzzy set is not a matter of affirmation or denial, as is required for classical sets, but a matter of degree.

In each particular application of set theory (classical or fuzzy), the set of all objects that are relevant to the application is called a *universal set* (or a *universe*). Regardless of whether we work with classical sets or fuzzy sets, the relevant universal set is always a classical set.

Fuzzy sets are defined on any given universal set as functions that are analogous to characteristic functions of classical sets. Each of these functions assigns to each object in the universal set a truth degree. If the truth degrees are real numbers in the unit interval [0,1], the defined fuzzy set is called a *standard fuzzy set*. Formally, a standard fuzzy set A in universe U is a function

$$A: U \to [0,1]$$

that assigns to each element x of U a number $A(x)$ from [0,1]. This number is called a degree (or grade) of membership of x in A and it is viewed as the degree (or grade) to which x is considered a member of the collection represented by fuzzy set A. That is, $A(x)$ is interpreted as the truth degree of proposition "x is a member of A."

In the literature on fuzzy sets, some authors distinguish between the notion of a fuzzy set and the corresponding function that assigns degrees of membership to elements of the universal set. They call the function a *membership function* of the fuzzy set. In doing so, they use two different symbols—one, such as A, for the fuzzy set, and another, usually μ_A, for the membership function. We do not make such an inessential distinction in this book and use the above-described notation in which a fuzzy set is defined as a function from the universal set to the set of truth degrees. Such notation is simpler and, by and large, more common in the current literature on fuzzy sets.

Recall that a characteristic function of a classical set in the universal set U is any function

$$A: U \rightarrow \{0,1\}$$

that assigns to each element x of U a truth-value 0 (if x is not a member of the set) or 1 (if x is a member of the set). That is, the concept of a fuzzy set differs from the concept of a characteristic function of a classical set only in that the set $\{0,1\}$ of truth-values is replaced by a general scale of truth degrees such as $[0,1]$.

Any special fuzzy set $A: U \rightarrow [0,1]$ for which $A(x) = 0$ or $A(x) = 1$ for each x from U is called a *crisp fuzzy set* or simply a *crisp set*. Clearly, every classical set can be represented by a crisp fuzzy set. Namely, a classical set C that is a subset of U is uniquely represented by a fuzzy set A_C in U such that $A_C(x) = 0$ if x is not a member of C and $A_C(x) = 1$ if x is a member of C. Conversely, every crisp fuzzy set in U represents a classical set that is a subset of U. This correspondence allows us to view classical sets as particular fuzzy sets and to identify classical sets with crisp sets.

Contrary to symbolic role of numbers 0 and 1 in characteristic functions of classical sets (as false and true, respectively), membership degrees assigned to objects by standard fuzzy sets have a numerical significance. For any object x in U, clearly, $A(x)$ defines the numerical degree of membership of x in fuzzy set A. In classical sets, 0 and 1 are considered as symbols; in fuzzy sets, 0 and 1, as well as other truth degrees, are viewed as numbers. An important consequence of this change is that fuzzy sets (including crisp sets) can be manipulated in various numeric ways that have no counterparts in classical set theory.

Unless stated otherwise, classical sets are viewed in this book as crisp fuzzy sets. We adopt the usual notation, according to which classical sets as well as fuzzy sets (including crisp sets) are denoted by uppercase letters. The underlying universal set is usually denoted by symbol U and its elements are denoted by lowercase letters.

A reasonable fuzzy set, *M*, representing the linguistic term *moderate humidity* (discussed in section 3.1) is defined by the graph in figure 3.1a. It is a standard fuzzy set that is defined on the interval [0, 100] of real numbers (i.e., *U* = [0,100]). A comparable classical set that represents the same linguistic term is defined in figure 3.1b by the graph of its characteristic function, which may also be viewed as a special (crisp) fuzzy set *M*. Clearly, this set is the interval [30, 70] of real numbers.

The problem of selecting (or constructing) an appropriate fuzzy set in a given application context for some purpose is discussed in chapter 6. Observe that selecting an appropriate classical set for representing a linguistic term depends equally on the purpose of using the term in a given application context. For example, the meaning of linguistic terms *normal temperature* or *high temperature*, regardless whether they are represented by classical sets or fuzzy sets, is very different in each of the following cases: (a) the terms refer to the body temperature of a patient and are employed for the purpose of medical diagnosis; (b) they refer to air temperature at some place on Earth, say in Antarctica, and are used for studying climate change; or (c) they refer to water temperature in a nuclear reactor and are used for the purpose of monitoring or control.

3.3   Basic Concepts of Fuzzy Sets

Given a fuzzy set *A* defined on a universal set *U*, the set of all elements of *U* for which $A(x) > 0$ is called a *support* of *A*, and the set of those for which $A(x) = 1$ is called a *core* of *A*. Fuzzy sets whose cores are not empty are called *normal* fuzzy sets; all other fuzzy sets are called *subnormal*.

Among the most important concepts associated with fuzzy sets is the concept of a *level cut* (also called an α-*cut*). Given a fuzzy set *A* defined on universal set *U* and any number α in the interval [0,1], the level cut at level α (or α-cut) of *A*, denoted by A_α, is a classical set of all objects *x* of *U* for which $A(x) \geq \alpha$. This can formally be written as

$$A_\alpha = \{x \in U : A(x) \geq \alpha\}, \tag{3.1}$$

where the standard symbol $x \in U$ means that a given object *x* is a member of universal set *U* (a classical set) and the colon denotes here (and throughout this book) the phrase *such that*. It follows immediately from this definition that for any fuzzy set *A* and any two numbers α and β in [0,1] such that

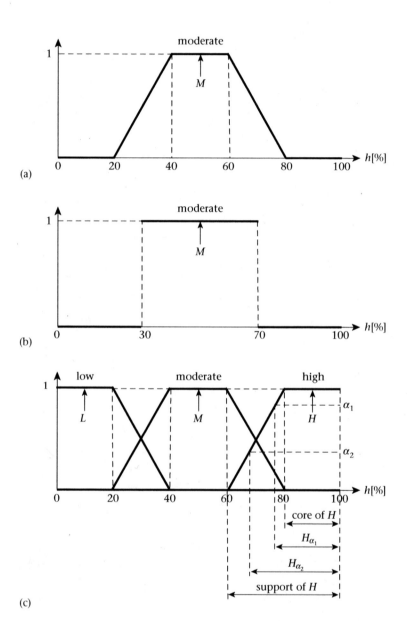

Figure 3.1
Illustrations of various examples discussed throughout this chapter.

$\alpha > \beta$, the set inclusion $A_\alpha \subseteq A_\beta$ always holds. That is, all distinct level cuts of any fuzzy set A form a family,

$$\mathbf{A} = \{A_\alpha : \alpha \in [0,1]\},$$

of nested classical sets. This means that for any sequence of numbers $\alpha_1 > \alpha_2 > \alpha_3 > \cdots$ in $[0,1]$, $A_{\alpha_1} \subseteq A_{\alpha_2} \subseteq A_{\alpha_3} \subseteq \cdots$. It has been mathematically established (Klir and Yuan 1995) that this family is an alternative representation of fuzzy set A.

Given the level-cut representation of fuzzy set A, its membership-function representation is uniquely determined for all $x \in U$ by the formula

$$A(x) = \sup\{\alpha : \alpha \in [0,1], x \in A_\alpha\}, \tag{3.2}$$

where "sup" denotes supremum (or maximum, if it exists).

The significance of the level-cut representation of fuzzy sets is that it connects fuzzy sets with classical sets. Whereas each classical set is a collection of objects that are conceived as a whole, each fuzzy set is a collection (potentially infinite) of nested classical sets that are also conceived as a whole. It is suggestive to compare this characterization of fuzzy sets as wholes of organized (nested) classical sets with the characterization of concepts in the classical book on holism by Smuts (1926, 17):

We have to return to the fluidity and plasticity of nature and experience in order to find the concepts of reality. When we do this we find that round every luminous point in experience there is a gradual shading off into haziness and obscurity. A "concept" is not merely its clear luminous centre, but embraces a surrounding sphere of meaning or influence of smaller or larger dimensions, in which the luminosity tails off and grows fainter until it disappears. The hard and abrupt contours of our ordinary conceptual system do not apply to reality and make reality inexplicable.

Examples of two level cuts, H_{α_1} and H_{α_2}, are shown in figure 3.1c for the fuzzy set representing high humidity (fuzzy set H). Observe that $\alpha_2 \leq \alpha_1$ and $H_{\alpha_1} \subset H_{\alpha_2}$. Also illustrated in this figure are the concepts of support and core for fuzzy set H.

Given two fuzzy sets, A and B, that are defined on the same universal set U, A is said to be a subset of B if and only if $A(x) \leq B(x)$ for all $x \in U$. If A is a subset of B, we write $A \subseteq B$. The set of all standard fuzzy subsets of U (sometimes called a *fuzzy power set*) is denoted by $[0,1]^U$, and the set of all crisp subsets of U is denoted by $\{0,1\}^U$.

The number of elements in set A defined on a finite universal set is called the *cardinality* of A. When A is a fuzzy set defined on a finite universal set U, its cardinality, $|A|$, is defined by the formula

$$|A| = \sum_{x \in U} A(x). \tag{3.3}$$

Important special fuzzy sets are *fuzzy intervals*. These are fuzzy sets defined on the set of real numbers $\mathbf{R}$ (i.e., $U = \mathbf{R}$) whose level cuts are classical intervals of real numbers for all levels in $(0,1]$. The concept of a fuzzy interval generalizes the concept of an interval of real numbers. It is convenient to represent any fuzzy interval E (extended classical interval of real numbers) for all $x \in \mathbf{R}$ by the following formula, often referred to as the *canonical representation* of fuzzy intervals:

$$E(x) = \begin{cases} f_E(x) & \text{when } x \in [a,b) \\ 1 & \text{when } x \in [b,c] \\ g_E(x) & \text{when } x \in (c,d] \\ 0 & \text{otherwise} \end{cases} \tag{3.4}$$

Symbols a, b, c, d in this formula denote real numbers such that $a \leq b \leq c \leq d$. Symbol f_E denotes usually a continuous and strictly increasing function ranging from 0 to 1, while symbol g_E denotes a continuous and strictly decreasing function ranging from 1 to 0. More general functions f_E and g_E are possible, but we do not consider them here. Special fuzzy intervals for which $b = c$ are usually called *fuzzy numbers*. The level-cut representation of E is expressed for all $\alpha \in [0,1]$ by the equation

$$E_\alpha = \left[f_E^{-1}(\alpha), g_E^{-1}(\alpha) \right], \tag{3.5}$$

where f_E^{-1} and g_E^{-1} are inverse functions of f_E and g_E, respectively. If f_E and g_E are linear functions, then $f_E(x) = (x - a)/(b - a)$ and $g_E(x) = (d - x)/(d - c)$. Fuzzy intervals of this kind, referred to as *trapezoidal fuzzy intervals*, are frequently used in applications of fuzzy set theory. Their advantage is that each of them is fully represented by the four real numbers a, b, c, d of its canonical representation. Level cuts of any trapezoidal fuzzy interval E are expressed for all $\alpha \in (0,1]$ by the convenient formula

$$E_\alpha = [a + (b-a)\alpha, d - (d-c)\alpha]. \tag{3.6}$$

All three fuzzy sets in figure 3.1c are examples of trapezoidal fuzzy intervals. The middle one, which represents moderate humidity, is defined by the following four numbers: $a = 20$, $b = 40$, $c = 60$, and $d = 80$.

3.4   Operations on Fuzzy Sets

Operations on fuzzy sets possess considerably greater variety than those on classical sets. In fact, many operations on fuzzy sets have no counterpart in classical set theory. The following five basic types of operations on fuzzy sets are generally recognized:

1. modifiers of fuzzy sets;

2. complements of fuzzy sets;

3. intersections of two or more fuzzy sets;

4. unions of two or more fuzzy sets; and

5. averaging operations of two or more fuzzy sets.

Modifiers and complements operate on one fuzzy set. Intersections and unions are defined on two sets, but their application can be extended to any number of fuzzy sets via their property of associativity. The averaging operations are not associative and must be defined, in general, for n fuzzy sets ($n \geq 2$). In addition to these five types of operations, fuzzy intervals are also subject to arithmetic operations of addition, subtraction, multiplication, and division.

As can be seen from this overall characterization of operations on fuzzy sets, this subject is extensive. It is a subject that has been investigated by many researchers and is now highly developed. Given the large scope of the subject, we are able to present in this tutorial only a brief characterization of each of the introduced types of operations. However, we provide the reader with references for further study.

All of these operations on fuzzy sets are induced by associated operations on the unit interval [0,1] in the following way. An n-ary operation on [0,1], say operation s, extends to an n-ary operation on fuzzy sets (which, for simplicity, we denote also by s) by assigning to fuzzy sets $A_1, A_2, \ldots, A_n$ a fuzzy set $s(A_1, A_2, \ldots, A_n)$ whose membership function is defined for all $x \in U$ by

$$\left[s(A_1, A_2, \ldots, A_n) \right](x) = s\left(A_1(x), A_2(x), \ldots, A_n(x) \right). \qquad (3.7)$$

We say that an operation on fuzzy sets defined in this way is based on the associated operation on [0,1].

3.4.1   Modifiers

Modifiers are unary operations whore primary purpose is to modify fuzzy sets to account for linguistic hedges. For example, if a fuzzy set represents, in the context of a given application, the concept of a *high temperature*, a suitable modifier would modify the fuzzy set to represent the concept of a *very high temperature*.

In general, each modifier, *m*, is based on a function of the form *m*: [0,1] → [0,1] that is order preserving. This means that, for all *a*, *b* ∈ [0,1], if *a* ≤ *b* then *m*(*a*) ≤ *m*(*b*). Among the great variety of possible modifiers, the most common modifiers either increase or decrease all values of a given membership function. A convenient class of functions, m_λ, that qualifies for representing both increasing and decreasing modifiers is defined for all *a* ∈ [0,1] by the simple formula

$$m_\lambda(a) = a^\lambda, \tag{3.8}$$

where λ denotes a parameter whose values range over the set (0, ∞) of real numbers. Each value of λ defines one particular modifier in this class, but the modifier for λ = 1 is degenerate and of no use since $m_1(a) = a$ for all *a* ∈ [0,1]. Each of the remaining values determines how strongly and in which way m_λ modifies each given membership function. Since *a* ∈ [0,1], two significant classes of modifiers m_λ can be distinguished:

1. For any value λ ∈ (0,1), $m_\lambda(a) > a$, so m_λ increases its argument *a*. They are thus suitable for representing linguistic hedges such as *fairly, moderately, somewhat*, and the like. The smaller the value of λ, the stronger the modifier.

2. For any value λ ∈ (1,∞), $m_\lambda(a) < a$, so m_λ decreases its argument *a*. They are thus suitable for representing linguistic hedges such as *very, highly, extremely*, and the like. The greater the value of λ, the stronger the modifier.

In addition to these two classes of modifiers, which are the simplest and most common, numerous other classes of modifiers have been introduced in the literature. Some of these involve more than one parameter. Which modifier is appropriate in each application context is basically an experimental issue. Given any data regarding the meaning of a linguistic hedge in a given context, we need to choose a class of modifiers that qualitatively conforms to the data and then determine a single modifier in this class that best fits the data.

3.4.2 Complements
Contrary to the unique operation of complement in classical set theory, the operation of complement in fuzzy set theory is not unique. In general,

each complement, c, is based on a function of the form c: $[0,1] \rightarrow [0,1]$ that is order reversing (i.e., for all a, $b \in [0,1]$, if $a \leq b$ then $c(a) \geq c(b)$) with $c(0) = 1$ and $c(1) = 0$. A complement $c(A)$ of fuzzy set A that is based on function c is defined for all $x \in U$ by the equation

$$[c(A)](x) = c(A(x)). \tag{3.9}$$

It is often desirable, although not necessary, to require also that $c(c(a)) = a$ for all $a \in [0,1]$, which means that complementing fuzzy set A twice results in A. That is, $c[c(A)(x)](x) = A(x)$ for all $x \in U$. Complements that satisfy this requirement are called *involutive complements*. A practical class of involutive complements, c_λ, is defined for all $a \in [0,1]$ by the formula

$$c_\lambda(a) = \left(1 - a^\lambda\right)^{\frac{1}{\lambda}}, \tag{3.10}$$

where λ denotes a parameter whose values range over the set $(0, \infty)$ of real numbers. Each value of λ defines one particular complement in this class. When $\lambda = 1$, the complement is usually referred to as the *standard complement*. The standard complement is thus defined for all $x \in U$ by

$$[c(A)](x) = 1 - A(x). \tag{3.11}$$

Various other classes of complements have been suggested in the literature. As with modifiers, the choice of a particular way of complementing fuzzy sets in each given application context is an experimental issue.

3.4.3   Intersections and Unions

Intersections and unions of fuzzy sets, denoted in this book by i and u respectively, are generalizations of the operations of intersection and union in classical set theory. Neither of these generalizations is unique. As in classical set theory, intersections and unions of fuzzy sets are defined as associative operations on two sets and can thus be extended to any number of sets. They are based on functions i: $[0,1] \times [0,1] \rightarrow [0,1]$ and u: $[0,1] \times [0,1] \rightarrow [0,1]$ that, in addition to associativity, are also required to be monotone nondecreasing in both arguments and commutative. The only distinction between them is that function i is required to collapse to the classical set intersection whereas function u is required to collapse to the classical set union within the restricted domain of crisp sets. All these requirements are formally expressed for all numbers a, b, $d \in [0,1]$ as follows:

Associativity—$i[a, i(b, d)] = i[i(a, b), d]$ and $u[a, u(b, d)] = u[u(a, b), d]$.

Monotonicity—$b \leq d$ implies $i(a, b) \leq i(a, d)$ and $u(a, b) \leq u(a, d)$.

Commutativity—$i(a, b) = i(b, a)$ and $u(a, b) = u(b, a)$.

Boundary conditions—$i(a, 1) = a$ and $u(a, 0) = a$.

The boundary conditions are needed to guarantee that, together with monotonicity and commutativity, $i(0, 0) = i(0, 1) = i(1, 0) = 0$, $i(1, 1) = 1$, $u(0, 0) = 0$, and $u(0, 1) = u(1, 0) = u(1, 1) = 1$, which means that i collapses to classical intersection and u collapses to classical union within the restricted domain of crisp sets.

For each pair of functions i and u, the intersection and union of fuzzy sets A and B are, respectively, fuzzy sets $i(A,B)$ and $u(A,B)$ defined for all $x \in U$ by the equations

$$[i(A,B)](x) = i(A(x), B(x)), \tag{3.12}$$

$$[u(A,B)](x) = u(A(x), B(x)). \tag{3.13}$$

If i and u are clearly understood from a given context, $i(A,B)$ and $u(A,B)$ may also be denoted by $A \cap B$ and $A \cup B$, resembling thus the operations of intersection and union on classical sets. Functions that satisfy the requirements on i are known in the literature as *triangular norms* (or *t-norms*), and functions that satisfy the requirements on u are known as *triangular conorms* (or *t-conorms*). That is, the class of t-norms captures all meaningful intersections of fuzzy sets, and the class of t-conorms captures all meaningful unions of fuzzy sets. These classes of functions have been extensively studied (Klement, Mesiar, and Pap 2000; Klir and Yuan 1995).

It is known that functions i and u are bounded by the inequalities

$$i_{\min}(a,b) \leq i(a,b) \leq \min(a,b), \tag{3.14}$$

$$\max(a,b) \leq u(a,b) \leq u_{\max}(a,b), \tag{3.15}$$

where

$$i_{\min}(a,b) = \begin{cases} \min(a,b) & \text{when } \max(a,b) = 1 \\ 0 & \text{otherwise,} \end{cases} \tag{3.16}$$

$$u_{\max}(a,b) = \begin{cases} \max(a,b) & \text{when } \min(a,b) = 0 \\ 1 & \text{otherwise.} \end{cases} \tag{3.17}$$

Operations min and max are usually called *standard operations*, while $i_{\min}$ and $u_{\max}$ are often called *drastic operations*.

Numerous classes of functions are now available that fully capture the ranges between standard and drastic operations described by the above inequalities. Examples are classes i_λ and u_λ that are defined for all $a, b \in [0, 1]$ by the formulas

$$i_\lambda(a,b) = 1 - \min\left\{1, [(1-a)^\lambda + (1-b)^\lambda]^{\frac{1}{\lambda}}\right\}, \qquad (3.18)$$

$$u_\lambda(a,b) = \min\left\{1, (a^\lambda + b^\lambda)^{\frac{1}{\lambda}}\right\}, \qquad (3.19)$$

where $\lambda \in (0, \infty)$ is a parameter whose values specify individual intersections or unions in these classes. The drastic operations are obtained in the limit for $\lambda \to 0$, while the standard operations are obtained in the limit for $\lambda \to \infty$ (Klir and Yuan 1995). Determining the most fitting intersection or union from these classes in each application context is again an experimental issue.

3.4.4 Averaging Operations

For two or more sets, intersections and unions produce one set. This means that they are special *aggregation operations*. Whereas classical sets can be aggregated only by these two operations and their combinations with the complement operation, fuzzy sets can also be averaging in many different ways. Since *averaging operations* are not associative, they must be defined as functions of n arguments for any $n \geq 2$. That is, averaging operations for fuzzy sets, denoted by h, are based on functions of the form $h: [0,1]^n \to [0,1]$. To qualify as averaging operations, these functions are required to be order preserving in all arguments, continuous, idempotent (i.e., $h(a, a,..., a) = a$ for all $a \in [0,1]$), and usually symmetric. It is well known (Klir and Yuan 1995), and significant, that

$$\min(a_1, a_2,...,a_n) \leq h(a_1, a_2,...,a_n) \leq \max(a_1, a_2,...,a_n) \qquad (3.20)$$

for any n-tuple $(a_1, a_2, ..., a_n) \in [0,1]^n$. This means that averaging operations fill the gap between the standard intersection (minimum operation) and the standard union (maximum operation).

One class of averaging operations, h_λ, where $\lambda \in (-\infty, \infty)$ is a parameter by which individual operations in this class are distinguished, is defined for all n-tuples $(a_1, a_2, ..., a_n)$ of the Cartesian product $[0,1]^n$ and for all $\lambda \neq 0$ by the formula

$$h_\lambda(a_1, a_2,...,a_n) = \left(\frac{a_1^\lambda + a_2^\lambda + \cdots + a_n^\lambda}{n}\right)^{\frac{1}{\lambda}}. \qquad (3.21)$$

For $\lambda = 1$, h_λ is clearly the arithmetic average. For $h_\lambda \to 0$, h_λ converges to the geometric average. For $\lambda \to -\infty$ and $\lambda \to \infty$, it converges to the minimum and maximum operations, respectively (Klir and Yuan 1995).

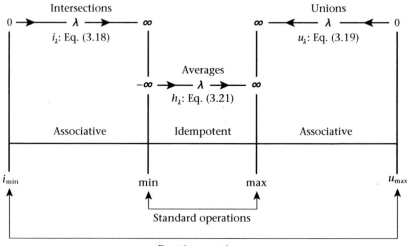

Figure 3.2
Ranges of classes of intersections, unions, and averages of fuzzy sets that are defined by equations (3.18), (3.19), and (3.21), respectively.

Other classes of averaging operations are now available, some of which are not symmetric. The latter employ weighting factors to express the relative importance of the individual fuzzy sets involved. For example, the function

$$h(a_1, a_2, ..., a_n, w_1, w_2, ..., w_n) = \sum_{i=1}^{n} w_i a_i, \qquad (3.22)$$

where the weighting factors w_i take usually values in [0,1] and $\sum_{i=1}^{n} w_i = 1$, expresses for each choice of values w_i the corresponding weighted average of values a_i ($i = 1, 2, ..., n$). Again, the choice of values w_i is an experimental issue.

Figure 3.2 illustrates ranges of the three parameterized classes of aggregation operations—intersections, unions, and averages—which are defined, respectively, by equations (3.18), (3.19), and (3.21). These operations belong to a broader class of aggregation operations (Grabisch et al. 2009). All recognized aggregation operations in this broader class are potentially useful for aggregating fuzzy sets.

3.4.5 Arithmetic Operations on Fuzzy Intervals

Any of the operations on fuzzy sets discussed in previous sections are applicable to fuzzy intervals as well. However, it is also meaningful to apply arithmetic operations of addition, subtraction, multiplication, and division to fuzzy intervals. See, for example, the books by Kaufmann and Gupta (1985) and Mareš (1994).

Employing the level-cut representation, arithmetic operations on fuzzy intervals are defined in terms of the well-established arithmetic operations on closed intervals of real numbers (Neumaier 1990; Moore, Kearfott, and Cloud 2009). However, there is a fundamental difference between arithmetic on real numbers and arithmetic on crisp or fuzzy intervals. Arithmetic operations on real numbers follow unique rules that are independent of what these numbers represent. On the contrary, arithmetic operations on intervals, regardless whether they are crisp or fuzzy, are dependent on what these intervals represent. As a consequence, they have to take into account any constraints that exist among the intervals involved (Klir and Pan 1998).

Fuzzy intervals and arithmetic operations on fuzzy intervals have been used to fuzzify various areas of mathematics that deal with real numbers.

3.4.6 Combinations of Complements, Intersections, and Unions

The fact that the primitive operations of complementation, intersection, and union are not unique in fuzzy set theory means that the generic term *fuzzy set theory* refers actually to a family of theories. These theories are distinguished from one another by their mathematical structure, which is induced by the three basic operations employed in each theory. As a consequence of the unsharp boundaries of fuzzy sets, some properties of classical set theory are inevitably violated in each of these fuzzy theories. However, it is important to realize that different theories may violate different properties. The proper choice of the three basic operations is thus particularly critical in some applications of fuzzy set theory, in which some properties of classical set theory are more important than others. In fact, various properties of classical set theory can be preserved in fuzzy set theory by an appropriate choice of the three basic operations. Choosing, for example, the standard operations, which are based on complement $c(a) = 1 - a$, t-norm $i(a,b) = \min(a,b)$, and t-conorm $u(a,b) = \max(a,b)$, some properties of the classical set theory are preserved, but the law of excluded middle and the law of contradiction are violated. If these laws are essential in some application, we can preserve them by choosing, for example, operations based on complement $c(a) = 1 - a$, t-norm $i(a,b) = \max(0, a + b - 1)$, and t-conorm $u(a,b) = \min(1, a + b)$. However, any chosen operations always violate some properties of classical sets. In this particular example, they violate distributivity and idempotence of classical intersections and unions.

3.5   Fuzzy Relations

When fuzzy sets are defined on universal sets that are Cartesian products of two or more sets, we refer to them as *fuzzy relations*. Individual sets in the Cartesian product of a fuzzy relation are called *domains* of the relation. When *n*-sets are involved in the Cartesian product, we call the relation *n*-ary (*n* is called the *arity* of the fuzzy relation). For example, a binary (2-ary) fuzzy relation between sets X and Y (or a fuzzy relation on $X \times Y$) is a function $R: X \times Y \rightarrow [0,1]$. That is, R is basically a fuzzy set in the universe $U = X \times Y$. This means that R is a function assigning to every pair (x,y) from $X \times Y$ (consisting of an element x from X and an element y from Y) a number $R(x,y)$ from [0,1], which is interpreted as the degree to which x is related to y. Note that fuzzy sets may be viewed as degenerate, 1-ary relations.

All concepts and operations applicable to fuzzy sets are applicable to fuzzy relations as well. However, fuzzy relations involve additional concepts and operations. The most important among the additional operations are projections, cylindric extensions, compositions, joins, and inverses.

3.5.1   Projections and Cylindric Extensions

Projections and cylindric extensions are applicable to any *n*-ary fuzzy relations ($n \geq 2$). However, for the sake of simplicity, we introduce them here in terms of 3-ary fuzzy relations R defined on the universal set $U = X \times Y \times Z$ with finite sets X, Y, and Z.

A *projection* of R is an operation that converts R into a fuzzy relation of a lower arity, which in this case is either a 2-ary or 1-ary (degenerate) relation. In each projection, some of the sets X, Y, and Z are suppressed (not recognized) and for the remaining sets, the projection is consistent with R in the sense that each level cut of the projection is a projection of the level cut of R in the sense of classical set theory. Formally, the three 2-ary projections of R on $X \times Y$, $X \times Z$, and $Y \times Z$, denoted by R_{XY}, R_{XZ}, and R_{YZ}, are defined for all $x \in X$, $y \in Y$, $z \in Z$ by the following formulas:

$$R_{XY}(x,y) = \max_{z \in Z} R(x,y,z),$$
$$R_{XZ}(x,z) = \max_{y \in Y} R(x,y,z),$$
$$R_{YZ}(y,z) = \max_{x \in X} R(x,y,z).$$

Each of these 2-ary projections can further be projected into one of the sets by similar formulas:

$$R_X(x) = \max_{y \in Y} R_{XY}(x,y)$$
$$= \max_{z \in Z} R_{XZ}(x,z),$$
$$R_Y(y) = \max_{x \in X} R_{XY}(x,y)$$
$$= \max_{z \in Z} R_{YZ}(y,z),$$
$$R_Z(z) = \max_{x \in X} R_{XZ}(x,z)$$
$$= \max_{y \in Y} R_{YZ}(y,z).$$

These projections are actually fuzzy sets, which can be viewed as degenerate relations.

Any fuzzy relation on $X \times Y \times Z$ that is consistent with a given projection is called an *extension* of the projection. The largest among them is called a *cylindric extension*. Let R_{EXY} and R_{EX} denote the cylindric extensions of projections R_{XY} and R_X, respectively. Then, R_{EXY} and R_{EX} are given for all triples $(x, y, z) \in X \times Y \times Z$ by the formulas

$$R_{EXY}(x, y, z) = R_{XY}(x, y),$$

$$R_{EX}(x, y, z) = R_X(x).$$

Cylindric extensions of the other 2-ary and 1-ary projections are defined in a similar way.

Given any set of projections of a given fuzzy relation R, the standard intersection of their cylindric extensions (expressed by the minimum operator) is called a *cylindric closure* of the projections. Regardless of the given projections of R, it is guaranteed that their cylindric closure contains R.

3.5.2   Compositions, Joins, and Inverses

Consider two binary fuzzy relations P and Q that are defined on $X \times Y$ and $Y \times Z$, respectively. Any such relations, which are connected via the common set Y, can be composed to yield a relation on $X \times Z$. The standard composition of these relations, which is denoted by $P \circ Q$, produces a relation R on $X \times Z$ defined by the formula

$$R(x,z) = [P \circ Q](x,z) = \max_{y \in Y} \min\{P(x,y), Q\{y,z)\} \qquad (3.23)$$

for all pairs $(x, z) \in X \times Z$. Other definitions of the composition of fuzzy relations, in which the min and max operations are replaced with other t-norms and t-conorms, respectively, are possible and useful in some applications. All these compositions are associative.

A similar operation on two connected binary relations, which differs from composition in that it yields a 3-ary relation instead of a binary one, is known as the relational join. For the same fuzzy relations P and Q, their *standard relational join*, denoted by $P * Q$, is a 3-ary relation on $X \times Y \times Z$ defined by the formula

$$R(x,y,z) = [P*Q](x,y,z) = \min\{P(x,y), Q(y,z)\} \tag{3.24}$$

for all triples $(x, y, z) \in X \times Y \times Z$. Again, the min operation in this definition may be replaced with another t-norm.

The inverse of a binary relation R on $X \times Y$, denoted by R^{-1}, is a binary relation on $Y \times X$ such that $R^{-1}(y,x) = R(x,y)$ for all pairs $(y, x) \in Y \times X$. Clearly, $(R^{-1})^{-1} = R$.

3.5.3 Binary Relations on a Single Set

Binary fuzzy relations in which elements of a set X are related to other elements of the same set have special significance and utility. Formally, these relations are 2-ary relations between X and X. That is, they are functions $R: X \times X \to [0,1]$. Such relations allow us to represent rigorously approximate equivalence, similarity, compatibility, or preference. Depending on the properties of R, the degree $R(x,y)$ may be interpreted as the degree to which x is equivalent to y, x is similar to y, x is compatible with y, or x is preferred to y.

Three of the most important types of classical binary relations on a single set—equivalence, compatibility, and ordering relations—are characterized in terms of four distinctive properties: reflexivity, symmetry, antisymmetry, and transitivity. We say that a fuzzy relation is:

reflexive if and only if $R(x, x) = 1$ for all $x \in X$;

symmetric if and only if $R(x, y) = R(y, x)$ for all $x, y \in X$;

antisymmetric if and only if $R(x, y) = 1$ and $R(y, x) = 1$ implies that $x = y$ for all $x, y \in X$; and

transitive (with respect to a t-norm i) if $i(R(x, y), R(y, z)) \le R(x, z)$ for all $x, y, z \in X$.

Note that other forms of antisymmetry have been studied in the literature, but the one above, which appears in several equivalent forms in the literature, has desirable mathematical properties (Belohlavek 2002). All of the above properties are proper generalizations of the corresponding properties of classical relations in that a classical relation is reflexive in the classical sense if and only if the corresponding crisp fuzzy relation is reflexive as a fuzzy relation. The same holds true for symmetry, antisymmetry, and transitivity.

Employing these definitions, we obtain the following fuzzy relations:

fuzzy equivalence relations—reflexive, symmetric, and transitive;

fuzzy compatibility relations—reflexive and symmetric; and

fuzzy partial orderings—reflexive, antisymmetric, and transitive.

3.6   Relevant Aspects of Fuzzy Logic in the Narrow Sense

3.6.1   An Overview

Fuzzy logic in the narrow sense (FLN), called also mathematical fuzzy logic (Hájek 2006), develops deductive systems of logic very much in the style of classical mathematical logic. That is, it studies propositional, predicate, and higher-order calculi; the concept of consequence, provability, axiomatization, completeness; complexity questions; and other topics. FLN is an outgrowth of various many-valued logics, which have been investigated in the area of symbolic logic since the beginning of the twentieth century (Rescher 1969; Dunn and Epstein 1977; Gottwald 2001). Many-valued logics differ from classical, two-valued logic by abandoning the assumption that there are exactly two truth values—*false* and *true*, usually denoted by 0 and 1, respectively. In particular, FLN allows additional, intermediary truth-values, called truth degrees, and assumes that the set of truth degrees is partially ordered and bounded by 0 and 1. In this sense, FLN uses a *comparative notion of truth* (Hájek 2006). A typical and perhaps the most important set of truth degrees is the real unit interval [0,1].

As in the case of classical logic, FLN uses connectives and quantifiers to build compound formulas from other, simple formulas. For example, if φ and ψ are formulas and "&" is a symbol of conjunction, then φ & ψ is a compound formula. Like classical logic, fuzzy logic uses formulas to formally represent statements about the world. Given an appropriate semantic structure (such as an evaluation of propositional symbols in the case of propositional logic, or a relational structure in the case of predicate logic), a truth degree of formula φ is denoted by $\|\varphi\|$. It is significant that the truth degree $\|\varphi\|$ of φ may in general be any element of the set of truth degrees. That is, formulas in fuzzy logic are *true to degrees*, not just *true* or *false* as in the case of classical logic. For example, $\|\varphi\| = 0.8$ means that φ is true to degree 0.8, $\|\varphi\| = 0$ means that φ is false (i.e., true to degree 0), and so on. An important feature of classical logic that most systems of fuzzy logic possess is *truth-functionality*. Truth-functionality means that the truth degree of a compound formula is determined by the truth degrees of the formulas from which the compound formula is built. For example, the truth degree of the compound formula φ&ψ is determined by the truth degrees of formulas φ and ψ by

$$\|\varphi \& \psi\| = i(\|\varphi\|, \|\psi\|), \tag{3.25}$$

where i is a suitable function, called a *truth function of conjunction*. Truth-functionality clearly distinguishes fuzzy logic from the various probability logics, as the latter are not truth-functional (the probability of φ & ψ is not determined by the probabilities of φ and ψ). Notice that, in principle, truth-functionality works the same way as in classical logic. The only difference is that in classical logic, the truth degrees $\|\varphi\|$ and $\|\psi\|$ can only be 0 or 1 and there is a unique truth function of conjunction, given by $i(0, 0) = i(0, 1) = i(1, 0) = 0$ and $i(1, 1) = 1$. In fuzzy logic, however, the truth function of conjunction is not unique and may be chosen from a specific class of admissible functions. In much the same way, if symbols $\Rightarrow$ and $\neg$ denote implication and negation, respectively, and if r and n are admissible truth functions of implication and negation, then the truth degrees of $\varphi \Rightarrow \psi$ and $\neg\varphi$ are given by

$$\|\varphi \Rightarrow \psi\| = r(\|\varphi\|, \|\psi\|), \tag{3.26}$$

$$\|\neg\varphi\| = n(\|\varphi\|). \tag{3.27}$$

3.6.2 Systems of Fuzzy Logic

Different systems of fuzzy logic are distinguished from one another by the sets of truth degrees and the truth functions of logical connectives. Because these systems use different truth functions of logical connectives, they have different logical properties. For example, they have different consequence relations and, in particular, different sets of tautologies, that is, different sets of formulas that are always true to degree 1. Many such systems of fuzzy logic have been studied in the literature (Gottwald 2001). The most studied ones are those in which the set of truth degrees is the real unit interval $[0,1]$ and the admissibility conditions for the truth functions of logical connectives are derived from logical considerations such as those involving the rule of modus ponens. Below, we discuss the admissibility conditions for the truth functions of the three most important logical connectives, namely, conjunction, implication, and negation. In the discussion, we assume that the set of truth degrees is the real unit interval $[0,1]$; but note that similar considerations apply to other important cases such as finite subsets of $[0,1]$ or sets of truth degrees that conform to the mathematical structure of a lattice.

For a function i on $[0,1]$ with two arguments to be considered an admissible truth function of conjunction, i is required to be a continuous (or at least left-continuous) t-norm (see section 3.4.3 for the definition of a t-norm). The arguments supporting such requirement may be summarized as follows. Since we require the truth degree of formula $\varphi \,\&\, \psi$ to be equal to the truth degree of $\psi \,\&\, \varphi$, that is, $||\varphi \,\&\, \psi|| = ||\psi \,\&\, \varphi||$, and since $||\varphi \,\&\, \psi|| = i(||\varphi||, ||\psi||)$ and $||\psi \,\&\, \varphi|| = i(||\psi||, ||\varphi||)$, we in fact require $i(a,b) = i(b,a)$ for any truth degrees a and b, that is, we require commutativity of i. In a similar way, the requirement that the truth degree of formula $(\varphi \,\&\, \psi) \,\&\, \gamma$ be equal to the truth degree of $\varphi \,\&\, (\psi \,\&\, \gamma)$ leads to the requirement of associativity of i. Consider now formulas $\varphi_1, \varphi_2, \psi_1,$ and ψ_2 such that $||\varphi_1|| \leq ||\varphi_2||$ and $||\psi_1|| \leq ||\psi_2||$, that is, the degree of the proposition represented by formula φ_2 is higher than or equal to that of the proposition represented by φ_1, and similarly for ψ_1 and ψ_2. The commonsense rule "the truer the propositions, the truer their conjunction" then leads to the requirement $||\varphi_1 \,\&\, \psi_1|| \leq ||\varphi_2 \,\&\, \psi_2||$, that is, to $i(||\varphi_1||, ||\psi_1||) \leq i(||\varphi_2||, ||\psi_2||)$. That is, we require that $||\varphi_1|| \leq ||\varphi_2||$ and $||\psi_1|| \leq ||\psi_2||$ implies $i(||\varphi_1||, ||\psi_1||) \leq i(||\varphi_2||, ||\psi_2||)$—that i be monotone nondecreasing. The last condition for t-norms, $i(a,1) = 1$ for each a, is required for truth functions of conjunction because we want the truth degree of a conjunction of any formula φ and a (fully) true formula $\underline{1}$ (i.e., a formula whose truth degree is 1) to be the same as the truth degree of φ; that is, we want $||\varphi \,\&\, \underline{1}|| = ||\varphi||$. The last condition required of a truth function of conjunction is continuity. The requirement of continuity comes from the requirement that as the truth degrees of formulas φ' and ψ' approach the truth degrees φ and ψ, respectively, the truth degree of conjunction $\varphi' \& \psi'$ approaches the truth degree of $\varphi \& \psi$.

To sum up, the above considerations show why continuous t-norms are considered admissible truth functions of conjunction. One important consequence of the definition of a t-norm is that when applied to classical truth degrees 0 and 1, every admissible truth function of conjunction in fuzzy logic coincides with the truth function of conjunction of classical logic, that is, $i(0,0) = i(1,0) = i(0,1) = 0$ and $i(1,1) = 1$. Note that if it is appropriate in a particular context of application, one may add further requirements and thus narrow down the class of admissible truth functions of conjunction.

When considering admissibility conditions for the truth functions of implication, it is important to realize that the connective of implication is closely related to that of conjunction and that this relationship must be taken into account. Various relationships between conjunction and implication are known from classical logic; for our discussion, the most important one is *adjointness*. In classical logic, adjointness says that if i and r are the truth functions of conjunction and implication, then for any truth-values a, b, and c (i.e., a, b, and c are 0 or 1), we have

$$i(a,b) \leq c \text{ if and only if } a \leq r(b,c).$$

In fuzzy logic, adjointness has the same form but a, b, and c denote arbitrary truth degrees (not only 0 or 1). Adjointness is the basic condition required in fuzzy logic to postulate a relationship between conjunction and implication. Its importance derives from the fact that, as demonstrated by Goguen (1968–69), it is equivalent to demanding that the rule of modus ponens works properly in fuzzy logic. For every given continuous t-norm i, there exists a unique function r such that i and r satisfy adjointness. Such a function, called the *residuum* of i, is given by

$$r(a,b) = \max\{c : i(a,c) \leq b\}. \tag{3.28}$$

Notice that if i is the truth function of classical conjunction, r as given by this formula is the truth function of classical implication, that is, the definition of the truth function of implication as the residuum is valid in classical logic as well. Residua satisfy various properties that make them natural truth functions of implications. For example, every residuum coincides with the truth function of classical implication when applied to classical truth degrees: $r(0,0) = r(0, 1) = r(1,1) = 1$ and $r(1,0) = 0$.

Negation in fuzzy logic is usually considered a derived connective. The truth function of negation is given by

$$n(a) = r(a,0). \tag{3.29}$$

This means that the truth degree of ¬φ (the negation of φ) equals the truth degree of $\varphi \Rightarrow \underline{0}$ (φ implies $\underline{0}$), where $\underline{0}$ represents a formula that is always false (its truth degree is 0). Again, note that this definition of negation is valid in classical logic as well.

We thus see two important aspects of fuzzy logic. First, fuzzy logic is a proper generalization of classical logic. Second, truth functions of logical connectives are no longer unique in fuzzy logic. Rather than providing definitions of particular truth functions, fuzzy logic provides requirements for these functions and considers all functions satisfying these requirements admissible truth functions of logical connectives. The various classes of admissible truth functions of logical connectives give rise to the corresponding logical calculi that may be axiomatized.

We now illustrate particular examples of truth functions of logical connectives by presenting the three most important examples of a continuous t-norm i, its residuum r, and negation n, called Łukasiewicz, Goguen (or product), and Gödel (or minimum) operations. Łukasiewicz operations are given by

$$i(a,b) = \max(0,\, a + b - 1),$$

$$r(a,b) = \min(1,\, 1 - a + b),$$

$$n(a) = 1 - a.$$

That is, with respect to Łukasiewicz operations, the truth degrees of φ&ψ, φ⇒ψ, and ¬φ are given by

$$\|\varphi\&\psi\| = \max(0, \|\varphi\| + \|\psi\| - 1),$$

$$\|\varphi \Rightarrow \psi\| = \min(1,\, 1 - \|\varphi\| + \|\psi\|),$$

$$\|\neg\varphi\| = 1 - \|\varphi\|.$$

Goguen operations are given by:

$$i(a,b) = a \cdot b,$$

$$r(a,b) = \begin{cases} 1 & \text{if } a \leq b \\ \dfrac{b}{a} & \text{otherwise,} \end{cases}$$

$$n(a) = \begin{cases} 1 & \text{if } a = 0 \\ 0 & \text{if } a > 0, \end{cases}$$

and Gödel operations are given by:

$$i(a,b) = \min(a,b),$$

$$r(a,b) = \begin{cases} 1 & \text{if } a \le b \\ b & \text{otherwise,} \end{cases}$$

$$n(a) = \begin{cases} 1 & \text{if } a = 0 \\ 0 & \text{if } a > 0. \end{cases}$$

Note that, for example, formula $\neg\neg\varphi \Rightarrow \varphi$ (the double negation of φ implies φ) is an example of a formula that is a tautology with respect to Łukasiewicz operations but is not a tautology with respect to Goguen or Gödel operations.

Hájek (1998) provides a basic monograph on fuzzy logic with continuous t-norms and their residua as the truth functions of conjunction and implication. He develops a so-called basic fuzzy logic, BL, provides a simple axiom system for BL, and shows that BL is complete, that is, a formula is provable in BL if and only if it is a tautology of BL. Fuzzy logics that are stronger than BL are obtained as axiomatic extensions of BL. That is, fuzzy logics stronger than BL are obtained by adding further axioms to the axioms of BL (or, equivalently, by strengthening the admissibility conditions for the truth functions of logical connectives). The three most important extensions of BL are Łukasiewicz logic, Goguen logic, and Gödel logic, in which the truth functions of logical connectives are given by the Łukasiewicz, Goguen, and Gödel operations described above.

Pavelka (1979) proposed a rather general approach to fuzzy logics that are not necessarily truth functional. This approach consistently pursues the idea of reasoning with degrees: Inferences are made from fuzzy sets T of formulas with $T(\varphi)$ representing a degree to which φ is assumed valid (more precisely, φ is assumed valid to degree at least $T(\varphi)$). Furthermore, provability and entailment are both a matter of degree in Pavelka-style fuzzy logic. That is, a given formula φ is provable from a fuzzy set T of formulas to a certain degree, rather than being just provable or not provable; likewise, φ follows from T to a certain degree, rather than either follows or does not follow. Note that entailment to degrees appears naturally in human reasoning. Suppose that $X \sim Y$ is a formula saying that X is approximately equal in size to Y, and that we assume for objects A, B, and C that $A \sim B$ at least to degree 0.8 and $B \sim C$ at least to degree 0.7. In this case, the fuzzy set of assumptions is given by $T(A \sim B) = 0.8$ and $T(B \sim C) = 0.7$. Rather than asking whether $A \sim C$ follows from T or not, it is intuitively far more natural to ask about the degree to which $A\sim C$ follows from T, that is, to consider entailment as a matter of degree. The completeness theorem in Pavelka-style fuzzy logic says that the degree to which a formula φ is provable from a fuzzy set T of formulas equals the degree to which φ follows from T. Gerla (2001) presents many results that have been obtained for Pavelka-style fuzzy logic.

3.6.3 Predicate Fuzzy Logic

Important components in formulas of predicate fuzzy logic are quantifiers. Several types of quantifiers have been studied in fuzzy logic (Gottwald 2001; Hájek 1998). They include the two classical quantifiers, universal and existential, as well as various nonclassical ones (Gottwald 2001; Hájek 1998). First, we illustrate how standard quantifiers are treated in fuzzy logic by presenting the semantics of the universal quantifier. Let $\varphi(x)$ be a formula with a free variable x. For example, the formula $Tall(x)$ could represent the proposition "x is tall." The truth degree of a universally quantified formula $(\forall x)\varphi(x)$, to be read "for every x: $\varphi(x)$," is defined by

$$\|(\forall x)\varphi(x)\| = \inf_{u \in U}\|\varphi(x/u)\| \qquad (3.30)$$

where U denotes a universe in which we evaluate the formula, and $\|\varphi(x/u)\|$ denotes the truth degree of φ given that element u is substituted for variable x. For example, if U consists of five persons denoted by A, B, C, D, E, who are considered tall to degrees 0.9, 1, 1, 0.2, 0.4, respectively, that is, $\|Tall(x/A)\| = 0.9, ..., \|Tall(x/E)\| = 0.4$, then the truth degree of $(\forall x)Tall(x)$, which represents the proposition "Every x is tall," is $\|(\forall x)Tall(x)\| = \min\{\|\varphi(x/A)\|,\|\varphi(x/B)\|,\|\varphi(x/C)\|,\|\varphi(x/D)\|,\|\varphi(x/E)\|\} = \min\{0.9, 1, 1, 0.2, 0.4\} = 0.2$. That is, the truth degree of proposition "Every x is tall" is 0.2.

   In addition to classical quantifiers, fuzzy logic works with various nonclassical quantifiers. The latter frequently occur and play an important role in natural language. An example of a nonclassical quantifier is the quantifier $Many$. The formula $(Many\ x)\varphi(x)$ is read "for many x: $\varphi(x)$." $(Many\ x)\varphi(x)$ may be interpreted as

$$\|(Many\ x)\varphi(x)\| = \frac{\sum_{u \in U}\|\varphi(x/u)\|}{|U|}, \qquad (3.31)$$

where $|U|$ denotes the number of elements of the universe. (If the universe is infinite, both the sum and $|U|$ need to be replaced by measure-theoretic concepts.) With the above example, the truth degree of $(Many\ x)Tall(x)$ is

$$\|(Many \; x)Tall(x)\| = \frac{\|\varphi(x/A)\| + \|\varphi(x/B)\| + \|\varphi(x/C)\| + \|\varphi(x/D)\|}{|U|}$$

$$= \frac{0.9 + 1 + 1 + 0.2 + 0.4}{5} = 0.7.$$

That is, the truth degree of the proposition "Many x are tall" is 0.7.

In very much the same way that classical logic is connected to classical set theory, fuzzy logic in the narrow sense is connected to fuzzy set theory. For example, operations with fuzzy sets, such as intersection or complement, are defined by means of logical formulas. For example, the degree $[i(A,B)](x)$ to which element x is a member of the intersection of standard fuzzy sets A and B that is based on a t-norm i (see section 3.4.3) is just the truth degree of formula "x is member of A & x is member of B" provided that i is the truth function of conjunction. It is important to mention that the counterparts of various relations well known from classical set theory naturally become fuzzy in fuzzy set theory. We illustrate this fact by the set inclusion relation. In classical set theory, set inclusion is defined as follows. For classical sets A and B which are subsets of a universe set U, we say that A is included in B, and denote this fact by $A \subseteq B$, if and only if the proposition

"for every element x from U, if x is a member of A then x is a member of B"

is true. However, if A and B are fuzzy sets in U, this proposition becomes a many-valued proposition, and, therefore, needs to be assigned a truth degree. This truth degree is interpreted as the truth degree to which fuzzy set A is included in fuzzy set B, which is denoted by $S(A,B)$. To see how $S(A,B)$ is calculated, one has to realize that (i) propositions "x is a member of A" and "x is a member of B" have truth degrees $A(x)$ and $B(x)$; (ii) that a given truth function r of implication needs to be applied to these truth degrees to obtain the truth degree of proposition "if x is a member of A then x is a member of B," which is given by $r(A(x),B(x))$; and (iii) that the rule for evaluating universal quantification "for every element x from U," which is given by $\inf_{x \in U} r(A(x),B(x))$, must be applied to obtain the truth degree of the proposition. In this way we obtain

$$S(A,B) = \inf_{x \in U} r(A(x),B(x)). \tag{3.32}$$

The particular case of $S(A,B) = 1$ means that the proposition is fully true. It can be shown that $S(A,B) = 1$ is equivalent to $A(x) \leq B(x)$ for each $x \in U$. In this case we say that fuzzy set A is (fully) included in fuzzy set B, and we denote this fact by $A \subseteq B$. In terms of membership functions, $A \subseteq B$ means that the membership function A lies below the membership function B. In general, $S(A,B)$ being less than 1 indicates that in some parts of universe U, the membership function B is below A. If $S(A,B)$ is less than 1 but close to 1, B is below A in some parts of U, but not too much. This illustrates what the degree $S(A,B)$ of inclusion tells us about the membership functions A and B. Clearly, $\subseteq$ is a crisp relation ($A \subseteq B$ can only be true or false) whereas S is a fuzzy relation ($S(A,B)$ may be an arbitrary truth degree).

3.7   Fuzzy Logic in the Broad Sense

When the term *fuzzy logic* is viewed in the broad sense, it refers to an on-going research program whose primary aim is to emulate commonsense human reasoning in natural language and utilize it in various applications. It is concerned with developing any conceptual and mathematical tools that are needed for pursuing this aim. Fuzzy sets are essential in this quest because of their capability to represent vague linguistic terms, which are typical of natural language.

To use the apparatus of fuzzy set theory in the domain of fuzzy logic, it is necessary to establish a connection between degrees of membership in fuzzy sets and degrees of truth of fuzzy propositions. This can only be done when the degrees of membership and the degrees of truth refer to the same objects. Let us examine first the simplest connection, in which only one fuzzy set is involved.

Consider a variable **V** with states (not necessarily numeric) in set V. Given a fuzzy set A defined on V, its membership degree $A(v)$ for any $v \in V$ may be interpreted as the degree of truth of the associated fuzzy proposition "v is a member of A." Conversely, given an arbitrary proposition of the simple form "v is a member of A," where v is a particular value of variable **V** and A is a fuzzy subset of V (representing an inherently vague linguistic term applicable to the variable), its degree of truth may be interpreted as the membership degree of v in A.

This simple correspondence between membership degrees and degrees of truth, which conforms well to our intuition, forms a basis for determining degrees of truth of more complex propositions. Truth degrees of negations, conjunctions, and disjunctions of fuzzy propositions are defined under this correspondence in exactly the same way as complements, intersections, and unions of fuzzy sets, respectively. For example, t-norms are functions used for defining not only intersections of fuzzy sets, but also, under this correspondence, truth degrees of conjunctions of fuzzy propositions.

The principal aim of fuzzy logic in the broad sense is to develop conceptual and mathematical tools for dealing with propositions expressed in natural language. The linguistic expressions involved in these propositions may contain linguistic terms of any of the following basic types:

fuzzy predicates—*tall, young, intelligent, expensive, high, low, beautiful,* etc.

fuzzy truth-values—*true, false, fairly true, very false, more or less true,* etc.

fuzzy probabilities—*likely, very likely, extremely unlikely, usually,* etc.

fuzzy quantifiers—*many, most, almost all, few, several, about one half, around 20%,* etc.

All of these linguistic terms are represented in each context by appropriate fuzzy sets. For fuzzy predicates, these fuzzy sets are defined on universal sets of objects to which the predicates apply. For fuzzy truth values and fuzzy probabilities, they are defined on the unit interval [0,1]. For fuzzy quantifiers, which are either absolute (*many, most, few, almost all*) or relative (*about one-half, around 10%, almost 100%*), they are defined either on the set of natural numbers or on the interval [0,1], respectively. For more information see Glöckner 2006.

3.7.1 Types of Fuzzy Propositions

It is useful to distinguish (albeit in a crude way) the following four types of fuzzy propositions.

Unconditional and unqualified propositions

Consider again a variable **V** whose states are in set V. Unconditional and unqualified fuzzy propositions of this type are based on the canonical form

$$\mathbf{V} \text{ is } A,$$

in which A denotes a fuzzy set on V that represents a fuzzy predicate relevant to states of V. A proposition, P_v, is obtained for each particular state of variable **V**. That is,

$$P_v: \mathbf{V} = v \text{ is } A.$$

The degree of truth of P_v, $T(P_v)$, is in this case the same as the degree of membership of v in fuzzy set A. That is,

$$T(P_v) = A(v).$$

As an example, let **V** be humidity, whose state set V is the closed interval $[0, 100]$, and let M be a fuzzy set representing *moderate* humidity, as defined in figure 3.1c. Consider the proposition P_v: **V** $= v$ is M and assume that the actual humidity value in a given context is $v = 65\%$. Proposition P_{65} is described in natural language as "humidity of 65% is moderate." Since $M(65) = 0.75$, we obtain that $T(P_{65}) = M(65) = 0.75$. Similarly, for fuzzy set H in figure 3.1c and the associated proposition P_v: **V** $= v$ is H, we obtain $T(P_{65}) = H(65) = 0.25$.

Unconditional and qualified fuzzy propositions

Unconditional and qualified fuzzy propositions can be truth qualified, probability qualified, or qualified in both ways. Truth-qualified propositions are based on the canonical form

$$\textbf{V} \text{ is } A \text{ is } Q_t,$$

where Q_t denotes a fuzzy truth-qualifier, which is always a special fuzzy set defined on $[0,1]$ that represents linguistic truth claims such as *true, false, fairly true, very false*, and so on. Denoting (for simplicity) individual fuzzy propositions based on this form again by P_v for all $v \in V$, we have

$$P_v: \textbf{V} = v \text{ is } A \text{ is } Q_t.$$

The degree of truth of P_v, denoted again by $T(P_v)$, is obtained in this case by composing function A with function Q_t. That is,

$$T(P_v) = Q_t(A(v)).$$

When Q_t represents the linguistic claim *true*, then it should clearly be the identity function on $[0,1]$. That is, $Q_t(a) = a$ for all $a \in [0,1]$ and, in this case, $T(P_v) = A(v)$, which is the same result as the one obtained for unconditional and unqualified fuzzy propositions. This means that unqualified fuzzy propositions are, in fact, special truth-qualified fuzzy propositions, in which the truth qualifier Q_t is tacitly assumed to represent the linguistic claim *true*. When Q_t represents the linguistic claim *false*, $Q_t(a) = 1 - a$. The two fuzzy truth qualifiers for linguistic truth claims *true* and *false* form a base from which other truth qualifiers are obtained by various fuzzy modifiers. For more details and examples, see Klir and Yuan 1995.

Probability-qualified propositions are based on the canonical form

$$\text{Pro}(\mathbf{V} \text{ is } A) \text{ is } Q_p,$$

where Pro($\mathbf{V}$ is A) denotes the probability associated with fuzzy set A (fuzzy event) and Q_p stands for a probability qualifier, which is always a fuzzy set defined on [0,1] that represents linguistic probability claims such as *likely*, *very likely*, *extremely unlikely*, and so on. For any given probability of fuzzy event A, say probability Pro(A) = p, we obtain the proposition

$$P_p: \text{Pro}(\mathbf{V} \text{ is } A) = p \text{ is } Q_p.$$

The truth-value of this proposition is

$$T(P_p) = Q_p(\text{Pro}(A)).$$

If this proposition were also truth-qualified by a truth qualifier Q_t, then its truth value would be

$$T(P_p) = Q_t(Q_p(\text{Pro}(A))).$$

When $\mathbf{V}$ has a finite number of states (V is finite) and a probability distribution function on V, say function f, is given, the probability of A is calculated by the formula

$$\text{Pro}(A) = \sum_{v \in V} A(v)f(v).$$

When V is the set of real numbers (or some interval of real numbers) and a probability density function on V, say function g, is given, the probability of A is calculated by the formula

$$\text{Pro}(A) = \int_V A(v)g(v)dv.$$

The calculation of probabilities for fuzzy sets was first introduced by Zadeh (1968).

For more information about truth-qualified and probability-qualified fuzzy propositions and examples illustrating details of computing the degree of truth of these propositions, see Klir and Yuan 1995.

Conditional and unqualified fuzzy propositions

Conditional and unqualified fuzzy propositions involve two variables, say $\mathbf{V}$ and $\mathbf{W}$, whose states are in sets V and W, respectively. They are based on the canonical form

$$\text{If } \mathbf{V} \text{ is } A, \text{ then } \mathbf{W} \text{ is } B,$$

where A and B are fuzzy sets defined on V and W, respectively. A convenient alternative form is

$$(\mathbf{V}, \mathbf{W}) \text{ is } R,$$

where R denotes a fuzzy relation on $V \times W$ that is determined for all $v \in V$ and $w \in W$ by the formula

$$R(v, w) = r[A(v), B(w)],$$

where r denotes a binary operation on $[0,1]$ that represents a suitable fuzzy implication in a given context of application. A proposition based on this alternative form, $P_{r,v,w}$, is obtained for the chosen fuzzy implication when $\mathbf{V} = v$ and $\mathbf{W} = w$. That is,

$$T(P_{r,v,w}) = r[A(v), B(w)].$$

For more information about fuzzy implications, see section 3.6.2 and also Klir and Yuan 1995, chapter 11.

Conditional and qualified fuzzy propositions

Conditional and qualified fuzzy propositions are based on any one of the following three canonical forms:

$$(\mathbf{V}, \mathbf{W}) \text{ is } R \text{ is } Q_t,$$

$$(\mathbf{V}, \mathbf{W}) \text{ is } R \text{ is } Q_p,$$

$$(\mathbf{V}, \mathbf{W}) \text{ is } R \text{ is } Q_p \text{ is } Q_t.$$

Individual propositions and their degrees of truth are determined as previously described.

3.7.2 Approximate Reasoning

Reasoning based on fuzzy propositions of the four types, possibly quantified by various fuzzy quantifiers, is usually referred to as *approximate reasoning*. In general, approximate reasoning draws on the methodological apparatus of fuzzy set theory, such as operations on fuzzy sets, manipulations of fuzzy relations, and fuzzy arithmetic.

The most fundamental components of approximate reasoning are conditional fuzzy propositions, which may also be truth qualified, probability qualified, quantified, or any combination of these. Special procedures are needed for each of these types of fuzzy propositions. This great variety of fuzzy propositions makes approximate reasoning methodologically rather intricate. This reflects the richness of natural language and the many intricacies of commonsense reasoning, which approximate reasoning based on fuzzy set theory attempts to model.

The essence of approximate reasoning is illustrated in this tutorial by explaining the *compositional rule of inference*—the best-known and widely applied rule of inference. For the sake of simplicity, we restrict the illustration to unqualified fuzzy propositions without quantifiers. The compositional rule of inference allows us to infer, from an approximate description of the value of an input variable and an approximate description of a relationship between the possible values of the input and output variables, an approximate description of the value of the output variable. Consider variables **V** and **W** with state sets V and W, respectively. Assume that there exists a constraint on the values of **V** and the values of **W**, which is represented by a fuzzy relation R on $V \times W$. Then, knowing that **V** is F (a fact), where F is a fuzzy set on V representing the approximate value of **V**, we can infer that **W** is C (a conclusion), where C is a fuzzy set on W representing the corresponding approximate value of **W** by the formula

$$C(w) = \max_{v \in V} \min[F(v), R(v,w)]$$

for all $w \in W$. This formula, which expresses the max-min composition

$$C = F \circ R,$$

is called a max-min compositional rule of inference (if max does not exist, it must be replaced with sup).

3.7.3 Fuzzy Systems

In general, each classical system is ultimately a set of variables together with a relation among states (or values) of the variables. When states of variables are fuzzy sets, the system is called a *fuzzy system*. In most typical fuzzy systems, the states are fuzzy intervals that represent linguistic terms such as *very small*, *small*, *medium*, *large*, and so on, as interpreted in the context of each particular application. If they do, the variables are called *linguistic variables*.

Each linguistic variable is defined in terms of a base variable, whose states are usually real numbers within a specific range. A base variable is a variable in the classical sense, as exemplified by any physical variable (temperature, pressure, tidal range, grain size, etc.). Linguistic terms involved in a linguistic variable are used for approximating the actual states of the associated base variable. Their meanings are captured, in the context of each particular application, by appropriate fuzzy sets (usually fuzzy intervals). That is, each linguistic variable consists of:

a *name*, which should reflect the meaning of the base variable involved;

a *base variable* with its range of states (usually a closed interval of real numbers);

a set of *linguistic terms* that refer to values of the base variable; and

a set of *semantic rules*, which assign to each linguistic term its meaning in terms of an appropriate fuzzy interval (or some other fuzzy set) defined on the range of the base variable.

Consider a linguistic variable **V** whose base variable has states (values) in set V. Fuzzy sets A_i (i = 1, 2, ...) that represent linguistic states of the linguistic variable are often defined in such a way that the sum of membership degrees in these fuzzy sets is equal to 1 for each $v \in V$. Such a family of nonempty fuzzy subsets of V is called a *fuzzy partition* of V. This concept is intuitively a natural generalization of the classical concept of partition and has wide applicability.

Fuzzy sets that represent states of a linguistic variable, which usually form a fuzzy partition, are often called *granules*. The process of constructing these fuzzy sets is called *granulation*. This process is a fuzzy counterpart of the classical process of *quantization* by which the set of all states of a variable is divided into subsets (quanta or aggregates) that form a classical partition of the whole set. Granulation is essential for a realistic mathematical representation of linguistic states of linguistic variables. It allows for a smooth transition between linguistic states (e.g., from *young* to *old*) that captures, at least in crude way, human interpretation and use of expressions in natural language.

An example of a linguistic variable is shown in figure 3.1c. Its base variable is humidity whose states are in the interval [0, 100]. The three fuzzy sets in the figure represent linguistic terms *low*, *moderate*, and *high*, and are states (granules) of the linguistic variable.

Three basic types of fuzzy systems are usually recognized: knowledge-based systems, model-based systems, and hybrid systems. In knowledge-based fuzzy systems, relationships between variables are described by collections of fuzzy inference rules (conditional fuzzy propositional forms). These rules attempt to capture the knowledge of a human expert, often expressed in natural language. Model-based fuzzy systems are based on traditional systems modeling, but they employ appropriate areas of fuzzy mathematics (fuzzy analysis, fuzzy differential equations, etc.). These mathematical areas, based on the notion of fuzzy intervals, allow us to approximate classical mathematical systems of various types via appropriate granulation to achieve tractability, robustness, and low computational cost. Hybrid fuzzy systems are combinations of knowledge-based and model-based fuzzy systems.

Model-based and hybrid fuzzy systems are outside the scope of this book. In knowledge-based fuzzy systems, the relation between input and output linguistic variables is expressed in terms of a set of fuzzy if-then rules (conditional propositional forms). From these rules and any information describing actual states of input variables, information regarding the actual states of the output variables is derived by an appropriate compositional rule of inference.

Assuming, for example, two input variables, $\mathbf{V}_1$ and $\mathbf{V}_2$, and one output variable, $\mathbf{W}$, we have the following scheme of inference to represent the input–output relation of the system:

Rule 1: If $\mathbf{V}_1$ is A_{11} and $\mathbf{V}_2$ is A_{21}, then $\mathbf{W}$ is B_1

Rule 2: If $\mathbf{V}_1$ is A_{12} and $\mathbf{V}_2$ is A_{22}, then $\mathbf{W}$ is B_2

. . . .

Rule n: If $\mathbf{V}_1$ is A_{1n} and $\mathbf{V}_2$ is A_{2n}, then $\mathbf{W}$ is B_n

Fact: $\mathbf{V}_1$ is F_1 and $\mathbf{V}_2$ is F_2

Conclusion: $\mathbf{W}$ is C

For more information, we recommend the books by Yager and Filev (1994), Babuška (1998), and Piegat (2001). For an easy-to-understand overview of the overall agenda of fuzzy logic in the broad sense, we recommend the paper by Zadeh (1996).

3.8 Overview of Applications

Although our focus in this tutorial is on the foundations of fuzzy logic, we also need to include a brief overview of the applications of fuzzy logic, for at least three reasons. First, fuzzy logic has by now been successfully applied in virtually all areas of human affairs, and research on the foundations of fuzzy logic has often been driven by applications. Second, applications of fuzzy logic may inspire some researchers in the psychology of concepts to explore the utility of fuzzy logic in their own field. Third, it is reasonable to assume that some readers of this book will be interested in developing an overall feeling for practical applicability of fuzzy logic.

Since the late 1980s, the literature dealing with applications of fuzzy logic has been growing so rapidly that it would not be realistic to strive for a comprehensive overview of all established applications of fuzzy logic. Our aim in this section is thus rather modest. We identify only the most visible applications and provide the reader with selective information for further study. The circumstances that led to the rapid increase of applications of fuzzy logic in the late 1980s and early 1990s have been well characterized by McNeil and Freiberger (1993).

Most applications of fuzzy logic that were developed prior to 1995 are described by Klir and Yuan (1995). About half of their book is devoted to applications and includes key references for each of the described applications. Moreover, the book has a bibliographical index, which helps the reader to quickly identify references in the various application areas. Some of the applications are generic in the sense that they are applicable to multiple disciplines, and some are developed for specific domains of individual disciplines. Among the generic applications described in the book are approximate reasoning, classification, cluster analysis, control, data analysis, decision making, design, diagnosis, image processing, optimization, pattern recognition, regression analysis, reliability analysis, risk analysis, scheduling, and systems modeling. Among the domain-specific applications are those in business, computer science (computer speech and vision, databases, expert systems, information retrieval, etc.), engineering (chemical, civil, electrical, environmental, mechanical, nuclear, industrial), earthquake studies (seismology), ecology, economics, medicine, meteorology, physics, psychology and behavioral sciences, robotics, and systems science. Zimmerman (1999) offers a more recent book devoted to applications of fuzzy logic.

Most of the applications of fuzzy logic described in the above-mentioned books have substantially expanded, and applications in some new areas have emerged. The following is a list of some of these new areas, each with a representative reference:

Chemistry (Rouvray 1997)

Finance (Peray 1999)

Geography (Petry, Robinson, and Cobb 2005)

Geology (Demicco and Klir 2004)

Management (Carlsson, Fedrizzi, and Fuller 2004)

Political science (Clark et al. 2008)

Sociology (Ragin 2000)

Transportation (Teodorović and Vukadinović 1998)

Two journals focusing on special applications of fuzzy logic should also be mentioned: *Fuzzy Economic Review* (published since 1995) and *Fuzzy Optimization and Decision Making* (published since 2002).

3.9 Principal Sources for Further Study

The areas of fuzzy logics in the broad and narrow sense have advanced enormously since the deceivingly simple notion of a fuzzy set was introduced by Zadeh (1965). Literature in these areas has been growing so rapidly and in so many different directions that it is very difficult for anyone who has not continuously followed developments in these areas to appreciate their scope and significance. It is even more difficult to comprehend all the intricacies of these areas. The aim of this section is to help the reader to expand on the material covered in this tutorial by further study.

The easiest way to approach further study is to use one of the available textbooks on fuzzy logic. The graduate textbook by Klir and Yuan (1995) is a natural extension of this tutorial since it employs virtually the same terminology and notation. It also contains a bibliography of over 1,700 entries and a bibliographical index. The following general textbooks are also recommended: Nguyen and Walker 2005, the third edition of a well-written, rigorous presentation with many examples and exercises; Pedrycz and Gomide 1998, a comprehensive coverage with a good balance of theory and applications; Bojadziev and Bojadziev 1995, a well-written undergraduate textbook; and Zimmermann 1996, the third edition of a classic textbook.

In the category of reference books, two important handbooks—Ruspini, Bonissone, and Pedrycz 1998 and Dubois and Prade 2000—are recommended as convenient sources of information on virtually any aspect of fuzzy logic; the latter is only the first, introductory volume of a series of handbooks on fuzzy sets that have been published by Kluwer. The reader should also be aware of two books of collected papers by Zadeh, edited by Yager et al. (1987) and Klir and Yuan (1996), that are indispensable for proper comprehension of fuzzy logic in the broad sense.

As far as journals in the areas of fuzzy logic are concerned, their number has been steadily growing. The following journals are, in our opinion, the most important ones to follow:

Fuzzy Sets and Systems—published since 1978 and sponsored by the International Fuzzy Systems Association (IFSA), this is undoubtedly the prime journal in the field;

International Journal of Approximate Reasoning—published since 1987 and sponsored by the North American Fuzzy Information Processing Society (NAFIPS), this is perhaps the second most important journal in the field;

IEEE Transactions on Fuzzy Systems—published since 1993 by IEEE, this is an important journal focusing primarily on theory and applications (not necessarily in engineering) of fuzzy systems;

International Journal of Uncertainty, Fuzziness, and Knowledge-Based Systems—published since 1993, this journal has developed an excellent reputation as a forum for research on combining fuzzy logic and various uncertainty theories in dealing with knowledge;

Soft Computing—published since 1997, this is the primary journal focusing on the broader area of soft computing, in which fuzzy logic is employed jointly with neural networks, evolutionary algorithms, and other areas.

Finally, we should mention that research and education in the area of fuzzy logic is now supported by numerous professional organizations. Many of them cooperate and interact via the International Fuzzy Systems Association (IFSA). In addition to publishing the prime journal in the field, *Fuzzy Sets and Systems*, IFSA has organized the biennial World IFSA Congress since 1985. The first professional organization supporting fuzzy logic was founded in 1981 under the name North American Fuzzy Information Processing Society (NAFIPS). In addition to publishing the *International Journal of Approximate Reasoning*, NAFIPS organizes annual meetings. Fuzzy logic is also supported by Institute of Electrical and Electronic Engineers (IEEE) in two ways: by organizing annually international conferences on fuzzy systems and by publishing the journal *IEEE Transactions on Fuzzy Systems*.

3.10 Summary and Conclusions

In this tutorial, we introduce basic ideas of fuzzy logic. The presentation is restricted, by and large, to the case when the set of truth-values is the unit interval [0,1]. Within this restriction, relevant elementary concepts are defined and the following key components of fuzzy logic are discussed at the introductory level sufficient for the purpose of this book:

five classes of operations on fuzzy sets: modifiers, complements, intersections, unions, and averaging operations;

level-cut representation of fuzzy sets and, in particular, of fuzzy intervals;

fuzzy relations and operations on fuzzy relations (projections, cylindric extensions, compositions, joins, and inverses);

fuzzy relations that represent approximate equivalence, similarity, compatibility and preference;

basic notions of fuzzy logic in the narrow sense (logical connectives and formulas, provability, completeness, tautology, and the like);

connections between fuzzy logic in the narrow sense and fuzzy set theory;

four basic types of fuzzy propositions;

basic ideas of approximate reasoning; and

linguistic variables and their role in knowledge-based fuzzy systems.

It is important to realize that the tutorial covers only a very small subarea of fuzzy logic, albeit the most relevant one to the purpose of this book. It seems thus appropriate to close the tutorial by presenting at least a partial list of those additional subareas of fuzzy logic that are not covered in the tutorial. They include the following:

all nonstandard fuzzy sets and the theories based on them;

fuzzified mathematical areas, such as arithmetic, mathematical analysis and differential equations, topology, geometry, abstract algebraic structures, graphs, hypergraphs, automata, etc.;

general principles of the fuzzification of mathematical theories;

general principles of defuzzifications of fuzzy sets (Martin and Klir 2007);

possibility theory based on a natural fuzzy-set interpretation by which information expressed in terms of fuzzy propositions can be represented and dealt with mathematically (Klir 1999);

the whole area of aggregating functions (Grabisch et al. 2009), which are in principle applicable for aggregating fuzzy sets; and

a category-theoretic treatment of fuzzy set theory (Rodabaugh, Klement, and Höhle 1992).

Readers interested in any of these subareas of fuzzy logic are referred to the overview of sources in section 3.9.

References

Babuška, R. 1998. *Fuzzy Modeling for Control*. Boston: Kluwer.

Belohlavek, R. 2002. *Fuzzy Relational Systems: Foundations and Principles*. New York: Kluwer.

Bojadziev, G., and M. Bojadziev. 1995. *Fuzzy Sets, Fuzzy Logic, Applications*. Singapore: World Scientific.

Carlsson, C., M. Fedrizzi, and R. Fullér. 2004. *Fuzzy Logic in Management*. Boston: Kluwer.

Clark, T. D., J. M. Larson, J. N. Mordeson, J. D. Potter, and M. J. Wierman. 2008. *Applying Fuzzy Mathematics to Formal Models in Comparative Politics*. Berlin: Springer.

Demicco, R. V., and G. J. Klir, eds. 2004. *Fuzzy Logic in Geology*. San Diego, CA: Academic Press.

Dubois, D. and H. Prade, eds. 2000. *Fundamentals of Fuzzy Sets*. Boston: Kluwer.

Dunn, J. M., and G. Epstein, eds. 1977. *Modern Uses of Multiple-Valued Logic*. Dordrecht: D. Reidel.

Gerla, G. 2001. *Fuzzy Logic: Mathematical Tools for Approximate Reasoning*. Dordrecht: Kluwer.

Glöckner, I. 2006. *Fuzzy Quantifiers: A Computational Theory*. Berlin: Springer.

Goguen, J. A. 1968–69. The logic of inexact concepts. *Synthese* 19:325–373.

Gottwald, S. 2001. *A Treatise on Many-Valued Logics*. Baldock: Research Studies Press.

Grabisch, M., J.-L. Marichal, R. Mesiar, and E. Pap. 2009. *Aggregation Functions*. Cambridge: Cambridge University Press.

Hájek, P. 1998. *Metamathematics of Fuzzy Logic*. Boston: Kluwer.

Hájek, P. 2006. What is mathematical fuzzy logic. *Fuzzy Sets and Systems* 157:597–603.

Kaufmann, A., and M. M. Gupta. 1985. *Introduction to Fuzzy Arithmetic: Theory and Applications*. New York: Van Nostrand Reinhold.

Klement, E. P., R. Mesiar, and E. Pap. 2000. *Triangular Norms*. Dordrecht: Kluwer.

Klir, G. J. 1999. On fuzzy-set interpretation of possibility theory. *International Journal of General Systems* 108:263–273.

Klir, G. J., and Y. Pan. 1998. Constraint fuzzy arithmetics: basic questions and some answers. *Soft Computing* 2:100–108.

Klir, G. J., and B. Yuan. 1995. *Fuzzy Sets and Fuzzy Logic: Theory and Applications*. Upper Saddle River, NJ: Prentice Hall.

Klir, G. J., and B. Yuan, eds. 1996. *Fuzzy Sets, Fuzzy Logic, and Fuzzy Systems: Selected Papers by Lotfi A. Zadeh*. Singapore: World Scientific.

Mareš, M. 1994. *Computation Over Fuzzy Quantities*. Boca Raton, FL: CRC Press.

Martin, O., and G. J. Klir. 2007. Defuzzification as a special way of dealing with retranslation. *International Journal of General Systems* 36:683–701.

McNeil, D., and P. Freiberger. 1993. *Fuzzy Logic: The Discovery of a Revolutionary Computer Technology—and How It Is Changing Our World*. New York: Simon & Schuster.

Moore, R. E., R. B. Kearfott, and M. J. Cloud. 2009. *Introduction to Interval Analysis*. Philadelphia: SIAM.

Neumaier, A. 1990. *Interval Methods for Systems of Equations*. Cambridge: Cambridge University Press.

Nguyen, H. T., and E. A. Walker. 2005. *A First Course in Fuzzy Logic*, 3rd ed. Boca Raton, FL: CRC Press.

Pavelka, J. 1979. On fuzzy logic I, II, III. *Zeitschrift für Mathematische Logic und Grundlagen der Mathematik* 25: 45–52, 119–134, 447–464.

Pedrycz, W., and F. Gomide. 1998. *An Introduction to Fuzzy Sets: Analysis and Design*. Cambridge, MA: MIT Press.

Peray, K. 1999. *Investing Mutual Funds Using Fuzzy Logic*. Boca Raton, FL: St. Lucia Press.

Petry, F. E., V. B. Robinson, and M. A. Cobb, eds. 2005. *Fuzzy Modeling with Spatial Information for Geographic Problems*. Berlin: Springer.

Piegat, A. 2001. *Fuzzy Modeling and Control*. Heidelberg: Physica-Verlag.

Ragin, C. C. 2000. *Fuzzy-Set Social Science*. Chicago: University of Chicago Press.

Rescher, N. 1969. *Many-valued Logic*. New York: McGraw-Hill.

Rodabaugh, S. E., E. P. Klement, and U. Höhle, eds. 1992. *Applications of Category Theory to Fuzzy Subsets*. Dordrecht: Kluwer.

Rouvray, G. M., ed. 1997. *Fuzzy Logic in Chemistry*. San Diego, CA: Academic Press.

Ruspini, E. H., P. P. Bonissone, and W. Pedrycz, eds. 1998. *Handbook of Fuzzy Computation*. Bristol: Institute of Physics Publishing.

Smuts, J. C. 1926. *Holism and Evolution*. London: Macmillan.

Teodorović, D., and K. Vukadinović. 1998. *Traffic Control and Transport Planning: A Fuzzy Sets and Neural Networks Approach*. Boston: Kluwer.

Yager, R. R., and D. P. Filev. 1994. *Essentials of Fuzzy Modeling and Control*. New York: John Wiley.

Yager, R. R., S. Ovchinnikov, R. M. Tong, and H. T. Nguyen, eds. 1987. *Fuzzy Sets and Applications: Selected Papers by L. A. Zadeh*. New York: John Wiley.

Zadeh, L. A. 1965. Fuzzy sets. *Information and Control* 8:338–353.

Zadeh, L. A. 1968. Probability measures of fuzzy events. *Journal of Mathematical Analysis and Applications* 23:421–427.

Zadeh, L. A. 1996. Fuzzy logic and the calculi of fuzzy rules and fuzzy graphs: A précis. *International Journal of Multiple-Valued Logic* 1:1–38.

Zimmermann, H.-J. 1996. *Fuzzy Set Theory and Its Applications*. Boston: Kluwer.

Zimmermann, H.-J., ed. 1999. *Practical Applications of Fuzzy Technology*. Boston: Kluwer.

4 "Slow Lettuce": Categories, Concepts, Fuzzy Sets, and Logical Deduction

Eleanor H. Rosch

4.1   Introduction

In James Thurber's story "Interview with a Lemming," a scientist is talking with a lemming who says that he has made a lifelong study of humans and knows all about them except for one thing that he doesn't understand. The scientist responds: "'It may interest you to know that I have made a life-long study of lemmings, just as you have made a lifelong study of people. Like you I have found but one thing about my subject which I don't under-stand.' 'And what is that?' asked the lemming. 'I don't understand,' said the scientist, 'why you lemmings all rush down to the sea and drown your-selves.' 'How curious,' said the lemming, 'The one thing I don't understand is why you human beings don't.'"

When two academic disciplines meet, it is somewhat like first contact between two cultures—or perhaps life forms. It may result only in the exchange of superficial artifacts and vocabulary, or perhaps in the colonization of one by the other. But at its best, though rarely, such contact might provide the impetus for a deep exploration of the assumptions and standard practices that underlie the areas where the two intersect. The stated aim of this book is to initiate dialogue between the field in mathematics that is called fuzzy logic (particularly fuzzy set theory) and the field in psychology that studies concepts and categorization. My aim in this chapter is to invite that dialogue toward the option of deep exploration. There has already been research and argument in the psychology of concepts that is very close to fuzzy set theory, though the two arose and developed independently. Inherent in both the psychological and mathematical work is a challenge to some fundamental assumptions of Western thought (whether that is recognized yet or not); might it be a challenge whose time has come? What can be added (and what cannot) by using the explicit formalisms of fuzzy logic for the psychological work?

Two characteristics seem to be required of the psychology of concepts if it is to interact fruitfully with fuzzy logic: (1) Since the essence of fuzzy sets is that their membership is a matter of degree rather than the all-or-none of classical sets, there should be reason to believe that degree of membership is psychologically meaningful for concepts. In the first part of this chapter, I will describe the research that introduced degree of membership in concepts into psychology, the further research that argues for its importance, and some of the ways in which the idea has been, perhaps unfairly, limited or resisted. (2) Since fuzzy logic is a generalization of classical logic, it is deductive; that is, once one has defined the appropriate form of the input and of operations on that input, the conclusion should follow without having to introduce extra material from knowledge about the world into each case. For example, if in order to get a reasonable goodness of membership gradient for *pet fish* from the conjunction of *pet* and *fish* you need to remove all the attributes of each that are incompatible with the other, whereas for *pet rock* you also have to add attributes to *rock* that are completely absent from rock outside of that conjunction (such as that it comes in a straw nest with a satiric set of instructions for its care and feeding), whereas the conditions are different yet for *pet peeve* . . . well, suffice it to say that applying the deductive aspect of fuzzy logic to concepts is a serious problem, to be discussed in the second part of the chapter. Finally, in the third part, I'll discuss why any of this matters and where we might go from here.

4.2   Concepts as Fuzzy Sets: Is the Internal Structure of Concepts Classical or Fuzzy?

What are concepts from the psychological point of view? (Chapter 2 of this volume provides a modern philosopher's take on the subject.) Concepts are the central constructs in most modern theories of the mind. Humans (and arguably other organisms) are seen as living in a conceptually categorized world. Objects and events (from household items to emotions to gender to democracy), although unique, are acted toward as members of classes. Some theories would say that without this ability to categorize, it would be impossible for us to learn from experience. Since at least the nineteenth century, it has been common to refer to the mental or cognitive aspect of categories as *concepts*. Concepts build into complex conceptual systems, and psychology, philosophy, computer science, and linguistics have all played a part in forming conceptual theory and research. In this chapter I will directly address only those views of the nature of concepts that are most relevant to fuzzy logic: (a) the classical view, because it mirrors classical set theory and shows the presuppositions that underlie much of our psychological and cultural thinking even now; (b) the graded structure and prototypes view because it directly challenges the classical view and is the closest to fuzzy set theory, thereby providing an opportunity for meaningful dialogue with fuzzy logic; and (c) the ecological approach, because it provides the context that encompasses concept use, thereby providing perspective on the issues of logic.

4.2.1   The Classical View

The classical view is the approach to concepts derived from the history of Western philosophy. When humans begin to look at their experience by means of reason, questions about the reliability of the senses and the bases for knowledge arise, as do more specific questions about how concepts and categories can have generality (called the *problem of universals*), how words can have meaning, and how concepts in the mind can relate to categories in the world. The Greeks, and most Western philosophers since, have agreed that experience of particulars as it comes moment by moment through the senses is unreliable ("a stick looks bent in water" has been a favorite example); therefore, only stable, abstract, logical categories can function as objects of knowledge and objects of reference for the meaning of words.

For Plato, the stable abstract essences behind concepts were metaphysical entities, the Forms, which one came to know by recollection. For Aristotle, universals were *in* particular objects and were learned by experience with the objects. The British empiricists Locke and Berkeley were basically Aristotelians but added theories about how these universals were learned from experience and in what form they were represented by the mind. The Aristotelian view of knowledge should sound familiar to us: Our biological classification system is based on his formula for organizing plants and animals according to the genus and species given by their universal qualities; our dictionaries are written according to the same principles; and our basic ideas about logic, explanation, and what is required of a theory of concepts stem from the same assumptions.

If only stable, abstract categories can function as objects of knowledge and meaning, those categories are required to have certain logical properties: (a) they have to be exact, not vague, that is, have clearly defined boundaries; (b) their members have to have attributes in common that are the necessary and sufficient conditions for membership in the category; and (c) it follows that all members of the conceptual category are equally good with regard to membership—either they have the necessary common features or they do not.

In short, such categories function as classical sets. An item is either in a category or it is not. Once you know an item's membership, you can make logical inferences about it without the need for recourse to anything in the external world; essentially the item becomes an abstract symbol. For example, if *All men are mortal* and *Socrates is a man*, you can conclude that *Socrates is mortal* without more ado about the state of his health or his relationships with the local government. It also doesn't matter what kind of category you are working with (animal, vegetable, mineral, or symbolic place-markers); it is only necessary and sufficient that the category obey these criteria to be a proper basis of knowledge and meaning.

In the 1950s and '60s the classical view became pervasive in the psychological investigation of concepts. In the work of Jerome Bruner and his associates (Bruner, Goodnow, and Austin 1956), subjects were asked to learn categories that were logical sets defined by explicit criterial attributes (such as *red*, *square*, or *number of borders*) combined by logical rules (such as *and* or *or*). Theoretical interest was focused on how subjects learned which attributes were relevant and which rules combined them. In developmental psychology, the theories of Piaget and Vygotsky were combined with the concept learning paradigms to study how children's ill-structured, thematic concepts develop into the logical adult mode. Artificial stimuli were typically used in experimental research at all levels, structured into microworlds in which the prevailing beliefs about the nature of categories were already explicitly built in. There is no way for a subject in an experiment to demonstrate a legitimate concept organized in a way other than that of classical sets if the only materials he is given to work with are classical sets.

The same kind of suppositions prevailed in linguistics. Most mainstream twentieth-century works in phonology, semantics, and syntax rested on the assumptions of the classical view. Phonemes were analyzed as sets of universal, abstract, binary features. Word meaning, the province of semantics, was likewise represented by a componential analysis of features; for example, *bachelor* was rendered as the features: human, male, adult, never married. A complex concept such as *bald bachelor* was considered the unproblematic union of the features of bachelor with those of bald. Synonymy, contradiction, and other relational aspects of word meaning were accounted for in a similar fashion. Syntax was analyzed by formal systems such as transformational grammar that also relied on decomposition into abstract features (for details and references to the linguistic material, see Taylor 2003).

The field of computer science also enthusiastically adopted a componential understanding of language. Treated in this way, meaning could be divorced from world knowledge and readily represented by the substitutable strings of symbols on which computers basically work. Even in anthropology, where there were claims by some for a complete relativity in the way cultures divided up the things of the world, when it came to linguistic anthropology and the study of concepts, componential analysis was prevalent (Taylor 2003).

4.2.2   Graded Structure and Prototypes

Consider the color red: Is red hair as good an example of your idea or image of red as a red fire engine? Is a dentist's chair as good an example of *chair* as a dining-room chair? Are you immediately sure how to classify and name every color you see?

As a graduate student in the late 1960s in an interdisciplinary department that combined psychology, anthropology, and sociology, the prevailing classical view of concepts and categorization did not seem to me to match the naturally occurring concepts of daily life or the word meanings of natural languages. All members of conceptual categories did not seem to be equally good members; many categories seemed to shade off gradually into nonmembers the way color names did; and the attributes given as criteria for membership in the standard examples of concepts in psychological experiments and in componential analysis (color, form, parts of objects, adjectives such as *bald* or *successful*) seemed to me obviously themselves conceptual categories whose application in the real world was not unproblematic. Was there a way to get hold of these issues experimentally?

Basic research on graded membership in categories

It is useful to begin with the initial research that established graded structure as an issue in psychology, because, since it takes place against the virtually universal acceptance of the classical view, it addresses the question of whether concepts can be considered fuzzy sets more directly than do later refinements.

My initial research was on color categories, a more tractable domain than concepts in general and one with both interesting physiological and cross-cultural dimensions. A series of studies on the naming, organization, memory, and learning of color categories included both subjects in the United States and among a stone-age people, the Dani of New Guinea, who have no basic hue terms in their language. The primary findings were that color categories do not have the properties of classical sets, but they do have structure. For English speakers, some colors are judged better examples of basic color names than others, and the better an example a color is, the shorter the time it takes to name it, the better the memory for the color in memory tests, and, for children, the earlier the color name is learned. Interestingly, such findings were mirrored in the Dani: They have a similar memory structure for the color space even without color names, and showed similar effects for learning and naming when I taught them color names (earlier research published under my former name in Heider 1971, 1972; later work in Rosch 1973a,b). From these data, I argued that color categories form around perceptually salient points in the color space and spread by means of stimulus generalization to adjacent colors, with the end result that the categories become structured into gradients with graded internal structure, no clear boundaries, but agreed-on best examples.

The data from the Dani fit nicely with earlier claims for a universal evolution of color names (Berlin and Kay 1969), with physiological evidence for unique hue points in the color space (DeValois and Jacobs 1968), and, importantly, with the kinds of generalization gradients obtained in classical conditioning studies. Pavlov's dogs produced decreasing amounts of saliva as tones grew farther from the tone originally combined with meat powder; they did not treat the category as a logical bounded set in which stimuli were either members or nonmembers. Generalization gradients were not thought of as relevant to concept formation, however; they violated all the classical view requirements. Reactions to my color work tended to be interest in the cross-cultural findings about color but resistance to claimed implications for concepts and categories as a whole, perhaps because, in the words of one reviewer, "we already know what concepts are."

The next set of experiments addressed a range of common English semantic categories: fruit, vegetable, vehicle, bird, furniture, clothing, weapon, science, sport, crime, disease, carpenter's tool, and toy. Such categories have the advantage for research of many nameable members; would those members also show gradients of category membership? In a series of initial experiments, subjects were asked simply to rate how good an example of the category each member was, that is, to judge how well each category member fit their "idea or image of the category name" (Rosch 1973b). People could easily and quickly perform this task, and there was high agreement among them. For example, an apple is rated a good example of fruit, a strawberry a middling example, and a fig a poor example; for vehicle, a car is a good example, a bicycle a middling example, and elevator a poor example. Subjects were not confusing the task with how well they liked the item, as liking did not correlate with goodness of example ratings (and was inversely correlated for crimes, as might be expected). It also did not correlate with overall word frequency (Mervis, Catlin, and Rosch 1976). For norms for these ratings, see Rosch 1973b, 1975b.

In fuzzy sets, one has numbers between 0 and 1 that indicate the degree of membership in the set, and these data provide just such numeric norms for subjects' judgments of degree of membership for common natural language semantic categories. In subsequent work, we obtained similar results for pictures of items for categories at a lower level of abstraction where the categories do not have many nameable members (Rosch and Mervis 1975) and for photographs of common objects taken from different perspectives (Palmer, Rosch, and Chase 1981). Since the initial research, goodness-of-membership rating scales have been obtained by many researchers for numerous, diverse kinds of concepts (see Murphy 2002).

Research on psychological importance of graded structure
Such scales can readily be called fuzzy sets, but a psychologist will not care what you call them unless these ratings tell us something meaningful about psychology.

In fact, gradients of membership have been shown to affect virtually every major method of study and measurement used in psychological research:

1. *Association* Association is taken as a key to the mind in many systems, for example, in approaches as diverse as British empiricist philosophy, connectionism in computer modeling, and psychoanalysis. Emotional reaction is believed to run along associative channels. The associative strength of a category name is highly correlated with ratings of goodness of example of category members. When asked to list members of a semantic category, subjects produce better examples earlier and more frequently than poorer examples; in fact, the best examples are almost always the first produced (Rosch 1973b, 1975b). Conversely, category names are higher associates of good than of poor members; for example, *fruit* is a high associate of *apple* but not of *fig*.

2. *Speed of processing* Reaction time has been considered a royal road to the study of mental processes in cognitive psychology. It was the use of reaction-time experimental designs that first demonstrated to behaviorist skepticism that it was possible to answer questions about internal mental events in a scientific manner. For both color and semantic categories, it is a robust finding that the better an example is of its category, the more rapidly subjects can answer "true" to the question of whether or not that item belongs to the category (Heider 1972; Rips, Shoben, and Smith 1973; Rosch 1973b, 1975b; see also Murphy 2002).

3. *Learning* Study of how humans and other organisms learn has been a central endeavor of psychology since its beginning. How good an example

is of its category has a major effect in the learning of the category. Artificial categories can be constructed in which goodness-of-example gradients are built in: for example, categories of dot patterns made by distortions of a central pattern, categories of stick figures in which an average figure is central, or categories of letter strings in which members have a family resemblance relationship. Such categories are learned faster if the better examples, particularly the most central members, are presented first, and the better examples are learned more quickly regardless of the order in which they are presented (Rosch 1973a; Rosch and Mervis 1975; Rosch, Simpson, and Miller 1976; Mervis and Pani 1980; see also Murphy 2002). Children acquire better examples of natural language categories earlier than poorer examples (Heider 1971; Rosch 1973b; Mervis 1987; Markman 1989; see also Murphy 2002, 336–341).

4. *Expectation and mental representation*   A traditional psychological experimental design called *priming* or *set* presents subjects with information briefly in advance of a task and measures what effect that has on their performance of the task. Presenting a word as the advance information has been used to study how the word is represented in the mind. We found that when subjects are presented a category name in advance of making a rapid judgment about the category, performance is improved (i.e., reaction time is faster) for good and actually hindered (slowed) for poor members of the category. This indicates that the mental representation of the category is in some ways more like the better than the poorer exemplars (Rosch 1975b).

5. *Probability judgments*   Probability is thought by many to be the basis of inductive inference and, thus, the basis of the way in which we learn about the world. Goodness of example is closely related to the variable called *representativeness* by Kahneman and Tversky (see Kahneman, Slovic, and Tversky 1982; Rosch 1983), which has been shown to distort probability judgments so strongly that the authors call it a cognitive illusion. For example, a sequence of coin tosses that more closely matches our idea of randomness (such as THHHHTH) will be judged more probable than one that is a poorer match (HHHHTH), even though the latter is shorter, less specific, and in fact contained within the former (see Kahneman, Slovic, and Tversky 1982; and Gilovich, Griffin, and Kahneman 2002, for many more examples).

6. *Natural language indicators of graded structure*   Natural languages themselves contain various devices that acknowledge and point to graded structure. One such device is that of hedge words like *technically, virtually,* and
really. The use of such words is linked to goodness-of-example ratings. It
sounds fine to say, "A tomato is technically a fruit," but it would need a
special context for "An apple is technically a fruit" not to sound peculiar.
On the other hand, "A _____ is a fruit *par excellence*" can be said of an apple
but not a tomato (Rosch 1975a, 1977; Lakoff 1987; Taylor 2003). Substi-
tutability of words for each other in sentences is another natural language
indicator of the role of goodness of example. We had subjects generate sentences using the category names for which we had goodness-of-example
ratings and had other subjects judge the naturalness and truth-value of
the resulting sentences when members of the category at different levels of
goodness of example were substituted for the category name. There was a
strong linear relationship between goodness of example and substitutabil-
ity. For example, in the sentence "Twenty or so birds often perch on the
telephone wires outside my window and twitter in the morning," the term
sparrow may be readily substituted for *bird*—but not *turkey* (Rosch 1977).

7. *Inference*   Inference is the name given to the way humans reach conclusions when they reason. In inductive reasoning, there is evidence that (in
the absence of any other information) people infer from more to less good
examples of categories more readily than the reverse. Rips (1975) found
that new information about a category member was generalized asymmetrically; for example, when told that the robins on an island had a disease,
subjects were more likely to decide that ducks would catch it than that
robins would catch a disease that the ducks had. (Obviously, if you have
more specific information or a causal explanation related to disease transmission, you will use that in your reasoning instead—Medin et al. 1997).
Developmentally, Carey (1982) found that young children generalize
asymmetrically in the domain of animals. When told that a human has an
organ called a spleen, 4-year-olds will assume that any animal, including a
bee, has a spleen, whereas when told that a bee has a spleen, they do not
infer that *any* animal, even a bug, has one. (See Murphy 2002, chapter 8,
for a general review of the categories and inductive inference literature.)

8. *Judgment of similarity and conceptual distance*   We structure the contents
of our minds in terms of the similarity and dissimilarity of things to each

other. In logic, similarity relations are symmetrical and reversible, as is distance in Euclidean space. However, goodness of example produces effects that violate these symmetries; less good examples of categories are judged more similar or closer to good examples than vice versa. For example, North Korea (which is rated a nonrepresentative example of a country by Americans) was judged more similar to China (a good example of a country) than China was judged similar to North Korea (Tversky 1977). The same kinds of asymmetries in judgment of distance were found for colors, numbers, and lines of particular orientations (Rosch 1975a).

In sum, gradients of category membership have demonstrably important effects across psychological functions. But the psychologist requires more. If the concept is not a classical set, with just necessary and sufficient features for membership, what is it? What is the mental representation of a concept, and how does it function?

Cognitive representation of graded concepts: Prototypes

The answer that I proposed to this question was that people form and use an idea and/or image of the category that represents the category to them, and which is more like (or more easily generates) the good than the poorer examples of the category. That representation often serves as the reference point to which people refer when performing tasks relevant to the category, such as identifying something as a member of the category or using the category in some other way. I called that representation a *prototype*, meaning the term in a general way (as a placeholder) with the assumption that different kinds of concepts would develop different types of prototypes. Obviously, while many concepts have default values for prototypes and degree of membership and these are what are typically evoked in psychological experiments, both prototypes and membership gradients can be rearranged or otherwise changed with circumstances. It is a matter of empirical investigation to determine what types of concepts and prototypes there are and how people use them. In short, *prototype* was originally meant in a way analogous to the manner in which Belohlavek and Klir (chapter 5, this volume) describe fuzzy logic as an abstract calculus rather than as a specific mathematical model.

If concepts were to be represented as fuzzy sets, would different types of graded structures and/or prototypes make a difference in those representations or in subsequent operations on those sets? The fate of the concept of prototypes at the hands of the psychological research community has been an interesting one and is sufficiently germane to the question of concepts as fuzzy sets that it is worth discussing prototypes at greater length.

Different degrees of concreteness–abstraction in prototypes

Prototypes for different kinds of categories differ in their concreteness or abstraction. For color categories, it is reasonable to suppose that the prototypes are images of the most salient best examples of the color (it certainly seems that way in consciousness for most people), something quite concrete and sensory. (For research on the nature of mental images, see Kosslyn 1980.) On the other hand, for superordinate semantic categories, the priming experiments (Rosch 1975b) indicated that the category name allowed subjects to generate a representation that facilitated simple operations on both words and pictures of the good examples of the category while hindering poor examples, clearly something more general and abstract than a simple image. For less abstract basic-level categories of physical objects such as *chair*, where members are characterized by shared nameable attributes, common motor movements when using the category, relative imageability, and an agreed-on best perspective from which the item should be viewed (Rosch, Mervis et al. 1976; Palmer, Rosch, and Chase 1981), the prototype appears to be more sensory (for the role of sensory imagery and symbol systems in concepts, see Barsalou 1999, 2008). But compare examples such as *chair* with more abstract superordinate categories such as *furniture*, whose members contain heterogeneous attributes, patterns of motor interaction, and appearances; there does not seem to be a vivid sensory prototype for *furniture* comparable to those for member subcategories such as *sofa* or *chair*.

Finally, some prototypes could be a specific episode or event. In the famous Hamill, Wilson, and Nisbett (1980) experiment, subjects were presented with a video interview with a supposed prison guard, in one case brutish, in another humane. Half the subjects were also given information about whether that type of guard was typical or atypical of prison guards. Subsequent tests showed the subjects to be highly influenced by the humane or inhumane interviews and completely unaffected by typicality information.

In sum, prototypes range along the concreteness–abstractness dimension.

Different types of prototypes and graded structures

How is it that gradients of category membership and their prototypical best examples are generated in the first place, and what does that mean for the different kinds of graded structures and prototypes that we can have? Below are some of the types:

1. *Salient stimuli or configurations in sensory domains* For some sensory domains such as color and form, there appear to be particular stimuli made salient by the physiology of perception that become the foci for the formation of graded categories. This was the case with color (as described earlier). Experiments on the learning of geometric form categories with the Dani, who neither had names for geometric forms in their language nor lived in a carpentered world, suggested that the good Gestalt forms of circle, square, and equilateral triangle might function in the same way as did prototypical colors. There are probably similar cases with the other senses.

2. *Central tendencies such as statistical means, modes, or family resemblances of the attributes of category members* Here the most prototypical members are those that have the most in common with other members as a whole and thus provide the most predictive power regarding the category. Much of my own research was on this kind of category with this kind of prototype. Unfortunately, the psychological research community has largely come to take the word *prototype* as having this and only this meaning and, by extension, has taken gradients of category membership or goodness of example to refer only to typicality gradients. (I will later show the problems that this creates both for the research performed on concepts and for the larger implications of that research.)

3. *Ideals where the prototype, that is, the reference point, is the extreme of one or more attributes rather than the central tendency* For American undergraduates, the best examples of cities ("Now that's a real city!") are the largest and most cosmopolitan, such as New York, Paris, and London, not average cities. Another example: Saints and saintliness are at the extreme, not the midpoint, of virtuousness.

4. *Idealizations of roles in social structures* Social structures create various roles (president, teacher, bus driver, mother, undertaker, daughter, student, customer, blogger, stoner, and so on), and cultures provide clusters of expectations of how the role is to be filled and stereotypes of the persons filling the roles. Both result in graded structure and prototypes.

5. *Stereotypes*   Social stereotypes are a type of prototype; it tends to be called a stereotype when it applies to a group of people (determined by factors such as race, ethnicity, gender, sexual orientation, religion, occupation or nationality), and it has social consequences. Such stereotypes can be elusive and difficult to change partly because they are the result of a natural aspect of the cognition of concepts.

6. *Precedent*   Anglo-American case law is based on precedent cases, not on principles alone. Precedent cases provide the reference points in arguing present cases with debate hinging on how much and in what respects the present case is similar to its precedents. (Notice how arguments between parents and children, especially about privileges, can often have this quality.)

7. *Categorization derived from goals*   Human life is structured around what we are trying to do at any given time. Communicative relevance of language is goal derived, as are such complex aspects of life as emotions, self-evaluations, and social interactions. Common material objects such as those typically studied in concepts research can have radically different goodness-of-membership ratings and prototypes when seen from the point of view of different goals: Compare *food, foods to eat on a diet*, and *foods to eat as a reward for having worked hard all day*. Ad hoc categories can be generated instantaneously for unusual goals: for example, things to take out of a house in case of a fire and places to hide from the mafia (Barsalou 1983). These also have prototypical best examples and gradients of membership.

8. *Reference points in formal structures*   Formal structures also create reference points, for example, multiples of 10 in the decimal system. These produce some of the same effects as other prototypes (Rosch 1975a).

9. *Easy-to-understand or easy-to-imagine examples illustrating abstract principles*   Think of classic textbook examples in any of the sciences. Think of examples that you yourself use when teaching or explaining. On the other hand, borderline cases are what tend to be used when one wishes to challenge a concept (is the pope a *bachelor?*) or produce difficult examination questions.

10. *Degree of fit to causal theories*   One example is sequences that "look" random. Since one of the activities humans do from infancy on is try to discover how they can control their environments and experiences, degree of fit to causal theories is of major importance.

11. *Early or most recent experiences with an item*   The sequence in which an item is encountered can be influential in the formation or change of

prototypes and membership gradients. This is especially true for concepts that name personal experiences such as falling in love. A related phenomenon is that the most recent experience can, at least temporarily, usurp prior information to become the reference point for classification and decisions, for example, doctors' reliance on their most recent cases for diagnosis (Brooks, Norman, and Allen 1991).

12. *A list of some of the best examples* For abstract categories, the prototype (i.e., that which is used as the reference point or representation for the category in a particular situation) may simply be a list of a few of the best examples. Speakers of the American Sign Language for the Deaf (ASL), which consists primarily of signs for basic-level categories (Rosch, Mervis et al. 1976), frequently use a list of three good members of the category to refer to the superordinate. For example, *furniture* could be expressed by the signs *table-chair-bed* and *fruit* by the signs *apple-orange-banana*. (That this is not evidence for an exemplar view of all of categorization will be discussed later.)

13. *Strong personal experience with particular member(s) of a category* Any personal experience with members of a category made particularly salient and memorable because they are emotionally charged, vivid, concrete, meaningful or interesting can influence the graded structure of that category and the prototype. Such experiences might or might not interact with early or recent encounters with an item.

14. *Idiosyncratic prototypes generated at a particular moment as a result of the confluence of an individual's past experience and present circumstances* In a real sense, this describes all prototypes as they are evoked and used in life activities and measured in psychological experiments (see section 4.3.1). The previous list of types of prototype indicates the origin of some common prototypes. Such commonalities make certain kinds of prototypes predictable enough for group data to be aggregated and for general, reportable results to be obtained.

Criticisms of graded structure and prototypes

The major forms of criticism draw their force from the assumption that the presuppositions underlying the classical view are unchallengeable and that any alternative theory of concepts must rest on the same grounds and fulfill the same functions as (were attributed to) the classical view. But neither fuzzy set theory nor the graded structure and prototypes view of concepts requires those assumptions; so it is not just the particular form of the classical view that is in question, but its base.

1. *Graded structure effects are too ubiquitous*   Graded structure effects are found for essentially every concept, including those that have a technical definition such as *odd number*. In psychology, this reliability would normally be described as *robustness*, a virtue. However, the logic in this case is that graded structure and prototypes cannot be the "real concept" since that is already provided by the definition (which subjects could readily give for such concepts when asked—Armstrong, Gleitman, and Gleitman 1983). Real concept? People relate with and use concepts in different ways at different times depending on the task they are engaged in and the purpose of the use (see section 4.3.1 for explication). But from within the classical view, a concept is only a real concept to the extent that it functions like a precise formal definition within a human-made formal system. This is a philosophical presupposition, not the product of observation.

2. *The empirical effects of graded structure are a mere processing heuristic*   This is an extension of the first criticism. The claim is that graded structure and prototype effects are the result of a processing heuristic that is unrelated to the core meaning of concepts. Specifically, prototypes provide a rapid recognition system for objects, whereas the true meaning of a concept is provided by its classically defined core (Smith, Shoben, and Rips 1974; Osherson and Smith 1981). The claim that prototypes constitute a faster processing system has not held up experimentally (see Murphy 2002), but the deeper problem is the philosophical precedence and inviolability assumed for a core.

3. *Criticism of the closest mathematical model, Zadeh's fuzzy logic*   The argument is that graded structure and prototypes cannot work as an account of concepts because Zadeh's fuzzy logic is flawed (Osherson and Smith 1981). Given that my and others' empirical work on concepts had developed without reference to fuzzy logic and that the few psychological researchers who had used the word *fuzzy* had not used the logic itself, this might seem an odd claim, but there are intermediate steps of reasoning that make it coherent: Anything that would replace the classical model of concepts must be the same class of thing that it is, a formal deductive model, and there must be something in the replacement that is able to fill the slot

occupied by criterial definitions in the classical model (the obvious candidate in the present case is prototypes) such that the formal model can still generate logical and linguistic functions such as contradiction and conjunction. But since the graded structure and prototype work does not provide such a formal model, we must turn to the nearest available model, which is fuzzy logic. As this line of reasoning continues, if Zadeh's fuzzy logic can be shown to produce incoherent results, it will follow that graded structure and prototypes can be dismissed. Belohlavek and Klir offer a refutation of Osherson and Smith's attack on fuzzy logic (chapter 5, this volume), but that is not the only issue at stake. It is an open question how the empirical work does or does not relate to a formal logic or model, fuzzy or otherwise; in fact, that is one of the reasons for this book and this chapter.

4. *Graded structure and prototypes change with context*   Graded structure, prototype effects, and related reasoning are not invariant; they can change with context and are affected by people's real-world knowledge (Barsalou 1987, 2008; Murphy 2002, chapter 6.) For example, if you are trying to move a piano, the attribute *heavy*, normally little thought of in relation to pianos, becomes very important. Also prototypes and graded structure can vary with culture. But of course! That's what this whole research enterprise was supposed to show by studying real-world (rather than artificial) categories and concepts that vary and change across experiences and circumstances. Why would anyone imagine the claim would be otherwise, unless he harbored the lingering assumption that knowledge (and thus any theory of concepts) must be about stable, unchanging structures?

5. *Prototypes are a-modal abstract structures whereas cognitive representations are verifiably concrete enough to include information from specific sensory modalities*   This is the critique from the "grounded cognition" view (Barsalou 2008). Actually prototypes generally contain much modality-specific sensory information (see the list of types of prototypes), and the prototype view is fully compatible with Barsalou's claim that concepts involve simulations. The prototypes view would simply add a prediction of graded structure and typicality effects to be found in the modality specific simulations for which Barsalou and others offer evidence.

6. *Prototypes and graded structure do not account for everything that people do with concepts*   This argument tends to be applied particularly with respect to studies of causal reasoning and inductive inference, but is also used

elsewhere. When experts or people in other cultures are shown to have rich practical knowledge and causal theories about a domain and to use that in reasoning, or to have culturally constructed meanings to their concepts, this is taken as a refutation of graded structure and prototypes (Atran and Medin 2008). But why would one insist that accounts of concepts be exclusive?

7. *Assimilation of graded membership to statistical probabilities*   In this tactic, graded structure is assumed to mean probability, and the graded structure and prototype view is called the *probabilistic view* of concepts (Smith and Medin 1981). This not only confuses vagueness at the boundaries of categories (see chapter 9, this volume) with goodness-of-example ratings, it also guts the force of graded structure as a phenomenon that both shows inadequacies in the classical view and points to many aspects of the way concepts function to which probabilities are blind. The fact is that subjects judge items that they are perfectly sure are members of a category as having differing degrees of membership.

8. *Defining prototype as only one of the types of prototype contained in the preceding list of fourteen different types (usually it is defined as an average), and pitting that experimentally against another type*   Exactly what a prototype or good example of a category is, as explained earlier, was left unspecified because prototypes can be of many types, depending on the category and situation of use. However, the research community has subsequently taken *prototype* to mean only the average of category member attributes, has pitted that type against stimuli that have different kinds of prototype structures, and has consequently concluded that the prototype theory is disconfirmed (see Murphy 2002 and chapter 2 of this volume for many examples). Particularly remarkable is when *prototype* is baldly defined as meaning a single specific image and then pitted against a more reasonably structured category, or when prototype theory is defined as the claim that physical similarity is the only dimension on which items are to be compared. Actually this development has a certain charm to it, since in the initial sets of studies of prototypes and graded structure, my own as well as others (*mea culpa*, Rosch 1978), that image of prototypes is the most prototypical, so prototype theory might predict something like this would follow.

In summary of section 4.2: The evidence is overwhelming that degree of membership in concepts is a meaningful and important psychological variable, and, thus, that fuzzy set theory might be quite relevant to concepts. There is also empirical evidence that the representation of a concept that serves as the reference point for use of the concept is akin to (in a variety of ways for different kinds of concepts) the best members of the category. It is also apparent that the psychological community feels that in order to be legitimate, concepts of this nature must fit into the functions that the classical view of concepts supposedly provided, that is, must fit into deductive models. In that case, operations on concepts are expected to yield results without recourse to extra world knowledge about the concept—or as linguists might say, on the basis purely of their syntax without recourse to semantics. We turn to that requirement next.

4.3   Deduction—Will It Work for Graded-Structure Concepts?

At this point, we need to step back and take a broader look at the context in which concepts occur. This can be called the *ecological view* of concepts (Rosch 1999; Gabora, Rosch, and Aerts 2008). The following are some of the principles of the ecological view that are most relevant to fuzzy sets and logic.

4.3.1   The Context of Concepts: The Ecological View

A concept occurs in use only at a given moment in the present. If it is part of a memory or plan, that memory or plan is happening in present time. Concepts occur not in isolation but in a context that includes both the circumstances in which the conceiver finds himself and everything in his knowledge base: his internal dictionary, encyclopedia, repertoire of habits and skills, emotions, desires, tacit knowledge, beliefs and theories (organized only semi coherently), expectations, values, autobiographical memories, and everything else comprising the vast pastiche of the human mind at a given point in time.

The use of a concept can happen only in a concrete situation—even if the situation is no more than a random thought, a philosophical example, or a psychology experiment. In the moment of use, the conceiver is acting with intentions and purposes, and his concepts are participating parts of such purposeful actions, not something outside of the situation that gains meaning solely by reference to the concept's extension. Another way to say this is that people are purposively participating in life games, the meaningful activities of life. Concepts, categories, and the rest of conceptualization are participating parts of these life games. There are life games in which referring to objects plays a role, but the reference always has some purpose; it occurs not in isolation, but as part of the game (see, e.g., Wittgenstein's [1953] famous discussion of "slab" in his *Philosophical Investigations*).

Each life game has a motive or motives (what the player is trying to do), and it has a loose set of rules for how it is to be played (parameters that instantiate what kind of a game it is). There are all kinds of life games at various levels of abstraction: survival, relating to people, marriage, playing social roles, predicting the physical world, playing an instrument, solving a math problem, reenacting childhood traumas, raking leaves, removing a splinter, seeking pleasure, following an ideal, teasing a friend, going to sleep, and so on. Structurally, life games are hierarchically nested; for example, participating in a concepts experiment may be nested within doing one's assignments in a class, which is nested within passing the class, which is nested within getting an education, which is nested within preparing for a career, and so on. Life games are also horizontally interpenetrating; for example, one is usually playing multiple life games by means of the same activity. For example, one can be exercising for both pleasure and health while perhaps simultaneously enacting an unconscious theme from earlier in life.

People have different modes of using their concepts, and they are quite flexible in switching among them. If asked to judge goodness of example, they will do so; if asked to give a definition, they will try to produce one; if asked to judge whether something does or does not belong to a category in an all-or-none manner, they will make the judgment (though probably taking longer if the item is a poorer member of the category); if asked to talk about particular experiences with or times they have encountered members of a concept, they will come up with them; if faced with a problem, they will try to avoid or solve it; and so on. Seen in this light, various theories of concepts are clearly not as contradictory as they are usually treated. More will be said about this in the concluding section.

Furthermore, all of this is open to change; humans can be creative. This is the context of categorization and concepts, the context in which fuzzy logic must operate if it is to be used on concepts in action.

4.3.2 Pet Fish, Striped Apples, and the Problems of Deduction

Looked at from the point of view of life games, intentions, the vast resources of human memory, the complexities of language, and the potentials for creative reorganization that are at a person's disposal each time that he performs an operation on a concept, it would not be surprising if problems arose in trying to model operations on concepts with the relatively impoverished information given only by degree of membership scales. There are different kinds of logical operations in both classical and fuzzy logic, but the operation of conjunction (intersection) has received almost all of the psychological attention in regard to concepts.

The research boom in conjunction appears to have been set off by one aspect of Osherson and Smith's (1981) attack on fuzzy logic and their subsequent paper (Osherson and Smith 1982) on conceptual conjunction. Conceptual conjunctions are almost always studied as two-word combinations, either noun-noun or adjective-noun. Here are the facts that launched a thousand ships (and, with reference back to no. 9 in the list of types of prototype, note their relative understandability and image-ability): A picture of a striped apple can be judged a very good example of a striped apple though a poor example of an apple and a very poor example of striped things; likewise, the best examples of pet fish (guppies and goldfish) are poor examples both of pets and of fish. However, the resultant research has pointed toward broader and more fundamental logical difficulties posed by conceptual combination.

The research on conceptual combination has already been extensively, clearly, and delightfully summarized both by Murphy (2002, chapter 12) and by Hampton in chapters 8 and 9 of this volume. From this work, I believe we can abstract four basic types of problems that conceptual combinations present for a fuzzy logic of concepts.

1. *Even classical operations don't work with conceptual conjunction* If you have classically defined groups of material objects, say balls and blocks, each of which is red or green, then the set of red balls will unproblematically be the logical intersection of balls and red things. But now let's assume that all of the concepts in the following example are classical—that each one in itself has necessary and sufficient criteria for membership, its boundaries are clear cut, and all of its members are equally good with respect to membership. Is there anything in the meaning of the concepts

themselves, each taken separately, that will tell us that: "corporate statio-
nery is *used by* the corporation and has the corporate logo on it; a corporate
account is an account that is *charged to* the corporation; a corporate car is
owned by a corporation and used for business travel; a corporate building is
where the business is carried out; a corporate lawyer is one who *works for* a
corporation; and a corporate donor is a donor who *is* a corporation" (Murphy 2002, 450). It is not the fuzziness of these concepts that makes it impossible for us to know the meaning of the combinations from each word
alone; it is that we have to know a great deal more than just each word.
There are numerous other such examples.

2. *Models of the conjunction of fuzzy concepts need more than degree of membership to produce their results*   There have been several attempts to model
conceptual combinations (see Hampton's chapters in this volume and
Murphy 2002, chapter 12), and at least four ingenious models have been
proposed: the Selective Modification Model (Smith et al. 1988), the Concept Specialization Model (Murphy 1988, 1990), the construal model of
Wisniewski (1997), and Hampton's models (chapter 8 of this volume). In
each case, there is a good deal of machinery besides goodness-of-example
ratings needed to characterize the two concepts of the combination (such
as schemas in which dimensions of variation and attributes interact), and
the functioning of that machinery is necessary for obtaining the desired
results. Furthermore, filling the slots in the schemas and prescribing how
the machinery is to function are dependent on world knowledge. Even
more distressingly from the point of view of a deductive logic, much of
that world knowledge is related to the interaction of the two concepts so
that it must be evoked uniquely for each conceptual pair.

Another problem with these models, from the psychologist's point of
view, is that they contain implicit processing assumptions—for example,
the order in which the conceiver fills slots, weights attributes, compares
alternatives, and makes decisions—which have gone largely untested. One
set of studies using reaction times for verification of specific features of
combined concepts yielded spectacularly disconfirming results for the concept specialization model and, by extension, other models that make the
same assumptions. (See Murphy 2002, 459–461, for details and references
for this intriguing work, and Barsalou 1990 for a discussion of the inherent

difficulty of distinguishing processing versus storage assumptions in tests of conceptual models.)

A final difficulty with these conceptual conjunction models: Although each model can account for a particular set of conceptual combinations, those for which it was designed all have classes of counterexamples obligingly pointed out by fellow researchers for which they cannot account. Murphy is forced to conclude his account with, "no model handles all the forms of combination that people can generate" (Murphy 2002, 469). Thus even were one or more of the models deemed an example of fuzzy logic, its scope would be limited.

3. *Emergent attributes: World knowledge enters ad hoc*   One of the most telling difficulties for a logic of conceptual combination is the case of emergent properties, that is, the many examples of conceptual combinations in which the conjoined concept has attributes possessed by neither of the concepts separately, and yet these are what determine goodness of example.

Emergent attributes can be produced from world knowledge of many sorts. People say that an *arctic bicycle* would have spiked tires, an attribute given for neither *arctic* nor *bicycle,* most likely generated by causal thinking (Johnson and Keil 2000). The attribute *long* is neither a property of *peas* nor of *unshelled things*, but is given as an attribute of *unshelled peas* (Murphy 1988) apparently from knowledge of what unshelled peas look like. *Talks* is not listed as an attribute for either *pet* or *bird*, but does show up for *pet bird* (Hampton 1987), perhaps from the subject's memory of a talking parrot—Hampton calls this "extensional feedback." And finally the knowledge that a *typewriter table*, unlike either of its constituents, must be of a proper height for typing and must have side space on which to put one's papers comes from functional knowledge about typing. The point of all this is that a deductive logic of any kind is not designed to incorporate memories or creative ideas from outside the system brought in ad hoc for each individual case in order to yield the proper results.

4. *Nonlogical and nonconsistent results for conjunctions, disjunctions, and negation*   From experiments using ingeniously worded phrases, Hampton (this volume) provides much evidence for the ad hoc intrusion of world knowledge and associations into reasoning about fuzzy concepts resulting in

subjects' endorsement of mutually inconsistent or nonlogical statements. It's easy to see the reasoning behind any given result after the fact (a clock is furniture, Big Ben is a clock, but Big Ben is not furniture), but hard to see how operations of a deductive fuzzy logic could encompass all such vagaries in a useful way.

One final word about negation: The very act of denial or of strong assertion appears to raise the truth-value of the complement. Thus the statement "John doesn't beat his wife" or "Twiggy doesn't use steroids" evokes the possibility of the truth of that which is being denied, something that might never have previously entered the mind of the listener. And "protesting too much" in the positive sense arouses the suspicion that the speaker means the opposite. These are delicate discourse effects of which there are many; if and how a fuzzy logic might handle them remains for future investigation.

In summary of section 4.3: There are many difficulties in applying an abstract deductive logic, fuzzy or otherwise, to concepts because of the repeated necessity to introduce ad hoc world knowledge to derive results. Can it be that we are asking the wrong questions and imposing the wrong demands on our "theories" of concepts?

4.4   General Discussion

We began with two basic questions about the relationship of fuzzy logic to the psychology of concepts: (1) Can concepts be treated as fuzzy sets? (2) Can the operations of fuzzy logic be applied to concepts? What can we conclude?

The answer to the first question appears to be a clear *yes*. People can assign degrees of membership to members of concepts, and those ratings have been shown to affect virtually every important psychological measure. The fact that for some concepts in some conditions, people can, will, and should treat the same concept as a classical set in no way invalidates fuzziness and is, in fact, provided for in fuzzy set theory (see the discussion of *crisp* sets in chapter 3 of this volume). Debates over the role of the best members of concepts in the mental representation of the concept (which I called *prototypes*) also do not invalidate the basic fuzziness of concepts;

in fact, the debate could not exist if the concepts did not have a graded structure.

The second basic question was whether the operations of fuzzy logic apply to concepts. Can information about the degree of membership of members of a concept be fed into a fuzzy logic operation and produce a valid and useful result without the further input of ad hoc information derived from real-world knowledge about the concept? Here the answer is more doubtful. Conjunctive concepts have been the most studied; the results so far are that the concept must be represented in a more complex manner than degree of membership (different models have different representations); that there is the constant need for input of relevant real-world knowledge into all aspects of the models; and that, even with that kind of "cheating," the models don't cover much territory. In short, the conceptual system appears to need to be porous to what humans know, perceive, and do in order to understand and perform operations on concepts.

This raises a further question: Is it reasonable or is it misleading to call concepts fuzzy sets if only degrees of membership apply to them, but they cannot be properly manipulated by the operations of fuzzy logic? Is there anything further that the mathematics of fuzziness has to offer the psychology of concepts under these conditions? After all, through its alliance with statistics, psychology is already reasonably sophisticated about scaling and other operations on distributions of numbers, and research on degree of membership in concepts began and has been proceeding without needing to refer to the mathematical work in fuzzy logic. Can this work be further enriched by technical input from the mathematics of fuzzy sets?

A second related question is about language; would we want to call concepts fuzzy sets, or just fuzzy, even without the use of fuzzy logic? In fact, prior to Osherson and Smith's (1981) critique, the word *fuzzy* was at times used, albeit informally, in research papers on concepts; afterward, use of the word largely disappeared even though there was an upsurge of research on conceptual combination. Other research on concepts with graded structure and prototypes also continued unabated. My fear is that if the word *fuzzy* were brought back other than within the context of fuzzy logic, it would soon lose its mathematical meaning. In ordinary usage, the word has, at best, a patronizing tone, as in *warm and fuzzy feeing*, and, at worst, a downright negative connotation, as in *fuzzy minded*—not a very welcoming signal that something psychologically and culturally important is in the offing.

The graded structure/fuzziness of concepts is important in its own right, whatever you call it—an importance that I don't think has yet been quite realized. Although the classical view of concepts, in the strict sense, has been overturned (or at least put out of fashion for now) by the accumulated evidence of graded structure, the ancient assumptions about what knowledge and understanding must be that underlie that view have remained in force. There remains a deep distrust of the temporal nature of the human mind and its modes of experience; the role of the senses is denigrated; knowledge is seen as something that must be stable and lasting beyond the flux of experience; words and concepts are seen as having to derive their meaning by reference to something beyond their usage within forms of life; and classical deductive logic is installed as the king of reasoning who provides cognitive and emotional security through clear rules and safe borders.

Both fuzzy set theory and the graded structure view of concepts challenge this set of premises. Classical presumptions may or may not have a metaphysical import beyond the conceptual mind, but this is not the realm in which science operates. Modern physics gets along perfectly well without something called *substance* behind material objects and without *causes* behind the connection between events. There is increasing evidence that cognition does not operate separately from the senses (Barsalou 1999, 2008, and see the wealth of other papers on his website, <http://psychology .emory.edu/cognition/barsalou/index.html>). Fuzzy logic and many other multivalent logics show that we need not adhere to classical definitions and rules to be reasonable. And language and concepts fulfill their various functions, such as communication, in a remarkably open and adaptable manner; for example, the case recounted by Gleitman, Armstrong, and Gleitman (1983) of blind children and their sighted mothers who did not notice for years that they were using words such as *see* and *look* somewhat differently. Why then are psychologists still trying to force graded structure and prototypes into an anachronistic mold? For example, why should the meaning and the degree-of-membership structure of a conceptual combination be necessarily determined by the meaning and structure of the two components singly?

I am often bemused at the way in which graded structure and prototypes (in at least some version) have by now become an accepted, even taken for granted, part of psychology, producing a cornucopia of experiments (far different from the desert in which I first began working), and yet the force of this as a new mode of understanding concepts is often difficult to discern. For example, the importance of a graded-structure-*cum*-fuzzy-set understanding of concepts also has cultural importance. People tend to reify and deify their concepts in a way that graded structure and fuzzy sets (and the ecological view) do not. People may live in a cocoon of concepts that they take as fixed and not-at-all fuzzy, may use concepts to bludgeon each other, may even be willing to die for concepts.

All that is far beyond the scope of this chapter, but I would like to close with mention of some issues in the psychology of concepts that bear the marks of reification and could possibly use help from some fuzzy mathematical thinking:

The Need for Levels of Abstraction Therapy   What abstract systems such as mathematics and particularly logic are good at is offering a language in which higher-order invariances and relations can be described and investigated. I believe that the psychology of concepts currently has a level-of-abstraction problem. It is no accident that fuzzy logic was misread by Osherson and Smith (1981) as a particular mathematical model rather than a general logic and that *prototypes* have been reduced to one kind of instantiation of one kind of prototype. Psychology likes to have its claims at just that middle level of abstraction at which there will be maximum disagreement and, henceforth, argumentative experiments—experiments being, after all, the coin of the realm. But experiments that pit the right hand against the left are unhelpful.

The following are some suggestions for where an abstract symbolic formulation, perhaps in terms of fuzzy logic or perhaps not, might open up new understanding.

Islands in a sea of fuzziness   Models in psychology of concepts operate by taking as given that everything is clear and definite except for the aspect that is being modeled. For example, if attributes are being counted or arranged into a schema, it is assumed that what we are calling attributes are unproblematic. But they themselves are fuzzy concepts. And generally they are also relative to the thing of which they are attributes. The legs of a chair are called legs rather than scrap lumber or bean poles because they are attached to the seat of the chair in a certain configuration, all of which is also fuzzy. It's fuzziness all the way down. Can fuzzy sets and perhaps fuzzy logic capture that kind of interlocking systemic fuzziness?

Gathering the lost tribes   There are many different types of goodness-of-example/degree-of-membership/fuzziness structures, each with different kinds of prototypes. These could be seen as a union of fuzzy sets each of which has different properties. Unions like that are difficult kinds of concepts for people to work with, but it generates much confusion to refuse to recognize that this is what we have. Expressing it in a symbolic language, perhaps the language of fuzzy sets, might help, especially in relation to the next issue.

Dissolving the exemplars versus prototypes battle   The battle between exemplar and prototype theories of concept learning has gone on for a long time and generated innumerable experiments. But it is not coherent. The exemplar view claims, basically, that we remember particular instances of a category and identify new members by matching to the old ones with no abstraction occurring. The opposing so-called prototype views claim that we abstract, usually a statistical average, and match to that. But a moment's contemplation of our own minds, if nothing else (psychology also shuns checking in with nonabstract immediate experience), makes it obvious that we do both. And research, both psychological and physiological, into the assimilation of new information (during sleep as well as waking) concurs. We have memories of particular events, and we have abstract knowledge (memory research distinguishes between episodic and semantic memory), and we have all manner of partially digested bits of memory in between. Even perception involves some abstraction (you don't have a red, apple-shaped first-order isomorphism in your brain when you see a red apple), and even an abstracted prototype involves a more concrete representation; it might even be in the form of a few best examples. Barsalou (1990), in an insightful but unfortunately much-ignored paper, has demonstrated how, because of the malleability of storage and processing assumptions, the two kinds of models become empirically indistinguishable. Murphy (2002) intelligently recognizes that we do both, but says that it would be impossibly difficult to develop a joint model. Is fuzzy logic up to it?

Back to world knowledge, goals, and the rest   If one is trying to turn graded structure and prototypes into a substitute for definitions in a universe conceived in the classical mold, then world knowledge, the interrelated-ness of concepts, the vast encyclopedic knowledge that humans bring to every task, and the creativity that can emerge in the simplest thought or speech act will be an enemy. But if graded structure/fuzziness is taken in its own right and concepts are seen as open rather than closed systems, all that becomes an uncharted fecund territory calling for exploration. One example: Can we map life games, their vertical and horizontal structures, how those fit together, the role of concepts in establishing and then chang-ing them, and the slots in life games into which different types of concepts fit? And what kinds of possibly fuzzy formal systems might be helpful in such an endeavor?

This brings us finally to *slow lettuce*. What do you think "slow lettuce" means? No, it's not lettuce that grows slowly or is served in salads by slow-food aficionados. It's a name that a bonobo named Kanzi, who has been taught language from birth, created for the vegetable kale (Kruger 2010). Why do you think he would call kale slow lettuce? I've only found one per-son who guessed. It was a man who had just gotten back from a meditation retreat where meals were eaten in a traditional ritualized manner called *oryoki* requiring that the food be consumed very rapidly with nothing in one's bowl left over. Kale from the garden had been served several times, and it was a problem for him because it took so long to chew. Ah, of course! Animals eat fast, "wolf down their food" as we say, with good reason in the wild. And, yes, Kanzi's trainers reported that he named kale "slow lettuce" because it takes longer to chew than regular lettuce. Maybe it is by means of similar objectives and similar experiences, rather than by ancient semi-metaphysical assumptions, that mathematicians, ordinary people, bono-bos, and maybe even lemmings (whose behavior our species does seem to be imitating these days) can come to communicate productively with one another.

References

Armstrong, S., L. Gleitman, and H. Gleitman. 1983. What some concepts might not be. *Cognition* 13:263–308.

Atran, S., and D. L. Medin. 2008. *The Native Mind and the Cultural Construction of Reality*. Cambridge, MA: MIT Press.

Barsalou, L. W. 1983. Ad hoc categories. *Memory & Cognition* 11:211–227.

Barsalou, L. W. 1987. The instability of graded structure: Implications for the nature of concepts. In *Concepts and Conceptual Development: Ecological and Intellectual Factors in Categorization*, ed. U. Neisser, 101–140. Cambridge: Cambridge University Press.

Barsalou, L. W. 1990. On the indistinguishability of exemplar memory and abstraction in category representation. In *Advances in Social Cognition III: Content and Process Specificity of Prior Experiences*, ed. T. K. Skull and R. S. Wyer, Jr., 61–88. Hillsdale, NJ: Lawrence Erlbaum.

Barsalou, L. W. 1999. Perceptual symbol systems. *Behavioral and Brain Sciences* 22:577–609.

Barsalou, L. W. 2008. Grounded cognition. *Annual Review of Psychology* 59:617–645.

Berlin, B., and P. Kay. 1969. *Basic Color Terms: Their Universality and Evolution*. Berkeley, CA: University of California Press.

Brooks, L. R., G. R. Norman, and S. W. Allen. 1991. The role of specific similarity in a medical diagnostic task. *Journal of Experimental Psychology: General* 120:278–287.

Bruner, J., J. Goodnow, and G. Austin. 1956. *A Study of Thinking*. New York: John Wiley.

Carey, S. 1982. Semantic development: The state of the art. In *Language Acquisition: The State of the Art*, ed. E. Wanner and L. R. Gleitman, 347–389. Cambridge: Cambridge University Press.

De Valois, R. L., and G. H. Jacobs. 1968. Primate color vision. *Science* 162:533–540.

Gabora, L., E. Rosch, and E. Aerts. 2008. Toward an ecological theory of concepts. *Ecological Psychology* 20:84–116.

Gilovich, T., D. Griffin, and D. Kahneman, eds. 2002. *Heuristics and Biases: The Psychology of Intuitive Judgment*. New York: Cambridge University Press.

Gleitman, L. R., S. L. Armstrong, and H. Gleitman. 1983. On doubting the concept "concept." In *New Trends in Conceptual Representation: Challenges to Piaget's Theory?* ed. E. K. Scholnick, 87–110. Hillsdale, NJ: Lawrence Erlbaum.

Hamill, R., T. D. Wilson, and R. E. Nisbett. 1980. Insensitivity to sample bias; generalizing from atypical cases. *Journal of Personality and Social Psychology* 39:578–589.

Hampton, J. A. 1987. Inheritance of attributes in natural concept conjunctions. *Memory & Cognition* 15:55–71.

Heider, E. R. 1971. Focal color areas and the development of color names. *Developmental Psychology* 4:447–455.

Heider, E. R. 1972. Universals in color naming and memory. *Journal of Experimental Psychology* 93:10–20.

Johnson, C., and F. C. Keil. 2000. Explanatory understanding and conceptual combination. In *Explanation and Cognition*, ed. F. C. Keil and R. A. Wilson, 328–359. Cambridge, MA: MIT Press.

Kahneman, D., P. Slovic, and A. Tversky, eds. 1982. *Judgment under Uncertainty: Heuristics and Biases*. New York: Cambridge University press.

Kosslyn, S. M. 1980. *Image and mind*. Cambridge, MA: Harvard University Press.

Kruger, J. 2010. Inside the minds of animals. *Time* 176 (7):36–43.

Lakoff, G. 1987. *Women, Fire, and Dangerous Things: What categories reveal about the mind*. Chicago: University of Chicago Press.

Markman, E. M. 1989. *Categorization and Naming in Children*. Cambridge, MA: MIT Press.

Medin, D. L., E. B. Lynch, J. D. Coley, and S. Atran. 1997. Categorization and reasoning among tree experts: Do all roads lead to Rome? *Cognitive Psychology* 32:49–96.

Mervis, C. B. 1987. Child-basic object categories and early lexical development. In *Concepts and Conceptual Development: Ecological and Intellectual Factors in Categorization*, ed. U. Neisser, 201–233. Cambridge: Cambridge University Press.

Mervis, C. B., J. Catlin, and E. Rosch. 1976. Relationships among goodness-of-example, category norms, and word frequency. *Bulletin of the Psychonomic Society* 7:203–284.

Mervis, C. B., and J. R. Pani. 1980. Acquisition of basic object categories. *Cognitive Psychology* 12: 496–522.

Murphy, G. L. 1988. Comprehending complex concepts. *Cognitive Science* 12: 529–562.

Murphy, G. L. 1990. Noun phrase interpretation and conceptual combination. *Journal of Memory and Language* 29:259–288.

Murphy, G. L. 2002. *The Big Book of Concepts*. Cambridge, MA: MIT Press.

Osherson, D. N., and E. E. Smith. 1981. On the adequacy of prototype theory as a theory of concepts. *Cognition* 9:35–58.

Osherson, D. N., and E. E. Smith. 1982. Gradedness and conceptual conjunction. *Cognition* 12:299–318.

Palmer, S., E. Rosch, and P. Chase. 1981. Canonical perspective and the perception of objects. In *Attention and Performance IX*, ed. J. B. Long and A. D. Baddeley, 135–151. Hillsdale, NJ: Lawrence Erlbaum.

Rips, L. J. 1975. Inductive judgments about natural categories. *Journal of Verbal Learning and Verbal Behavior* 14:665–681.

Rips, L. J., E. J. Shoben, and E. E. Smith. 1973. Semantic distance and the verification of semantic relations. *Journal of Verbal Learning and Verbal Behavior* 12:1–20.

Rosch, E. 1973a. Natural categories. *Cognitive Psychology* 4:328–350.

Rosch, E. 1973b. On the internal structure of perceptual and semantic categories. In *Cognitive Development and the Acquisition of Language*, ed. T. M. Moore, 111–144. New York: Academic Press.

Rosch, E. 1975a. Cognitive reference points. *Cognitive Psychology* 7:532–547.

Rosch, E. 1975b. Cognitive representations of semantic categories. *Journal of Experimental Psychology. General* 104:192–233.

Rosch, E. 1977. Human categorization. In *Advances in Cross-Cultural Psychology I*, ed. N. Warren, 1–49. London: Academic Press.

Rosch, E. 1978. Principles of categorization. In *Cognition and Categorization*, ed. E. Rosch and B. B. Lloyd, 27–48. Hillsdale, NJ: Lawrence Erlbaum.

Rosch, E. 1983. Prototype classification and logical classification: The two systems. In *New Trends in Conceptual Representation: Challenges to Piaget's Theory?* ed. E. K. Scholnick, 73–86. Hillsdale, NJ: Lawrence Erlbaum.

Rosch, E. 1999. Reclaiming concepts. *Journal of Consciousness Studies* 6:61–77.

Rosch, E., and C. B. Mervis. 1975. Family resemblances: Studies in the internal structure of categories. *Cognitive Psychology* 7:573–605.

Rosch, E., C. B. Mervis, W. D. Gray, D. M. Johnson, and P. Boyes-Braem. 1976. Basic objects in natural categories. *Cognitive Psychology* 8:382–439.

Rosch, E., C. Simpson, and R. S. Miller. 1976. Structural bases of typicality effects. *Journal of Experimental Psychology. Human Perception and Performance* 2:491–502.

Smith, E. E., E. J. Shoben, and L. J. Rips. 1974. Structure and process in semantic memory: A featural model for semantic decisions. *Psychological Review* 81:214–241.

Smith, E. E., and D. L. Medin. 1981. *Categories and Concepts*. Cambridge, MA: Harvard University Press.

Smith, E. E., D. N. Osherson, L. J. Rips, and M. Keane. 1988. Combining prototypes: A selective modification model. *Cognitive Science* 12:485–527.

Taylor, J. 2003. *Linguistic Categorization*. Oxford: Oxford University Press.

Tversky, A. 1977. Features of similarity. *Psychological Review* 84:327–352.

Wisniewski, E. J. 1997. When concepts combine. *Psychonomic Bulletin & Review* 4:167–183.

Wittgenstein, L. 1953. *Philosophical Investigations*. New York: Macmillan.

5 Fallacious Perceptions of Fuzzy Logic in the Psychology of Concepts

Radim Belohlavek and George J. Klir

5.1   Introduction

After the emergence of fuzzy logic in the 1960s, literature on the psychology of concepts reveals two distinct periods as far as attitudes toward fuzzy logic are concerned. In the 1970s, some cognitive psychologists and linguists started to make occasional remarks about fuzzy logic in their publications dealing with concepts. In general, these remarks expressed positive attitudes toward fuzzy logic, as is partially documented in chapter 1. However, these positive attitudes abruptly changed to negative ones in the early 1980s, and fuzzy logic has ever since been portrayed as unsuitable for representing and dealing with concepts. It has been virtually abandoned in the psychology of concepts, contrary to its use and impressive successes in many other areas of human affairs (see chapter 3, section 3.8, for an overview of applications of fuzzy logic). What happened in the psychology of concepts in the early 1980s that resulted in this drastic change in attitudes toward fuzzy logic?

In this chapter, we show that this abrupt change in attitudes toward fuzzy logic was, by and large, a result of a number of negative claims regarding fuzzy logic that were advanced in a paper by two highly influential cognitive psychologists (Osherson and Smith 1981). For convenience, we refer to this paper as OSP throughout this chapter, and we refer to the authors, Osherson and Smith, as O&S.

Our principal aim in this chapter is to demonstrate that the negative claims in OSP are all either formally or conceptually erroneous and that, in spite of this major deficiency, the paper has decisively influenced the entire field of the psychology of concepts. (This chapter is loosely based on Belohlavek et al. 2002, 2009.)

The amount of influence that a critical publication by reputable scholars has on a field of research should not be underestimated. A paradigm case from a different field is that of Minsky and Papert's book *Perceptrons*, published in 1969 by the MIT Press. Minsky and Papert were interested in exploring the potential and limitations of early neural networks, principally known at that time through Frank Rosenblatt's work on the perceptron. Their book is a thorough mathematical analysis of the kinds of functions a two-layer perceptron is capable of computing. The well-known and devastating result of this analysis is that there are important functions that the perceptron cannot perform. Although Minsky and Papert considered the possibility of extending the perceptron to multilayer neural networks, they concluded that it was their "intuitive judgment that the extension is sterile" (Minsky and Papert 1969, 232). Because of their excellent reputation and the rigor of their analysis, most researchers relied on their "intuitive judgment" and did not pursue any further research on artificial neural networks. This resulted in virtual demise of the research program in this area until the mid-1980s. As we all now know, Minsky and Papert's misguided "intuitive judgment" delayed for more than twenty years the development of what is now an important research area. Surely there is a lesson to be learned here.

The chapter is structured as follows. In section 5.2, we describe, using our notation and terminology, each of the negative claims regarding fuzzy logic made in OSP. In section 5.3, we document the enormous influence of these negative claims and, in particular, how they were uncritically accepted as correct. In section 5.4, we scrutinize these claims (and a few additional ones) in detail and show that all of them represent fallacies of several different types. In section 5.5, we summarize the principal issues discussed in this chapter.

5.2 Osherson and Smith's (1981) Paper (OSP)

As the title of OSP suggests, the primary aim of O&S is to examine the adequacy of one of the main theories of concepts, namely, the prototype theory, as a viable theory of concepts. The authors state in the abstract:

Prototype theory construes membership in a concept's extension as graded, determined by similarity to the concept's "best" exemplar (or by some other measure of central tendency). The present paper is concerned with the compatibility of this view of concept membership with two criteria of adequacy for theories of concepts. The first criterion concerns the relationship between complex concepts and their conceptual constituents. The second concerns the truth conditions for thoughts corresponding to simple inclusions. (OSP, 35)

For their examination to be sufficiently concrete, O&S make two choices. First, from the various versions of prototype theory available in the literature, they select one particular version. Second, they use "fuzzy-set theory as a means of implementing the prototype approach" (OSP, 36). On page 41, they write:

We may now investigate the compatibility of prototype theory with the facts of conceptual combination, in particular, with the relationship between the characteristic functions of complex concepts and the characteristic functions of their conceptual constituents. Combinatorial principles germane to this problem have been supplied by Zadeh (e.g., 1965) under the name of *fuzzy-set theory*. . . . It is possible that principles other than those provided by Zadeh can better serve prototype theory in accounting for conceptual combination, but no suitable alternative has yet been suggested. . . . Since, in addition, fuzzy-set theory is a natural complement to prototype theory, and the former is an appealing theory in its own right, we shall evaluate prototype theory exclusively in the context of fuzzy-set theory.[1]

After a brief overview of the concept of a fuzzy set and the operations of (standard) intersection, union, and complement of fuzzy sets in section 2.3, O&S write in section 2.4:

We are ready to demonstrate that prototype theory in conjunction with fuzzy-set theory contradicts strong intuitions we have about concepts. (OSP, 43)

O&S carry out their demonstration in section 2.4 and in section 3 by considering four problem areas they call *conjunctive concepts, logically empty* and *logically universal concepts, disjunctive concepts,* and *truth conditions of thoughts.* We present O&S's considerations and conclusions regarding these areas in the rest of this section.

5.2.1 Conjunctive Concepts

O&S consider the set of all fruits as a domain F and three relevant concepts in this domain: *apple, striped,* and *striped apple.* In their discussion, O&S use a drawing of a normal apple with stripes on it (OSP, 44) and refer to this striped apple as a. They argue that the membership degree of a in the fuzzy set of striped apples, SA, should be, from the psychological point of view, greater than the membership degree of a in the fuzzy set of apples, A. That is, they argue that the inequality

$$SA(a) > A(a) \qquad (5.1)$$

(inequality (2.11) in OSP) should hold for the striped apple a. Assuming that SA is a standard intersection of A and the set of all striped fruits, S, they argue that the intersection of A and S violates (5.1). That is, according to O&S,

$$SA(a) = \min[(S(a), A(a)]$$

and, consequently,

$$SA(a) \leq A(a)$$

(inequality (2.12) in OSP), which contradicts (5.1). O&S then conclude (OSP, 45):

Given the above, it becomes clear that prototype theory conjoined to fuzzy set theory will lead to a contradiction whenever an object is more prototypical of a conjunction than of its constituents. . . . We conclude that prototype theory *cum* fuzzy-set theory is not compatible with strong intuitions about conjunctive concepts.

5.2.2 Logically Empty and Logically Universal Concepts

In section 2.3.2 of OSP, O&S argue that the concept *apple that is not an apple* is logically empty and, similarly, that the concept *fruit that either is or is not an apple* is logically universal, and that, as a consequence, the sets representing these concepts are, respectively, the empty set and the universal set. These properties are, of course, correct in terms of classical logic and classical set theory, where they are called the *law of contradiction* and the *law of excluded middle*, respectively. O&S demonstrate that these properties do not hold when standard operations of complement, intersection, and union are employed as follows. The fuzzy set *ANA* representing the concept *apple that is not an apple* is a (standard) intersection of the fuzzy set *A* representing the concept *apple* and the fuzzy set *NA* representing the concept *not an apple*. In addition, *NA* is the (standard) complement of *A*. As a consequence, the membership degree of a particular fruit x in *ANA* is given by

$$ANA(x) = \min(A(x), NA(x)) = \min(A(x), 1-A(x)).$$

If a is a fruit, such as the one shown in figure 1(a) in OSP, for which $0 < A(a) < 1$, then it follows that

$$ANA(a) > 0,$$

showing that *ANA* is not logically empty (note that for the logically empty fuzzy set *E*, we have $E(x) = 0$ for every element in the universe). In a similar way, O&S demonstrate that the fuzzy set *F* representing the concept *fruit that either is or is not an apple* is not logically universal, that is, does not fulfill $F(x) = 1$ for every fruit x in the universe. O&S then claim (OSP, 46):

We conclude that fuzzy-set theory does not render prototype theory compatible with strong intuitions pertaining to logically empty and logically universal concepts.

5.2.3 Disjunctive Concepts

In section 2.4.3 of OSP, O&S discuss an example involving the concept *financial wealth* and its connection to concepts *liquidity* and *investment*:

Table 5.1

Person	Liquidity	Investment
A	$105,000	$5,000
B	$100,000	$100,000
C	$5,000	$105,000

As an example of a disjunctive concept, consider (financial) wealth. It seems clear that wealth is conceptually connected to liquidity and investment in this way: the degree to which one enjoys either or both of the latter determines the degree to which one is wealthy. (OSP, 46)

They consider three persons, A, B, C, whose assets are given in table 5.1. O&S describe the concepts *liquidity*, *investment*, and *wealth*, respectively, by fuzzy sets L, I, and W (our notation), and argue correctly that the following inequalities should be satisfied on intuitive grounds:

$$L(A) > L(B)$$

$$I(C) > I(B)$$

$$W(B) > W(A)$$

$$W(B) > W(C)$$

The basic issue now is how $W(x)$ is determined for any $x \in X$ in terms of $L(x)$ and $I(x)$. That is, we want to find a function f such that

$$W(x) = f[L(x), I(x)]$$

is, for any $x \in X$, sensible on intuitive and/or experimental grounds. O&S argue that "if fuzzy-set theory is to represent the conceptual connection among liquidity, investment, and wealth, it would seem that the only option is to employ fuzzy union" (OSP, 47), and what they mean is the standard union. That is, they obtain

$$W(x) = \max[L(x), I(x)],$$

which is, as O&S show, in contradiction to the assumptions $L(A) > L(B)$, $I(C) > I(B)$, $W(B) > W(A)$, $W(B) > W(C)$. O&S then write (OSP, 48):

We conclude that fuzzy-set theory renders prototype theory incompatible with strong intuitions about disjunctive conceptual combination.

5.2.4   Truth Conditions of Thoughts

The last example discussed in OSP (48–53) concerns the so-called truth conditions of thoughts. What O&S mean by this term is basically the issue of determining the truth degree of a proposition of the form

$$\text{All } As \text{ are } Bs. \tag{5.2}$$

The authors claim that propositions of this form are normally assigned the truth condition

$$(\forall x \in U)(A(x) \le B(x)), \tag{5.3}$$

where U is a universe of discourse and A and B are membership functions of fuzzy sets representing the terms A and B in (5.2), respectively.[2] Then, they present a "counterintuitive result" (OSP, 49–51): Let U be the universe of all animals and let A and B be, respectively, the fuzzy sets representing concepts *grizzly bear* and *inhabitant of North America*. That is, (5.2) becomes "All grizzly bears are inhabitants of North America." Then, if there is a squirrel (call it Sam) who lives on Mars and if $A(\text{Sam}) = a > 0$ and $B(\text{Sam}) < a$, it follows that $A(\text{Sam}) \le B(\text{Sam})$ is not the case, and thus the existence of a squirrel on Mars makes the truth value of "All grizzly bears are inhabitants of North America" 0 (false). The authors conclude that (OSP, 51):

fuzzy-set theory does not render prototype theory compatible with the truth conditions of inclusions.

In section 5.4.2, we analyze the arguments by O&S presented in this section, as well as a few other arguments put forward in OSP. We show that the conclusions arrived at by O&S are erroneous and that they are based on various types of fallacies. In spite of that, OSP has had a lasting, negative influence on the use of fuzzy logic in the psychology of concepts. This is demonstrated in the next section.

5.3   Influence of Osherson and Smith's (1981) Paper

Although the overall conclusions of O&S are based on several types of errors and misunderstandings, as we show in detail in section 5.4, the paper has been highly influential. Since the publication of OSP in 1981, there has scarcely been any article or book on concepts that does not refer to the criticism of fuzzy logic in this paper, and it is routinely taken for granted that this criticism is valid.

In the following, we demonstrate by several quotations from publications of highly respected scholars how the conclusions presented in OSP have been uncritically accepted and propagated. Note how quickly the conclusions go from those made by O&S to critical conclusions about fuzzy set theory as a whole.

Armstrong, Gleitman, and Gleitman (1983, 270) write:

Osherson and Smith, 1981, have described this kind of prototype model formally, and distinguished it from the featural interpretations of prototype theory. For both types of models, these authors demonstrate that prototype theory, amalgamated with combinatorial principles from fuzzy-set theory (Zadeh, 1965), cannot account for our intuitions about conceptual combination.

The following quote is from a paper by Roth and Mervis (1983, 522) in which they refer to OSP and a follow-up paper by Osherson and Smith (1982):

Recent work of Osherson and Smith (1982) suggests additional problems in applying fuzzy set theory to semantic categories. Osherson and Smith point out a number of logical inconsistencies that arise when fuzzy set theory is used to form complex concepts from simpler ones. These results taken in combination with our own results suggest that fuzzy set theory is limited in its usefulness as a formal model of the semantics of natural categories.

In a review of work on human concepts and concept formation in the mid-1980s, Medin and Smith (1984, 133) write:

More recent studies provide extensive arguments against the use of fuzzy-set theory as an account of complex concepts (see Jones 1982, Osherson & Smith 1981, 1982, Roth & Mervis 1983).

Kamp and Partee (1995, 130) write:

Osherson and Smith appeal to fuzzy-set theory (Zadeh, 1965) as the most likely means for extending prototype theory to deal with conceptual combination. O&S then succeed in clearly showing that fuzzy-set theory cannot support a compositional semantics whose input consists of prototype concepts.

And (ibid., 129):

[M]any of the problems O&S discovered are due to difficulties that are intrinsic to fuzzy set theory.

Hampton (1997, 139) writes:

Although fuzzy logic had some success in accounting for intuitions about the conjunction of unrelated statements (Oden, 1977), it soon became clear, following a key article by Osherson and Smith (1981), that not only the minimum rule, but in fact any rule that takes as input solely the truth value of the two constituent statements is doomed to failure.

In a book edited by Margolis and Laurence (1999), which consists of 652 pages of selected important writings on concepts, starting with Plato and going to modern treatments of concepts, the editors refer to OSP in their introductory chapter (38):

In a seminal discussion of the Prototype Theory's reliance on fuzzy sets, Daniel Osherson and Edward Smith presented a number of forceful objections to this treatment of compositionality (Osherson and Smith 1981).

The following quote is a footnote in a paper by Fodor and Lepore (1996) (which is also reprinted in Fodor and Lepore 2002, 30):

An alternative ("fuzzy logic") treatment assumes that there are infinitely many truth values between T and F, and that "wall-to-wall carpets are furniture" has one of them. However, Osherson and Smith (1981) have shown that this approach leads to apparently insoluble problems in the case of concepts that are built out of the Boolean connectives.

Let us now mention two papers that argue with some of the conclusions of OSP. The first one is a paper by Zadeh (1982), which was published in *Cognition* as a direct response to OSP. This paper addresses in general terms most of the arguments made by O&S. However, it is a rather short paper, in which only two pages are devoted to these arguments. Moreover, their refutation is not presented in sufficiently specific terms. The rest of the paper deals with Zadeh's own proposal for a model of prototypes. This, perhaps, is why his arguments were misunderstood or misinterpreted. This can be seen from Osherson and Smith's (1982) reply to Zadeh's paper, on which we comment in section 5.4. The second paper is by Fuhrmann (1988b). Both Zadeh 1982 and Fuhrmann 1988b, which are discussed in section 5.4, have been virtually ignored within the community of cognitive psychology and thus did not change the attitude toward fuzzy logic.

5.4   Fallacies Regarding Fuzzy Sets and Fuzzy Logic in the Literature on the Psychology of Concepts

In this section, we address in detail the claims of OSP, presented in section 5.2, as well as various other critical claims regarding fuzzy logic that were made in the literature on the psychology of concepts. We show that these claims are not sustainable. They are based on various misunderstandings, misconceptions, or oversights, and represent fallacies of different types. These types are categorized and described in the rest of this section. In particular, the claims from OSP presented in section 5.2 are analyzed in sections 5.4.2–5.4.5.

5.4.1 Ill-Conceived Assumption That Fuzzy Set Theory Is a Theory of Concepts

Several erroneous and misleading claims made in the literature on the psychology of concepts stem from confusing fuzzy set theory with a theory of concepts/categories and concept manipulation. Fuzzy set theory is a mathematical theory. As any mathematical theory, fuzzy set theory has no fixed interpretation. Rather, it is open to many interpretations. That is, fuzzy set theory provides us with a calculus, in a similar manner to, for example, the theory of differential equations or probability theory. Mathematical theories can be used to build models for various applications. Differential equations can be used to build models of physical processes, employed, for example, for weather forecasting. Likewise, probability theory can be used to build models of economic processes, employed, for example, for risk assessment. If a particular model does not perform well in experiments, then it is the model that has to be rejected and reconsidered, not the mathematical theory in terms of which the model is described. Note that the identification of fuzzy set theory with the prototype view of concepts was criticized already by Fuhrmann (1988b, 352).

The following quotations show that, surprisingly, the above simple facts are not recognized, by and large, in the literature on the psychology of concepts. That is, fuzzy set theory is often presented as a theory of conceptual combinations. For instance, Laurence and Margolis (1999, 38) write in their introductory chapter:

> The standard model for composing graded categories was a version of fuzzy set theory—a modification of standard set theory that builds on the notion of graded membership (see esp. Zadeh 1965).

Fuzzy set theory is not a model for composing categories. As explained above, it is a calculus that can be used for formalizing our intuitions about compositions of graded categories and other issues.

Cohen and Murphy (1984, 30–31), in explaining the concept of a fuzzy set, write:

For each object x and concept C in question, Zadeh's system assigns a value in $[0,1]$, called a characteristic value, or a degree of typicality. . . . Zadeh's rules (including recent developments, 1978, 1981) seem to be the only systematic attempt to describe how prototype-based concepts should be combined and evaluated.

Then, when discussing extensional and other models of concepts on page 33, they make the following statement:

A paradigm case of an extensional model is the fuzzy set model (Zadeh, 1965).

Later, on page 35, they make the same statement even more explicitly:

The standard extensional model of fuzzy concept theory is the original fuzzy set model proposed by Zadeh (1965) and formalized by Osherson and Smith (1981).

Here, referring to the "fuzzy set model proposed by (Zadeh, 1965)" as an extensional model of concepts is incorrect. Zadeh did not propose any model of concepts. He proposed a mathematical theory—a theory of fuzzy sets. Neither did he propose rules for "how prototype-based concepts should be combined and evaluated." He only proposed basic operations with fuzzy sets, such as union, intersection, and so on, as possible generalizations of the corresponding operations of classical set theory.

Osherson and Smith (1982, 303–304), when speaking of conjunctive concepts, introduce a so-called *simple functional hypothesis* (SFH):

The gradient theorist may reasonably expect that $c_{A\&B}$ is related to c_A and c_B in the simple functional manner described in the (SFH):

(SFH) There is some function, f, such that for all conjunctive concepts,

$A\,\&\,B : (\forall x \in D)\; c_{A\&B}(x) = f(c_A(x), c_B(x))$.

Specification of the function, f, of (SFH) would solve the problem of conjunctive concepts within the gradient framework. Zadeh (1965) proposed that the function in (SFH) is *min* (the minimum); Goguen (1968–1969) suggested it is the product. Both of the hypotheses are open to counterexamples discussed in Osherson and Smith (1981, Section 2.4.1).

Neither Zadeh (1965) nor Goguen (1968–1969) proposed any function for the simple functional hypothesis about how conjunctive concepts are combined. Zadeh and Goguen proposed *min* and *product* as possible functions for the definition of an intersection of fuzzy sets. It is Osherson and Smith who came up with (SFH), a hypothesis about conceptual combination, and suggested testing whether Zadeh's min (or Gogen's product) satisfies (SFH).

The following quotation is taken from the abstract of Roth and Mervis (1983, 509). It summarizes the main conclusion of their paper:

It is argued that fuzzy set theory, in principle, cannot specify the relationships among representativeness values in different categories, because the theory does not take the attributes of exemplars directly into account.

By the same logic, one could argue that probability theory and statistics, in principle, cannot specify the relationships among personal income and spending, because the theory does not take the inflation rate into account. Needless to say, such an argument is absurd. It is the economist, not the theory of probability and statistics, who proposes that a model of income and spending needs to take inflation rate into account. In the same spirit, it is the psychologist using fuzzy set theory, and not fuzzy set theory itself, who proposes that a model of representativeness values in categories needs to take the attributes of exemplars directly into account.

A similar misconception is presented in the following two quotations. The first is from Roth and Mervis (1983, 511):

The first experiment was designed to examine in detail the representativeness of exemplars in categories within the animal taxonomy to determine if fuzzy set theory makes accurate predictions for that domain.

The second is from Medin and Smith (1984, 133):

Zadeh's (1965) fuzzy set theory claims that typicality in the composite is the minimum of the typicalities in the constituents, which means that something cannot be a better example of *pet fish* than it is of *pet* or *fish*.

To examine this misconception is particularly important. First, the misconception confuses fuzzy set theory with a theory of conceptual combination (and perhaps with theories of other topics in the psychology of concepts), which is certainly not correct. Second, and more importantly, the misconception leads to the conclusion that fuzzy set theory is not appropriate for modeling several issues in the psychology of concepts. Let us demonstrate this by the last quotation from Medin and Smith (1984). If the quotation is right, fuzzy set theory is not appropriate for modeling typicalities in composite concepts and is to be rejected for this purpose. However, fuzzy set theory does not claim (and, in principle, cannot claim) anything about typicality in a composite concept, since it is not a theory of typicality. The correct statement of the intended objection is the following: A model M in which typicalities are modeled by membership functions of fuzzy sets, and in which typicalities of a composite are modeled by a membership function of intersection of fuzzy sets corresponding to the constituents, claims that typicality in the composite is the minimum of the typicalities in the constituents. It was argued by several psychologists (using for example the concept of *pet fish*) that this claim is wrong. This implies that what has to be rejected is model M, not fuzzy set theory itself. In other words, the problem is in the model, not in the mathematical theory used.

5.4.2   Claims Concerning Inclusion of Fuzzy Sets and Universal Quantification

One of the notions of fuzzy logic that seems to be grossly misunderstood in the literature on the psychology of concepts is the notion of inclusion of fuzzy sets. Recall that for classical sets A and B we say that A is a subset of B (A is included in B), written $A \subseteq B$, if each object that belongs to A belongs also to B. If A and B are fuzzy sets, then an appropriate notion that generalizes the classical subsethood relation is the notion of a degree of subsethood (degree of inclusion). Recall from chapter 3 that a degree of inclusion of a fuzzy set A in a fuzzy set B is a truth degree $S(A,B)$ given by (3.32), that is,

$$S(A,B) = \inf_{x \in U} (r(A(x), B(x))),$$

where U is the universal set, r is a truth function of implication as defined by (3.28), and "inf" denotes infimum in $[0,1]$ (infimum coincides with minimum if U is finite). This formula for S has a clear meaning. As explained section 3.6.3, $S(A,B)$ is the truth degree of the proposition:

For every element $x \in U$, if x is a member of A then x is a member of B.

A natural requirement for S is that $S(A,B) = 1$ if and only if $A(x) \le B(x)$ for each x in U. As explained in section 3.6.3, S satisfies this requirement and induces a crisp binary relation between fuzzy sets defined on U. This relation is usually denoted by $\subseteq$ and it is defined for each pair A, B of fuzzy sets in the fuzzy power set of U by the following statement:

$A \subseteq B$ if and only if $A(x) \le B(x)$ for each $x \in U$.

In terms of fuzzy logic, $\subseteq$ is the level cut of S at level 1. When $A \subseteq B$, A is said to be fully included in B.

The misunderstanding of inclusion of fuzzy sets is best illustrated by the example from OSP presented above in section 5.2.4, to which several authors have referred. The conclusion by O&S that the existence of squirrel Sam who lives on Mars makes the truth-value of "All grizzly bears are inhabitants of North America" equal to 0 (false) is wrong. The mistake in this case stems from the failure to recognize that (5.3) is not the definition of the truth degree of (5.2). Since "All As are Bs" means "for all x in U, if x belongs to A then x belongs to B," the truth degree of (5.2) is equal to the degree $S(A,B)$ of inclusion of A in B. For example, if the Łukasiewicz implication (see chapter 3, section 3.6.2) is used for r, that is,

$$r(a,b) = \min(1, 1 - a + b),$$

we get

$$S(A,B) = \inf_{x \in U} \min(1, 1 - A(x) + B(x)).$$

That is, the truth degree of "All As are Bs" is

$$\|\text{All As are Bs}\| = \inf_{x \in U} \min(1, 1 - A(x) + B(x)).$$

Sam's existence thus implies that the truth degree of "All grizzly bears are inhabitants of North America" is at most $\min[1, 1 - A(\text{Sam}) + B(\text{Sam})]$. If, for instance, $A(\text{Sam}) = 0.1$ and $B(\text{Sam}) = 0.05$, then the truth degree of (5.2) is at most 0.95 (the existence of other animals that count to a certain degree for grizzly bears and live outside North America can make $S(A,B)$ still smaller). The meaning of (5.2), when interpreted correctly, therefore satisfies the intuitive requirements of O&S.

Note that in his reply to the grizzly bears example from OSP, Zadeh (1982, 293) suggested:

An alternative way of resolving the difficulty is to fuzzify the concept of inclusion, as is done in the papers by Bandler and Kohout (1980), Gottwald (1979) and Wilmott (1981).

As is shown above, this suggestion removes the difficulty caused by O&S's misunderstanding of inclusion of fuzzy sets. Note also that the definition of $S(A,B)$, which we use, is covered by Goguen (1968–1969), a classical paper that is included in the reference list of OSP. Nevertheless, O&S state the following (their eq. (3.2) is our eq. (5.3)):

To replace (3.2) with a "partial falsification" scheme so as to allow for truth values between *truth* and *falsity* requires nontrivial theory construction of a kind apparently not yet undertaken. (OSP, 51)

In their reply to Zadeh (1982), Osherson and Smith (1982, 312) write:

Zadeh (1982) states that an alternative approach to inclusion is to embrace fuzzy truth (*via* the fuzzification of inclusion itself). We have already expressed our misgivings about this approach (Osherson and Smith, 1981, Section 3.5); the papers cited by Zadeh (1982) do not allay these anxieties.

There is another interesting issue regarding statement (5.2) and the grizzly bears example. This issue is briefly addressed by Zadeh (1982, 293):

in a natural language the quantifier *all* is usually not meant in its strict logical sense. Thus, in general, *all* in a proposition in a natural language should be interpreted as a fuzzy proportion which is close to unity.

The point here is that *all* is very often used with the meaning of *almost all* or *many*. This is particularly the case if one feels that the more squirrels on Mars, the smaller the truth degree of (5.2) should be, which is an issue discussed by O&S. In this case, one actually has in mind a proposition of the form "Almost all *As* are *Bs*" or "Many *As* are *Bs*." (Quantifiers like *many*, *almost all*, and the like are studied in logic under the name "generalized quantifiers" and are discussed in chapter 3, section 3.6.3.) Consider, for example, the quantifier *many*. The proposition "Many *As* are *Bs*" means "for many *x* in *U*, if *x* belongs to *A* then *x* belongs to *B*." Taking into account that the truth degree of a proposition quantified by *many* is obtained by equation (3.31), and assuming as above that the Łukasiewicz implication is used for *r*, the truth degree of "Many *As* are *Bs*" is

$$\|\text{Many } As \text{ are } Bs\| = \frac{\sum_{x \in U} \min(1, 1 - A(x) + B(x))}{|U|}. \tag{5.4}$$

Another approach, based on the notion of a cardinality of a fuzzy set, was proposed by Zadeh (1982). For a finite universe *U*, the cardinality |*A*| of a standard fuzzy set *A* in *U* is defined by equation (3.3). Then, according to Zadeh (1982), the truth degree of "Many *As* are *Bs*" can be defined by

$$\|\text{Many } As \text{ are } Bs\| = \frac{|A \cap B|}{|A|},$$

where ∩ denotes the minimum-based intersection of fuzzy sets or, more specifically, by

$$\|\text{Many } As \text{ are } Bs\| = \frac{\sum_{x \in U} \min(A(x), B(x))}{\sum_{x \in U} A(x)}. \tag{5.5}$$

Equations (5.4) and (5.5) describe two possible interpretations of "Many As are Bs." It is easy to see that both of them satisfy the following intuitive requirements, which are implicitly present in the arguments of O&S. First, if $A(x) \leq B(x)$ for each $x \in U$ then $\|$Many As are Bs$\| = 1$. Second, $\|$Many As are Bs$\|$ decreases as the number of x for which $A(x) > B(x)$ increases. In more detail, the greater the difference $A(x) - B(x)$, the smaller the truth degree of the proposition "Many As are Bs." Zadeh (1982) suggested this approach, with references to the literature, as well as its modification by considering only those x in U for which A exceeds some threshold k. This proposal was again misunderstood by Osherson and Smith (1982), who formalized Zadeh's proposal by stating that (5.2) is true if $(\forall x \in U)(A(x) > k) \Rightarrow A(x) \leq B(x))$. That is, they assigned again only 0 or 1 to (5.2), and then argued that this did not work either.

The confusion about fuzzy set inclusion and quantifiers is spread throughout in the literature on the psychology of concepts. For example, Cohen and Murphy (1984, 42), in a section entitled "Objections to Fuzzy Models," write (in the quote below, $TYP_A(x)$ denotes a typicality value):

The fuzzy set rule for universal quantification is given by this test for "All A's are B's"

$$(\forall x \in U)[Ax \to Bx] \text{ iff } (\forall x \in U)[TYP_A(x) \leq TYP_B(x),$$

where U is some domain.

Here, in addition to erroneously replacing a degree $S(A,B)$ of inclusion of fuzzy sets with the crisp inclusion relation $\subseteq$, the authors confuse readers as to what a rule of universal quantification in fuzzy logic says. In fact, as discussed in section 3.6.3, the rule says that the truth degree of a universally quantified formula is given by equation (3.30).

5.4.3   Misunderstandings of Logically Empty and Logically Universal Concepts

A widespread claim concerning the alleged inadequacies of fuzzy set theory is based on what were termed *logically empty* and *logically universal* concepts in OSP (see section 5.2.2 above). The argument goes as follows. Consider a concept *red apple* and a fuzzy set R such that $R(x)$ is a degree to which x is a red apple. Then, using the standard operations for negation and conjunction (chapter 3, section 3.4), we find that the sentence "x is a red apple and x is not a red apple" has the truth degree $\min(R(x), 1-R(x))$ when we use the standard operations of conjunction and negation. For instance, for an apple x such that $R(x) = 0.7$, we get $\min(R(x), 1-R(x)) = 0.3$. Therefore, the conjunctive concept of *object that is both a red apple and not a red apple* is not empty since it contains x to degree 0.3. A similar argument can be used to show that the disjunctive concept of *object that is a red apple or is not a red apple* is not universal since it contains x to degree 0.7. This argument leads several authors to reject fuzzy set theory. In addition to the quote from OSP presented above in section 5.2.2, we include the following examples. Johnson-Laird (1983, 199):

[T]he conjunction of the two is greater than zero. This consequence is absurd, because a self-contradiction surely merits a truth value of zero.

Kamp and Partee (1995, 134):

According to the most familiar versions of fuzzy logic the degree to which a satisfies the conjunctive concept *apple which is not an apple* is then the minimum of the c-values values of the conjuncts, and thus greater than 0. Clearly this is not the right result.

Requiring that the concept *object which is both a red apple and not a red apple* be empty (i.e., that the corresponding membership function is equal to 0 for every element) and that the concept *object which is a red apple or is not a red apple* be universal (i.e., that the corresponding membership function is equal to 1 for every element) is equivalent to requiring the well-known *law of contradiction* and the *law of excluded middle*, two of the basic laws of classical logic. The authors of the above quotations require, in fact, that these laws hold in fuzzy logic and fuzzy set theory in order to correctly represent concepts. To require this, however, demands a justification that they do not provide. The requirement that both these laws be valid has already been disputed in numerous ways (e.g., Fuhrmann 1988a, 323–324, 1988b, 353; Lakoff 1987, 141; Zadeh 1982, 292). For example, Zadeh (1982, 292) writes:

The principle of the excluded middle is not accepted as a valid axiom in the theory of fuzzy sets because it does not apply to situations in which one deals with classes which do not have sharply defined boundaries.

Instead of presenting here the various arguments against the requirement, we would like to point out the fact that contrary to classical logic, the truth degree $\min(R(x), 1-R(x))$ of "x is a red apple and x is not a red apple" provides us with nontrivial information about x. Namely, in classical logic, this truth degree is always 0 and, hence, not informative. In fuzzy logic, if we know that $\min(R(x),1-R(x))$ is, say, 0.4, we know that x is a borderline case. That is, in such a situation, either $R(x) = 0.4$ (x is red to degree 0.4) or $1-R(x)$ = 0.4 and thus $R(x) = 0.6$. If, on the other hand, $\min(R(x),1-R(x)) = 0$, we know that x is not a borderline case at all. That is, in such a situation, either $R(x) = 0$ (x is not red at all) or $1-R(x) = 0$ and thus $R(x) = 1$ (x is fully red). In other words, $\min(R(x),1-R(x))$ ranges between 0 and 0.5, and the closer it is to 0.5, the more x is a borderline case of *red apple*.

Another important remark is the following. If, for some reason, we have to require that the law of contradiction and the law of the excluded middle hold, fuzzy set theory is capable of satisfying this requirement. Although the two laws do not hold under some combinations of operations (such as the standard operations of complement, intersection, and union), they hold for numerous other combinations that fuzzy logic offers. For instance, if we take the Łukasiewicz operations introduced in chapter 3, section 3.6.2, then both the law of contradiction and the law of the excluded middle are satisfied. It is important to realize that for each chosen combination of operations, some properties of the algebra of classical set theory are inevitably violated. This is a consequence of the imprecise boundaries of fuzzy sets. However, different combinations violate different properties, and this is crucial for our argument. The standard operations, for example, violate the law of contradiction and the law of the excluded middle. Some other combinations preserve these laws, but violate other properties, usually distributivity and idempotence. There is a well-established procedure (Klir and Yuan 1995, section 3.5) by which classes of operations can be constructed that satisfy the two laws. Hence, fuzzy logic can represent cognitive situations in which the laws of contradiction and/or excluded middle should hold according to experimental evidence. Thus, O&S are wrong in their conclusions.

5.4.4 Failure to Recognize the Expressive Power of Fuzzy Logic

Many erroneous and mistaken claims about the inadequacies of fuzzy logic have been made because the full expressive power of fuzzy logic was not recognized. By fuzzy set theory, for example, the authors of these claims often mean just the notion of a standard fuzzy set plus the standard operations of complement, intersection, and union, which are based on $1-x$, min, and max, as proposed in Zadeh's (1965) seminal paper. As is well known and mentioned in chapter 3, fuzzy logic has considerably more expressive power than its fragment based on 1–x, min, and max. The following three examples demonstrate in detail two of the many oversights regarding fuzzy set theory that can be found in the literature on the psychology of concepts.

Our first example is the well-known one from OSP described above in section 5.2.3. A crucial point in analyzing this example is O&S's argument regarding the choice of function f (OSP, 47):

[I]f fuzzy-set theory is to represent the conceptual connection among liquidity, investment, and wealth, it would seem that the only option is to employ fuzzy union.

As mentioned in section 5.2.3, what O&S mean is one particular union, namely, the one based on the max operation. This argument is, however, unwarranted, since f can be chosen from an infinite set (a continuum) of aggregation functions. Moreover, it is easy to see that the right function in this example should be an averaging function (see chapter 3, section 3.4.4). If there is no special experimental evidence to use some particular averaging function (possibly weighted), we may as well choose the arithmetic average, so that

$$W(x) = \frac{L(x) + I(x)}{2}$$

for all $x \in X$. This function satisfies the inequalities required in OSP. This example is particularly illuminating: It shows that fuzzy logic has some capabilities that have no counterparts in classical set theory. Indeed, classical sets cannot be averaged.

Our second example, again taken from OSP, is that of the striped apples, described above in section 5.2.1. In this example, O&S employ a drawing of a striped apple, shown in their paper as figure 1a. They correctly argue that this picture of a striped apple, a, is psychologically more prototypical of a striped apple than of an apple. They express this fact in terms of relevant fuzzy sets A, S, and SA (introduced above in section 5.2.1) by inequality (5.1). So far, so good. However, prior to stating this reasonable requirement, they assume, without any justification, that the adjective-noun concept *striped apple* is a conjunctive concept and, consequently, that fuzzy set SA should be expressed as an intersection of fuzzy sets A and S. O&S then use the standard intersection and show that SA obtained in this way violates the required inequality (5.1). They are correct, and, moreover, it is trivial to show that any other intersection operation (t-norm; see chapter 3, section 3.4.3) would in fact violate the inequality as well.

The problem with O&S's argument in this example is their assumption, presented without any justification, that adjective-noun concepts are conjunctive. In fact, the adjective is usually viewed as a modifier of the noun, and there is no reason to assume that SA must be expressed as an intersection of A and S. According to Lakoff (1987, 142), for example, "The assumption that noun modifiers work by conjunction is grossly incorrect."

One possible solution was outlined briefly by Zadeh in his response to OSP (Zadeh 1982, 291–292). Zadeh's arguments, applied to the *striped apple* example, are as follows. Since the intersection $A \cap S$ is a subnormal fuzzy set (i.e., the maximal degree of membership in $A \cap S$ is less than 1) and since we focus our attention on $A \cap S$, we are tacitly normalizing with respect to the greatest degree of membership in $A \cap S$ and are working with a normalized fuzzy set $N(A \cap S)$. There are several possible ways to normalize fuzzy sets. For example, one could use the formula

$$[N(A \cap S)](a) = [(A \cap S)(a)]/M,$$

where M is the greatest degree of membership $(A \cap S)(a)$ for a ranging over all conceivable apples (or the supremum of the degrees, if the greatest one does not exist). In this view, the appropriate choice for fuzzy set SA is $N(A \cap S)$ rather than $A \cap S$. O&S's objection then no longer applies, because the degree of membership of a particular apple in $N(A \cap S)$ is greater than the degree of membership of the same apple in $A \cap S$. Clearly, whether or not the approach based on normalization of fuzzy sets or other approaches, such as the one based on considering "striped" as a modifier, are appropriate remains to be determined experimentally. In any case, to propose a simplistic fuzzy logic model of SA and to reject fuzzy logic because the model does not work, as O&S did, is clearly wrong.

Our third example concerns the concept of a stack, introduced by Jones (1982). To avoid the supposed inability of fuzzy set theory to represent conjunctive concepts presented by O&S, which we explained above in section 5.2.1, Jones introduces the concept of a stack and operations with stacks and argues that:

It was shown that systematization of the stack view allowed the construction of a form of prototype theory of concepts that has important advantages over one that is based on fuzzy-set theory. Unlike fuzzy-set theory, stack theory represents appropriately both conceptual conjunction and disjunction, and furthermore provides a coherent account of certain phenomena raised by a consideration of binary taxonomy. (Jones 1982, 289)

Jones's main arguments are based on the operations on stacks that he defines. Jones demonstrates that these operations meet the expectations about conjunctive concepts presented in OSP. In the following, we show that a stack is, in fact, a fuzzy set defined by a particular formula. Furthermore, we show that Jones's operation on stacks does, in fact, coincide with a normalization of product-based intersection of fuzzy sets. Interestingly, using the normalization of an intersection of fuzzy sets to meet the intuitive requirements of O&S for conjunctive concepts was proposed by Zadeh (1982). Nevertheless, in a reply to Zadeh (1982) and Jones (1982), Osherson and Smith (1982, 313) remark that: "Stack theory ingeniously avoids many of the problems encountered by the earlier hypotheses."

According to Jones, a stack is given by assigning to any so-called instantiation x a value $C(x)$ from $(0,1]$, which Jones calls *characteristicness*, by

$$C(x) = I(R(d(x,p))).\qquad (5.6)$$

Here, p is a prototype, $d(x, p)$ is a distance of x from p, R is a so-called ranking function, and I is an inverse transformation. The ranking function R maps distances into ranks. Ranks are natural numbers 1, 2, ... , and it is required that R maps distances to ranks in an order-preserving way: the larger the distance, the larger the rank assigned to it, and the smallest distance is assigned rank 1. The inverse transformation I maps the ranks to values from $(0,1]$ in an order-reversing way: the smaller the rank, the larger the value from $(0,1]$ assigned to it. As an example of I, Jones proposes to take $I(n) = 1/n$; he writes, "However, this particular transformation appears unduly restrictive in practice since, for example, it excludes the existence of C-values between $1/2$ and 1" (Jones 1982, 283). Jones also proposes an operation that should account for the conjunctive combination of concepts. For two concepts, A and B, represented by characteristicness functions C_A and C_B, given by

$$C_A(x) = I(R(d(x,p_A))) \text{ and } C_B(x) = I(R(d(x,p_B))),$$

the characteristicness function C corresponding to the conjunctive concept is given by

$$C(x) = I(R(-\text{prod}(C_A(x), C_B(x)))), \qquad (5.7)$$

where "prod" denotes the usual product. Note that there is a technical difficulty in Jones's model with the ranking function R: When discussing (5.6), Jones requires R to be order preserving and to assign the last rank 1 to the smallest value of the distance function d. The smallest value s of d is a nonnegative number (possibly $s = 0$, but Jones does not say it explicitly). In equation (5.7), however, R assigns ranks also to negative values, namely to values of the form $-\text{prod}(C_A(x), C_B(x))$, and is required to do this in an order-preserving way to ensure that "it is high-characteristic instantiations that receive low-value ranks" (Jones 1982, 283). This implies that for the smallest distances d, and for negative values, say

$$-0.25 = -\text{prod}(C_A(x_1), C_B(x_1)) \text{ and } -0.9 = -\text{prod}(C_A(x_2), C_B(x_2)),$$

one should have $R(-0.9) < R(-0.25) < R(s)$, which is impossible since $R(s) = 1$ is the smallest rank-value. We consider this only a technical difficulty of Jones's model. In fact, it can be removed by, for instance, using the ranking function R in equation (5.7), which is different from R in equation (5.6).

Let us now analyze Jones's proposals. Clearly, equation (5.6) is only one particular way of defining a membership function of a fuzzy set C. Equation (5.6) defines C as a function assigning a value from $(0,1]$ to any element x (instantiation). In fact, Jones's formula defines the fuzzy set in a way that is well known in fuzzy logic and is used in the definition of triangular fuzzy sets, which are a particular case of trapezoidal fuzzy intervals (explained in chapter 3, section 3.3): The membership degree of an element x in a fuzzy set C is inversely related to the distance of x from a fixed element (reference point, denoted by p in Jones's formula), expressed by a suitably defined distance function. The essence of equation (5.7) can be described as follows: One takes the product, $\text{prod}(C_A(x), C_B(x))$, of the membership degrees of x in C_A and C_B and assigns to it a number from $[0,1]$ obtained by applying an order-reversing function $-$ (minus), an order-preserving function R, and an order-reversing function I. The role of R is to accomplish that value 1 be assigned to x for which the value $\text{prod}(C_A(x), C_B(x))$ is the largest one over all xs (or the supremum of them, if there is no largest one). Since applying an order-reversing function two times yields an order-preserving function, the point is actually to map, in an order-preserving way, values of $\text{prod}(C_A(x), C_B(x))$ to values from $[0,1]$ in such a way that the largest value (or supremum) is mapped to 1. But this is exactly what one obtains if C is defined to be a normalization of the intersection of fuzzy sets C_A and C_B, that is,

$$C = N(C_A \cap C_B),$$

where N is a suitable normalization function that depends on R and I, and $C_A \cap C_B$ is an intersection of fuzzy sets C_A and C_B based on the product t-norm (see chapter 3, sections 3.4 and 3.6), that is, $(C_A \cap C_B)(x) = C_A(x) \cdot C_B(x)$. Note that it is not possible to present here an explicit definition of N because it depends on R and I, and Jones does not present any specific definitions of R and I.

Therefore, while Osherson and Smith (1982) appeal to the ingenuity of Jones's proposal and, at the same time, argue against Zadeh's proposal of taking normalization of fuzzy sets, Jones's model is in fact a special case of Zadeh's proposal.

5.4.5   Erroneous and Misleading Claims Regarding Fuzzy Logic in the Narrow Sense

Erroneous or misleading claims regarding fuzzy logic in the narrow sense have also arisen in the literature on concepts. We illustrate them by two examples. The first example is taken from OSP (51–52), where the authors express their general distrust of a calculus that allows propositions with intermediate truth degrees. They claim, without any serious justification (52):

The problem is that infinite valued logics generally violate strong intuitions about truth, validity, and consistency.

The following is the only example by which O&S illustrate what they mean (OSP, 52, n. 15):

To illustrate with an influential system, consider Lukasiewicz's infinite valued logic L-aleph. The intuitively valid sentence

If John is happy, and if John is happy only if business is good, then business is good.

is ruled nontautologous in L-aleph.

However, this is not true. If p denotes "John is happy" and q denotes "business is good" then the above sentence corresponds to a propositional formula $\varphi = (p \,\&\, (p \Rightarrow q)) \Rightarrow q$. If $\|p\|$ and $\|q\|$ are truth degrees of p and q, then the truth degree assigned to φ in Łukasiewicz's calculus is

$$\min\{1, 1 - \max[0, \|p\| + \min(1, 1 - \|p\| + \|q\|) - 1] + \|q\|\},$$

which is always equal to 1. This means that φ is a tautology, contrary to what O&S claim.

The second example is expressed by the following quote taken from another paper by Osherson and Smith (1997, 200–201):

It is useful to note how committed fuzzy logic is to the non-standard reading of contradictions. Suppose that fuzzy truth-assignment μ over a propositional language has the well-known properties:

(14)(a) $\mu(\theta \wedge \varphi) = \min[\mu(\theta), \mu(\varphi)]$.

   (b) $\mu(\neg\theta) = 1 - \mu(\theta)$.

Then it is easy to prove the following: Suppose that $\mu(\theta \wedge \neg\theta) = \mu(\varphi \wedge \neg\varphi)$, for every pair of propositions θ, φ. Then the range of μ is limited to no more than two values. In other words, in the presence of (14), contradictions must admit a range of truth values on pain of μ collapsing to a non-fuzzy, two-value truth assignment. (A similar argument is presented in Elkan (1993).)

However, fuzzy logic is the wrong target here, because a system satisfying (14a), (14b), and $\mu(\theta \wedge \neg\theta) = \mu(\varphi \wedge \neg\varphi)$, is not a system of fuzzy logic. The assumption that $\mu(\theta \wedge \neg\theta) = \mu(\varphi \wedge \neg\varphi)$ is foreign to fuzzy logic. As far as we know, such an assumption has never been used in any theory or applications of fuzzy logic. Thus, the authors miss the point and commit the fallacy of *ignoratio elenchi*. To see how unnatural the assumption that $\mu(\theta \wedge \neg\theta) = \mu(\varphi \wedge \neg\varphi)$ is, recall the above observation regarding what the truth degree of "*x* is a red apple and *x* is not a red apple" tells us about *x*. We can see from (14a) and (14b) that the value of $\mu(\theta \wedge \neg\theta)$ can range from 0 to 0.5. In fact, $\mu(\theta \wedge \neg\theta) = 0$ if $\mu(\theta) = 0$ or $\mu(\theta) = 1$, that is, if θ is what is sometimes called a crisp proposition, while $\mu(\theta \wedge \neg\theta) = 0.5$ if $\mu(\theta) = 0.5$, that is, if θ is what is considered a fuzzy proposition. Therefore, $\mu(\theta \wedge \neg\theta)$ can be seen as measuring the fuzziness of proposition θ. The closer $\mu(\theta \wedge \neg\theta)$ is to 0.5, the fuzzier θ is. Now, the assumption that $\mu(\theta \wedge \neg\theta) = \mu(\varphi \wedge \neg\varphi)$ for every pair of propositions θ and φ says that the fuzziness of any two propositions is the same. Needless to say, such an assumption is absurd.

For completeness, we should also remark on the paper by Elkan (1993) to which Osherson and Smith refer in the above quote. Elkan (1993) defines a formal system of fuzzy logic by the standard operations of conjunction, disjunction, and negation. However, he also requires that degrees of truth of arbitrary propositions in this formal system be equal if the propositions are "logically equivalent according to the rules of classical two-valued propositional calculus" (Elkan 1993, 698) and presents a theorem showing that "only two different truth values are in fact possible in the formal system" (ibid.). This treatment is somewhat problematic since the defined formal system is clearly a system of "nonfuzzy logic," so Elkan (1994) revised it. In this second paper, he again defines a formal system of fuzzy logic by the standard operations of conjunction, disjunction, and complementation, but he includes a weaker additional requirement. He requires, as part of his Definition 1, that degrees of truth of arbitrary propositions in the formal system be equal if the propositions are logically equivalent. Then, he asserts and proves the following theorem, where A and B are assertions whose truth values are denoted by $t(A)$ and $t(B)$ and $\land$, $\lor$, $\neg$ denote the standard operations of conjunction, disjunction, and complementation, respectively:

Theorem 1   Given the formal system of Definition 1, if $\neg(A \land \neg B)$ and $B \lor (\neg A \land \neg B)$ are logically equivalent, then for any two assertions A and B, either $t(B) = t(B)$ or $t(B) = 1 - t(B)$.

This treatment is not problematic. However, Definition 1 together with the condition that $\neg(A \land \neg B)$ and $B \lor (\neg A \land \neg B)$ be logically equivalent (stated in Theorem 1) again defines a system of "nonfuzzy logic" (a system that does not allow any intermediate truth degrees). Belohlavek and Klir (2007) provide a formal analysis of both Elkan's papers.

5.5   Conclusions

In this chapter, we discuss and correct the many misunderstandings, misconceptions, and oversights regarding the role of fuzzy logic in the psychology of concepts that are repeated again and again in the literature of this field, and are accepted, by and large, uncritically. We identify an appreciable number of them, including those presented in OSP, and we categorize and analyze them in section 5.4. The following list summarizes the principal issues:

1. Fuzzy set theory is not a theory of concepts, but it can be utilized for representing and dealing with concepts, regardless of the theory of concepts

that one employs. Some critics do not recognize this fact, and, as a consequence, fuzzy set theory is conflated with various theories of concepts. As a result, fuzzy set theory is often criticized as a presumed theory of concepts.

2. Many critics do not recognize fuzzy set theory as a generalization of classical set theory. Instead, they wrongly view these two theories as mutually exclusive.

3. Some aspects of fuzzy logic remain overlooked or misunderstood and, as a consequence, critics make unjustified arguments to reject this area of mathematics.

4. Some critics' conclusions are either formally incorrect or are based on unjustified assumptions.

Notes

1. The claim that "fuzzy-set theory is a natural complement of prototype theory" is misleading here since prototype theory emerged from research completely independent of fuzzy set theory (see chapter 4, this volume). Moreover, the particular model based on fuzzy set theory that O&S use to interpret prototype theory is only one of many possible models. To derive general arguments against prototype theory from this particular interpretation, as O&S do, is incorrect. However, these are separate issues that are not of our concern in this chapter (see chapter 4).

2. In their examples, O&S use D to denote a universe of discourse. To be consistent with the notation introduced in chapter 3, we denote a universe of discourse by U rather then D in our discussion as well as in the quotes from OSP.

References

Armstrong, S. L., L. L. Gleitman, and H. Gleitman. 1983. What some concepts might not be. *Cognition* 13:263–308.

Bandler, W., and L. J. Kohout. 1980. Fuzzy power set and fuzzy implication operators. *Fuzzy Sets and Systems* 4:13–30.

Belohlavek, R., and G. J. Klir. 2007. On Elkan's theorems: Clarifying their meanings via simple proofs. *International Journal of Intelligent Systems* 22:203–207.

Belohlavek, R., G. J. Klir, H. W. Lewis, III, and E. Way. 2002. On the capability of fuzzy set theory to represent concepts. *International Journal of General Systems* 31 (6):569–585.

Belohlavek, R., G. J. Klir, H. W. Lewis, III, and E. Way. 2009. Concepts and fuzzy sets: Misunderstandings, misconceptions, and oversights. *International Journal of Approximate Reasoning* 51 (1):23–34.

Cohen, B., and G. L. Murphy. 1984. Models of concepts. *Cognitive Science* 8:27–58.

Elkan, C. 1993. The paradoxical success of fuzzy logic. In *Proceedings of the Eleventh National Conference on Artificial Intelligence* (AAAI'93), 698–703. Menlo Park, CA: AAAI Press.

Elkan, C. 1994. The paradoxical success of fuzzy logic. *IEEE Expert* 9 (4):3–8.

Fodor, J. A., and E. Lepore. 1996. The pet fish and red herring: Why concepts aren't prototypes. *Cognition* 58:243–276.

Fodor, J. A., and E. Lepore. 2002. *The Compositionality Papers*. Oxford: Oxford University Press.

Fuhrmann, G. Y. 1988a. "Prototypes" and "fuzziness" in the logic of concepts. *Synthese* 75:317–347.

Fuhrmann, G. Y. 1988b. Fuzziness of concepts and concepts of fuzziness. *Synthese* 75:349–372.

Goguen, J. A. 1968–1969. The logic of inexact concepts. *Synthese* 19:325–373.

Gottwald, S. 1979. Set theory and fuzzy sets of higher order. *Fuzzy Sets and Systems* 2:125–151.

Hampton, J. 1997. Conceptual combinations. In *Knowledge, Concepts, and Categories*, ed. K. Lamberts and D. Shank, 485–527. Cambridge, MA: MIT Press.

Johnson-Laird, P. N. 1983. *Mental Models*. Cambridge, MA: Harvard University Press.

Jones, G. V. 1982. Stacks not fuzzy sets: An ordinal basis for prototype theory of concepts. *Cognition* 12:281–290.

Kamp, H., and B. Partee. 1995. Prototype theory and compositionality. *Cognition* 57:129–191.

Klir, G. J., and B. Yuan. 1995. *Fuzzy Sets and Fuzzy Logic: Theory and Applications*. Upper Saddle River, NJ: Prentice Hall.

Lakoff, G. 1987. *Women, Fire, and Dangerous Things*. Chicago: University of Chicago Press.

Laurence, S., and E. Margolis. 1999. Concepts and cognitive science. In *Concepts: Core Readings*, ed. E. Margolis and S. Laurence, 3–82. Cambridge, MA: MIT Press.

Margolis, E., and S. Laurence. 1999. *Concepts: Core Readings*. Cambridge, MA: MIT Press.

Medin, D. L., and E. E. Smith. 1984. Concepts and concept formation. *Annual Review of Psychology* 35:113–138.

Minsky, M. L., and S. A. Papert. 1969. *Perceptrons: An Introduction to Computational Geometry.* Cambridge, MA: MIT Press.

Oden, G. C. 1977. Fuzziness in semantic memory: Choosing exemplars of subjective categories. *Memory & Cognition* 5 (2):198–204.

Osherson, D. N., and E. E. Smith. 1981. On the adequacy of prototype theory as a theory of concepts. *Cognition* 9:35–58.

Osherson, D. N., and E. E. Smith. 1982. Gradedness and conceptual combination. *Cognition* 12:299–318.

Osherson, D. N., and E. E. Smith. 1997. On typicality and vagueness. *Cognition* 12:299–318.

Roth, E. M., and C. B. Mervis. 1983. Fuzzy set theory and class inclusion relations in semantic categories. *Journal of Verbal Learning and Verbal Behavior* 22:509–525.

Wilmott, R. 1981. Mean measures of containment and equality between fuzzy sets. In *Proceedings of the International Symposium on Multiple-Valued Logic,* 183–190. Los Alamitos, CA: IEEE Computer Society Press.

Zadeh, L. A. 1965. Fuzzy sets. *Information and Control* 8 (3):338–353.

Zadeh, L. A. 1982. A note on prototype theory and fuzzy sets. *Cognition* 12:291–297.

6 Representing Concepts by Fuzzy Sets

Jay Verkuilen, Rogier A. Kievit, and Annemarie Zand Scholten

6.1 Introduction

As is discussed in detail in chapter 5, fuzzy set theory itself cannot provide a descriptive model for how humans reason about concepts, but it can be used as a mathematical tool for building such models or any other models in psychology (Smithson and Oden 1999). In this chapter, we focus on preconditions for this use of fuzzy set theory: constructing fuzzy sets for representing concepts.

The problem that fuzzy sets are designed to handle involves the issue of *degree-vagueness* (Ackerman 1994). By this we mean the lack of firm boundary between objects to which a given concept applies and objects to which it does not. The problem is an old one, with the most notable example being the well-known Sorites paradox. There are many variants, but the essential component is that membership in a given set does not have a sharp demarcation. Often this is the result of perceptual limitation, when the units that make up the whole are very small. For instance, a heap of sand is made up of many grains. Removing one grain does not change its "heapness," but if one continues this process, we will reach a point at which any observer would agree that a heap is no longer present. In other cases, degree-vagueness occurs not because of our inability to discriminate the state of the world, but because we cannot discriminate at the level of consequences. For instance, the addition of an extra student to a class is certainly discriminable to the instructor, but it hardly changes the membership of the class in terms of its perceived size. However, the addition of multiple students to the class definitely changes its perceived size. To speak of an application of fuzzy set theory, both categorical endpoints and gradation between these endpoints are essential. It is important that both properties be present. Many constructs of interest to behavioral scientists can be thought of as being subject to degree-vagueness between categorical endpoints. Here are some examples:

• Brehm and Gates (1993), in a study of principal–agent relations in a bureaucracy, considered the degree to which an individual agent (in their case a police officer) was working or shirking, that is, engaged in behavior consistent with the principal–agent relationship or defecting from it. The data used in this study were part of a larger study by Reiss (1971). This proportion, as a value between 0 and 1, was judged by an observer assigned to the officer. It makes little sense to consider this proportion as a probability in the conventional sense. This proportion is better interpreted as a meaningful position between "fully shirking" and "fully working." Brehm and Gates model this proportion by using regressors that predict compliance or defection, allowing them to test different game-theoretic accounts of principal–agent behavior.

• The United Nations Development Programme's Human Development Index (HDI) scores nations on the general concept of development, as defined by combining three key variables: wealth, health, and literacy (UNDP 2009). The HDI was not constructed specifically as a fuzzy set, but it can be thought of in those terms (Verkuilen 2005; Smithson and Verkuilen 2006).

• Participants in cognitive psychology experiments frequently make choices between two objects in a two-alternative forced-choice paradigm. Often they are asked in addition to rate their confidence in their decision, usually on a scale that has well-defined endpoints ranging from "not at all confident" to "totally confident." Confidence ratings are often used to provide additional information about discriminable stimuli and could be the object of study themselves. Other so-called graphical ratings are used in similar contexts, such as preference studies. One successful model for these data is the fuzzy logical model of perception (FLMP), which has been tested in great detail by Massaro and colleagues (e.g., Friedman and Massaro 1998).

• The concept of physical maturity summarizes the ensemble of specific measurements that could be made about a child, regarding bone development, secondary sex characteristics, dental development, and so on, all of which start in an immature state and eventually develop to a mature state, although at different paces. However, this concept ranges from "not mature" to "mature" in degrees. Healy and Goldstein (1976) showed how to generate a scoring system that maps measurements to a maturity scale in an optimal way. Although they did not refer directly to a fuzzy set interpretation of their results, interpreting their optimal maturity scale in such a light is quite natural.

• Conventional psychiatric diagnosis schemes (e.g., the *Diagnostic and Statistical Manual of Mental Disorders*, DSM-IV) can be seen as crisp set membership assignment functions that assign a 1 if a person fits a certain criterion or 0 if he or she does not. However, this does not sit well with the nuances of clinical practice; it ignores an intuition shared by experts and lay persons alike, namely, that it makes sense to entertain the possibility that a person is "more depressed" than some other person. A better perspective might be to consider psychiatric disorders as fuzzy, that is, to devise membership functions that assign values to individuals to represent a degree of depression, with meaningful endpoints ("Fully depressed" to "Not depressed"). This example will be considered in more detail later.

All of these examples illustrate continuous variation between qualitative poles of full membership or nonmembership. In each case a single number represents the state of a subject at a given point in time. For instance, a child scored according to physical maturity will start at 0 (not mature) and end up at 1 (fully mature). Determining this value depends on combining the values of the various physical measurements under question by means of some procedure. Other times, subjective judgments of the subjects or of external judges are involved, as is the case for the confidence rating and police examples given above, respectively.

As Bilgiç and Türkşen (1999) note, getting things to work in practice requires facing up to two related but distinct issues. The first is that of *membership assignment*. Is it possible to provide meaningful values of membership for objects in a fuzzy set? This question depends, of course, on the purpose to which the membership values are meant to be put. Obtaining meaningful, or at least useful, membership functions is essentially a unidimensional scaling problem. In this case, the disciplines of psychometrics and mathematical psychology offer potential solutions to the problem of assigning membership, and also provide insight into limitations on what can be expected. Presuming it is possible to assign meaningful fuzzy set values, the second problem relates to comparisons *between* sets, which is known as *property ranking*. Claims such as "object x is more in fuzzy set A than it is in fuzzy set B" require that we can make meaningful comparisons between the memberships in A and B. The property ranking issue is necessary for handling many uses to which fuzzy sets might be put. It is also somewhat of an Achilles' heel, because it is difficult to establish empirically meaningful relationships between sets unless the membership of objects in the sets can be compared.

To illustrate our points, we pursue two concepts that have broad implications throughout psychology. The first is the concept of utility (Shafir and LeBoeuf 2002) seen through the lens of fuzzy set theory. Models for choice behavior based on utility (or related concepts) have a long and voluminous tradition in psychology and economics and are widely used across the behavioral sciences. Utility theory has been extensively formalized. For this reason, utility represents a useful case in which the findings are quite clear about what is and is not likely to be possible for the membership function. The second concept we examine is that of major depressive disorder (MDD), a serious type of depression. This is a widely experienced psychopathological phenomenon for which a strong definition does not yet exist and for which, it is becoming clear, standard statistical measurement models do not seem particularly appropriate. Reasoning based on fuzzy sets may be able to shed light on this important problem.

6.2   Membership Assignment

To make use of fuzzy set theory, it is necessary to address some intertwined but nevertheless distinct issues. We organize these into three basic parts. First is the *interpretation of membership* and the purpose for which the scale will be used. What does partial membership in a set mean? There is no unique answer to this question, as it depends strongly on the context of application. The second involves the *measurement level* question. At what level of measurement do the membership values lie? That is, what sort of numerical properties can we consider a membership level to have? For instance, are memberships to be concatenated by an operation such as the arithmetic average? If so, this requires an interval level of measurement. By contrast, using the min operator for intersection requires only that the memberships be comparable ordinally. This is discussed further in section 6.2.2. Although these issues are distinct, decisions about one have implications for the other. Different interpretations are associated with different scaling procedures, which in turn result in different levels of measurement. Conversely, which measurement level is necessary depends on the use to which the memberships will be put, and what computations are to be performed on them. Third and finally, we will consider several methods of *assigning membership*. The interpretation of membership and the associated measurement level will be discussed for several examples of these assignment methods. (Further discussion of membership interpretation and assignment can be found in Bilgiç and Türkşen 1999; Verkuilen 2005; Smithson and Verkuilen 2006.)

6.2.1   Interpretation of Membership

To determine what the appropriate measurement of membership should be, it is important to consider the interpretation of membership that the investigator intends. Here we lay out the different ways that have been proposed in the past, though it should be noted that there might be others. Five different views of membership have been identified. These views were neatly exemplified by Bilgiç and Türkşen (1999, 196, with slight edits to make notation consistent):

The vague predicate "John (x) is tall (T)" is represented by a number t in the unit interval $[0,1]$. There are several possible answers to the question "What does it mean to say $t = 0.7$?":

1. Likelihood view: 70% of a given population agreed with the statement that John is tall.

2. Random set view: when asked to provide an interval in height that corresponds to "tall," 70% of a given population provided an interval that included John's height in centimeters.

3. Similarity view: John's height is away from the prototypical object which is truly "tall" to the degree 0.3 (a normalized distance).

4. Utility view: 0.7 is the utility of asserting that John is tall.

5. Measurement view: When compared to others, John is taller than some and this fact can be encoded as 0.7 on some scale.

The first two interpretations have probabilistic underpinnings. The likelihood view essentially asserts that fuzziness equals probability in the sense that the membership here is a sample proportion from a given population. Under this interpretation, there is no vagueness within a single judge, just across judges, with probabilistic uncertainty appearing as a result of sampling variability. The random set view of fuzzy set theory identifies level sets as the crucial quantity. It focuses on the interval of the support of the fuzzy set, identifying membership with level cuts of a particular width of the support. The level cut defines the proportion of the population that asserts that the given object falls into the given interval. These two concepts of fuzziness seem rather distant from likely theoretical applications in the behavioral sciences.

The next three views are much closer in spirit to concepts in the psychological literature. The similarity view identifies membership of 1 with a prototypical object in the set of objects under consideration and considers membership as a normalized distance from this ideal. For instance, given object x, a distance d_x of x from the ideal object in set T, and some nonnegative, usually weakly monotone, function f, membership might be assigned as:

$$t_x = \frac{1}{1+f(d_x)}.$$

There is a long tradition in psychological research regarding similarity-based theories, and it is expected that the similarity view will be the most natural to most psychologists. The problem of defining an appropriate distance is by no means trivial, and it has been the subject of voluminous and sophisticated research (Takane and Shibayama 1992, and references therein). The utility view considers membership to be the utility of asserting that the object is in a given set. In a sense, it is a variant of the similarity view, if one is willing to assume there exists at least one object for which this utility would be maximal and another for which this utility would be minimal. (The originally proposed utility view made some rather extreme claims, e.g., regarding the lack of context-specificity of membership, but we believe that there is no reason to maintain these specific claims.) The measurement view considers membership through the lens of representational measurement theory, which formally describes if, and to what extent, relations between numbers (scales) can be used to represent certain qualitative relations between empirical objects. From the measurement perspective, degree of membership is considered a property with specific measurement characteristics. These characteristics are important when statistical operations are performed on the membership values in order to conclude something about this underlying property. The measurement can be considered more of a methodological approach than an independent view on the ontological status of membership values.

The different views described above are not mutually exclusive. For instance, elicited binary judgments regarding similarity to a prototype may be used to define the empirical relations, which are in turn considered by way of representational measurement axioms. As it stands, this typology is an undifferentiated "laundry list." A better typology of interpretations of the membership function with formal backing would be a welcome addition to the literature.

6.2.2 The Measurement Level Question

It is important to be clear about the *measurement level* associated with membership in a fuzzy set: What properties of numbers do membership functions possess? Considering the measurement level of membership forces us to think about membership structure and assignment. Also, when the purpose is to draw conclusions about membership based on statistical operations, the level of measurement determines whether conclusions will depend on the arbitrarily chosen scale or not. For example, strictly speaking, operations such as the arithmetic mean require numerical structure at the level of an interval scale, whereas the median or min-max operators require only ordinal measurement. To give some idea why measurement level is important in this respect, we discuss the development of measurement theory below. For a more extensive overview see Michell 1999 or Hand 2004.

Theories of measurement

During the first part of the twentieth century, the status of psychological measurement was challenged by physicists like Campbell (1920). It was thought that true measurement requires the demonstration of additive structure in the property of interest. The term *fundamental measurement* was coined to refer to measurement of properties that show additivity directly (length, mass, and elapsed time) or by derivation of directly additive properties (density and electrical resistance). There are three basic types of scales obeying these axioms. The *absolute scale* has no degree of freedom for transformation. An example would be a count or normalized count such as a probability. A *ratio scale* such as mass, distance, or elapsed time from a defined starting point has only an arbitrary unit (e.g., meters or feet for distance are both valid units) but has a well-defined zero. In this case both ratios and differences of a ratio scale are meaningful. An *interval scale* is one that allows for transformation of a unit and also translation of the origin. Common examples include Celsius temperature or calendar time. Only differences of interval scales are meaningful. The *log-interval scale* is a variant of the interval scale in which ratios are meaningful but not differences. Examples include measures such as fuel usage as measured in miles per gallon. *Ordinal measurement*, where only ordering relations are meaningful, does not satisfy the additivity requirements for fundamental measurement.

Unsurprisingly, few psychological variables are amenable to fundamental measurement. One of the few examples is the von Neumann–Morgenstern utility function. Even when physical measurements such as reaction times or evoked potential are available, it is unclear how these relate to psychological properties, such as mental capacity or emotion, which are thought to underlie them. Townsend (1992) discusses this issue in the context of reaction time, which is commonly used in cognitive psychological studies to determine properties of underlying mental representation of tasks. Although reaction time is on a ratio scale, there are some subtleties involved in maintaining this interpretation. However, as Townsend notes, the cost of losing the ratio measurement properties of reaction time mitigates most of the interesting empirical results derived from studying it.

Stevens (1946) proposed that the definition of measurement should follow the empirical structure of properties and redefined measurement as the assignment of numbers to objects according to a rule. The rule corresponds to the type of relation between objects that is captured, determining the level of measurement. If the rule is "assign different numbers to distinguish different types of objects," representing only category information, we can speak of measurement at the nominal level. The ordinal measurement level entails ordering the objects on the property of interest, the interval level entails the comparability of differences, and the ratio level entails the direct comparability of quantities.

Associated with these levels are types of transformations that leave intact the type of information captured by the data. A statistic, or the inference based on it, should remain invariant under permissible transformations that represent the underlying property equally well. Strictly speaking, statistics that make use of interval information, such as parametric t- and F-tests should therefore not be used with ordinal data. The proposed permissibility of statistics evoked a fierce debate (Lord 1953; Gaito 1980; Townsend and Ashby 1984; Zand Scholten and Borsboom 2009). This debate was never truly settled, in part because Stevens's theory was subsumed into a more sophisticated theory, which emphasizes the legitimacy of inferences, not statistics.

This theory, known as *representational measurement theory*, axiomatizes whether consistent assignment of numbers to objects is possible for some property, and what the associated measurement level is (Krantz et al. 1971). For a measure to be of the interval level, the objects under study are required to obey a number of axioms. Additive conjoint measurement (ACM) is a highly relevant representational structure for psychological properties, because it allows indirect demonstration of additivity. The most important ACM axiom is *double cancellation*, a complex of simultaneous order restrictions, which ensures that transitivity requirements hold. Not many psychological variables obey such axioms perfectly, although they may do so approximately.

One option is to acquiesce, accept that the ordinal level is the best we can do for now, and focus on methods that ensure unambiguous inference. As noted above with regard to reaction time, this often requires giving up too much of what can be studied empirically. Another approach is to adopt a pragmatic definition of measurement, one that entails a sizable amount of interpretation. Measurement by fiat refers to numerical assignment based primarily on theory and the intuitions of researchers, not on tested axioms. The term was coined by Torgerson (1958), who rightly noted that there is nothing inherently wrong with measurement by fiat, particularly in the early days of inquiry. For the behavioral sciences, measurement by fiat is the only workable definition in the foreseeable future. Nearly any practical measurement task, will involve some combination of representational and pragmatic aspects (Hand 2004). One hopes that, as a field of inquiry develops, better validated measures will be developed.

What level is needed?

What measurement level is needed depends on the use to which one wants to put the membership values. If categorization into a trichotomy—*not a member, partial member, full member*—is all that is needed, the ordinal level of measurement is sufficient. Furthermore, as discussed by Smithson (1987) and Smithson and Verkuilen (2006), much of fuzzy set theory is essentially ordinal, so it is possible to get a lot done with just ordinal membership assignment. As mentioned before, the min-max operators rely only on ordinal comparisons. Even then, interset relations depend on property ranking. For instance, Smithson (2005) shows that it is possible to develop an ordinal measure of fuzzy inclusion.

Often, however, a higher measurement level is needed. For instance, anyone intending to use fuzzy set modifiers based on power transformations such as Zadeh's (1972) linguistic hedges needs numerical membership values. Exactly what level of measurement required is somewhat unclear. Wakker (2008) explores the measurement properties of power transformations in great detail. He shows that power transformations require interval measurement, but higher levels have been claimed. More generally, if the membership values are to be subjected to statistical operations that make use of quantitative properties, then an interval level is needed. Measures such as fuzzy cardinality require even higher measurement. Although only very few fuzzy sets will hold up under the harsh scrutiny of axiomatic measurement theory, this does not mean that the entire enterprise is hopeless. There are indeed examples of fuzzy set membership assignment methods that can be argued to show quantitative structure.

6.2.3 Assignment Methods

As one might expect, there are many ways of obtaining membership values. These methods have their strengths and weaknesses.

Direct scaling

Several direct scaling procedures have been developed over the years. These rely on a judge (broadly defined) providing a direct assignment of a membership value to an object. What can be done with ratings so acquired varies greatly, ranging from taking them at face value to subjecting them to verification of the axioms of representational measurement theory. A substantial number of direct scaling methods exists (Bilgiç and Türkşen 1999). All are variants of well-known methods of data gathering used in the behavioral sciences. *Polling* interprets sample proportions gathered from many judges as membership. In the terminology of scaling theory, this is referred to as *single stimulus response*. One weakness of this strategy is that it is unlikely to be workable when one wishes to consider an individual judge's membership values. *Direct rating* elicits membership values from one or more judges by presenting objects to them and gathering some sort of numerical response, possibly subject to subsequent transformation. Graded response formats can, in principle, provide more information than binary ones, especially about discriminable objects, but at the cost of stronger assumptions and more potential for interjudge heterogeneity. Polling and direct rating are simply variants of each other, with polling providing judges with a binary response format and the gradation for membership being derived from aggregates of these binary responses, whereas direct rating elicits this gradation immediately. Two related strategies are mentioned by Bilgiç and Türkşen (1999). *Reverse rating* reverses the process of direct rating by having judges assign objects to given values of membership. The method of *interval estimation* naturally matches the random set view, by asking a judge to assign objects to intervals of the support set that match a given membership level. A generally useful reference on direct scaling is Torgerson 1958.

Indirect scaling

Several scaling models have been developed that could be used to build membership functions up from more elemental responses provided by one or more judges. We consider one of the simplest and best-studied examples, the von Neumann–Morgenstern utility function, in some detail. This provides a scaling procedure that can generate interval scales based on choices made over a sequence of gambles (Luce and Raiffa 1957). Much like additive conjoint measurement, the von Neumann–Morgenstern procedure comes down to testing crucial assumptions about transitivity. Consider a hypothetical decision maker, Rose, who has to decide between three alternative vacations, each lasting a week: stay home (*S*), trip to Paris (*P*), and trip to London (*L*). Assume further that it has been established for Rose that she prefers Paris to London, Paris to staying home, and London to staying home. Without loss of generality, we may assign $u(S) = 0$ and $u(P) = 1$. By providing Rose gambles *SpL*, *SqP*, and *LrP*, where *XyZ* denotes "receiving option *X* with probability *y*, else receiving option *Z*," it is possible to assign a numeric utility for the trip to London such that $0 < u(L) < 1$, assuming her choices are transitive. (The procedure can, of course, be generalized to more than three objects.) It should be noted that a given decision maker's choices may not satisfy the von Neumann–Morgenstern axioms and thus not be scalable. This would happen if transitivity conditions were violated, for instance, if she preferred Paris to London, London to staying home, but staying home to Paris. To assess membership this way, we identify utility with membership. Researchers in behavioral decision making have found a number of systematic anomalies to von Neumann–Morgenstern utility theory, including a relatively greater aversion to loss than preference for gain, but it still represents a useful first approximation and scaling method.

A number of other scaling models provide similar insight. For instance, the well-known paired comparisons procedures allow the generation of an interval scale of utility, assuming that choices made by judges satisfy stochastic transitivity conditions, which are probabilistic generalizations of the von Neumann–Morgenstern transitivity conditions. Böckenholt (2006) presents a substantial review of the probabilistic utility scaling literature, which he connects to the behavioral decision-making literature. Another approach can be found in the well-known Rasch model. The Rasch model is an item-response theory model that relates latent ability to the probability of answering an item correctly via a logistic function. The model can be used to estimate latent values based on ordinal item scores. The Rasch model can be seen as an instantiation of ACM (Perline, Wright, and Wainer 1979) and thus provides a method for generating an interval scale. If data fit this model, then the underlying property can be said to display quantitative structure, at least according to some (Embretson and Reise 2000; Bond and Fox 2007). The Rasch model is very strict, however, and in many cases only a small set of items will show adequate fit. Even if good fit is achieved, the latent ability scale in the model varies over the entire real line. There are bounded representational structures that address this problem, but the Rasch model as a form of ACM is not one of these. One way to establish relatively natural endpoints, however, could be to assign a 0 to respondents who answered all items incorrectly, a 1 to respondents who answered all items correctly, and to rescale the latent ability values of all other respondents accordingly. This sits well with the fact that these extreme scores are not used in the estimation of the Rasch model since they result in an infinitely small or large latent value when conditional maximum likelihood estimation is used.

Unfortunately, although an interval scale is useful for many purposes, it lacks the defined endpoints desired in fuzzy set theory. While the example above has $u(S) = 0$ and $u(P) = 1$, any other two numbers would do just as well because utility is an interval scale. Something extra is necessary to identify these anchor points. Often this can be done by considering other aspects of the choice set. For instance, option P may represent for this decision maker the ideal week's vacation, better than all other possibilities. In this case it makes sense to identify it as Rose's ideal point, which means that it becomes reasonable to assume $u(X) < 1$ for all other choices X less preferred than P, without loss of generality. Similarly, she could definitely want to take some trip, in which case $u(X) > 0$ for all other choices X preferred to S. A different person, Colin, might have a different preference ordering. Böckenholt (2004) shows how to identify, given some judicious addition of information and reasonable assumptions, the origin of the scale in a paired-comparisons scaling context that provides natural statistical tests for consistency. He provides numerous examples and code to fit his models. Lootsma (1999) also discusses using reasonable anchor points such as the status quo policy or an ideal policy to help set the origin in a useful way.

However, a fair degree of confusion remains in the scaling literature. For example, one popular method of indirect scaling that has been used in the fuzzy set literature is the *analytic hierarchy process*, or AHP (Saaty 1977). AHP is itself a reinvention of techniques found in the scaling literature of the 1950s (Torgerson 1958) and is related to magnitude ("ratio") scaling, common in psychophysics. But ratio scaling of the psychophysical variety should not be thought of as generating a genuine ratio scale. That is, this kind of ratio scaling does not yield a scale that is invariant up to multiplication by a constant and for which both ratios and differences are meaningful. Birnbaum has shown that ratio judgments are not consistent in the way that would be required for them to provide a ratio scale. (See Hardin and Birnbaum 1990 for a summary of this line of research.) Instead, ratio scaling works on log-interval scales, which are simply exponentiated interval scales for which there should be no expectation that both differences and ratios be consistent, as there would be for a true ratio scale. However, Lootsma (1999) criticizes AHP, which has been widely applied in fuzzy set applications on similar grounds. Another example of this confusion involves the Fuzzy Logic Model of Perception (e.g., Friedman and Massaro 1998), which models binary choice and rating data using a transformation of membership functions. Crowther, Batchelder, and Hu (1995) show that it is equivalent to the Rasch model.

Transformation/measurement by fiat

Frequently, values for an existing variable can be obtained, and the investigator has some idea—based on theory, prima facie validity, or intuition—as to how this existing variable aligns with the concept embodied by the fuzzy set. For instance, a preexisting interval scale with identifiable endpoints can, without loss of generality, be linearly transformed into the unit interval. Also, other nonlinear transformations might be chosen to represent the sorts of qualitative features believed to underlie the concept of membership.

Hybrid strategies

In practice it is often necessary to adopt a hybrid of the above methods. For instance, values generated from indirect scaling may satisfy the requirements of an interval scale, but measurement by fiat may be necessary to set the maximal and minimal values. This was exactly what was done to set the endpoints of the membership function in the utility scaling example given previously.

Validation

Validation of membership assignment is a necessary but difficult task. Scaling models and axiomatic measurement theory provide routes for verifying internal properties of scales. For instance, the double cancellation axiom and other axioms of conjoint measurement verify that an additive representation for the given empirical system is possible and a number of different models, for example, the Rasch model, obey these axioms. It is important to note that verification of measurement level assumptions via Rasch modeling requires an acceptable model fit. Such fit is often achieved only after step-wise exclusion of items that show bad fit. This procedure can lead to an artificial unidimensional scale. Validation therefore requires replication of results using identical but also different tests. However, internal verification is not the only task one might want to undertake. A great deal of the power of fuzzy sets comes from the use of connectives such as intersection or union or operations such as negation, which allow sets to be derived from more basic sets. However, it is not clear a priori whether, for fuzzy sets A, B, if derived and directly obtained membership agree. In this case it seems quite reasonable to elicit membership values a, b, $a \cap b$, $a \cup b$, and so on, over a set of objects X and see whether these agree with those derived from the chosen connectives and operations. Research in behavioral decision making suggests that agreement is unlikely to hold, given the well-documented inability of judges to correctly guess probabilities of compound events (e.g., Wolfe and Reyna 2010). This is clearly an area for further research.

6.3 Property Ranking

We have already discussed property ranking to some degree. To continue our exploration of insights from utility theory, we examine the problem of *interpersonal comparison of utility*. It is widely held that a decision maker may have a utility function, assuming her decisions are sufficiently consistent to satisfy the von Neumann–Morgenstern axioms, and probabilistic utility theories have relaxed the requirements to allow a certain level of inconsistency likely to be inherent in real choices. In a sense it seems that interpersonal comparison of utility ought to be possible—a pithy quote illustrating this, taken from Sen 1970, p. 199, is "it should not be difficult to say that Emperor Nero's gain from burning Rome did not outweigh the loss of the rest of the Romans"—but formalizing this comparison has proven to be elusive.

Luce and Raiffa (1957, chapter 6) provide a thought-provoking example of the property ranking problem in the context of a two-person game first proposed by philosopher R. B. Braithwaite. The "story" of this game involves two neighbors, our hypothetical decision makers, Rose and Colin,

Table 6.1

	Colin Plays	Colin Doesn't Play
Rose Plays	(0,0.11)	(1,0.22)
Rose Doesn't Play	(0.50,1)	(0.33,0)

who live in adjoining apartments and have to allocate time playing musical instruments. Braithwaite asked whether it would be possible to generate a fair allocation of time, taking into account players' strength of preference. Each player can choose either to play or not play. Utility functions are obtained for both and are normalized by assigning a value of 0 to each player's least preferred policy and 1 to each player's most preferred policy, permissible for an interval scale. That is, the best option is assigned one utile, the worst option zero utiles, and all others fractionally in between. These utiles are player specific. The purpose is to determine if it is possible to equate them across players. The resulting normal form game with normalized utilities for each player is given in table 6.1. For instance, if both Rose and Colin are playing, she receives 0 utiles and he receives 0.11 utiles.

Luce and Raiffa examine two related solutions to the interpersonal comparison of utility. The simpler of the two takes Nash's bargaining solution and works backward to convert to units of the original measurement scales, while the other elaborates this procedure slightly. Doing this shows that Rose is indifferent between the arbitrated solution and a lottery that weights her most-preferred alternative with probability 0.652 and her least-preferred alternative with probability 0.348. Similarly, Colin achieves 0.763 utiles. To achieve this result, Colin should play while Rose remains silent 16 out of 23 nights, and Rose should play on the remainder. This method is shown to satisfy all axioms of the Nash equilibrium except the independence of irrelevant alternatives (IIA), which states that the addition of objects to the choice set should not change relationships among existing objects. Unfortunately, the normalization used above depends on the objects given here, even if the choices added are dominated or otherwise irrelevant alternatives. Although the set of alternatives might be able to be pruned down only to the set of meaningful choices, in general we cannot assume this is so.

This lines up with prior empirical research in utility theory. For example, Wallsten et al. (1986) provide a thorough, systematic study that aimed to formalize common linguistic quantifiers. The goal of their study was to determine if subjects (economics and social science graduate students at a major research university) could provide membership functions for probability words such as "doubtful," "probable," or "likely." Membership assignment was done by way of a conjoint measurement method based on paired comparisons of the degree to which each word applied to a pair of gambles presented. Membership values were assigned as estimated parameters from the scaling models based on axioms of ratio measurement. These models were shown to have acceptable fit. In particular, they showed that subjects appear to be internally consistent in the sense that their understanding of the probability words satisfactorily predicted the same relationships among words that the measurement model did (up to sampling variability), which amounts to satisfying ordering conditions among the comparisons. However, membership functions between subjects were not very consistent. Similarly, subjects in an experiment performed by Böckenholt (2004) were additive at the individual level, but there appear to be nonnegligible individual differences, very much in line with those found by Wallsten et al. More advanced procedures that have been explored in the literature on probabilistic scaling with hierarchical nonlinear models might improve this situation, at least in the sense of being able to better quantify the amount of between-subject heterogeneity.

How does this relate to fuzzy set theory? The solution to interpersonal comparison of utility (or lack thereof) is essentially the same problem as property ranking. A number of proposed fuzzy-set-based techniques are essentially premised on property ranking or consequences of it. For instance, the measurement of fuzzy inclusion proposed by Ragin (2000) depends strongly on the margins of the distribution of the two fuzzy sets being compared. This in turn depends on comparability across sets, that is, property ranking. Sometimes this seems plausible given the content of the sets to be compared, but by no means is it always so, and depends strongly on the membership assignment in a manner that a different measure of inclusion would not. For instance, Ragin's proposed procedure will declare two stochastically independent variables to be fuzzy subsets if the margins are sufficiently skewed.

6.4   Example: Major Depressive Disorder

We now consider an example in some detail. Here, we show how fuzzy set theory can be relevant to the assessment of psychopathological disorders such as depression. Most formalizations of psychiatric diagnosis schemes have an implicit method of membership assignment that does not concur with the subtlety of actual diagnosis by practitioners. Take, for instance, an archetypical psychopathological disorder, major depressive disorder (MDD). Conventional clinical assessment of MDD, following the guidelines of DSM-IV, takes on the following form. There are nine major symptoms of clinical depression: depressed mood, diminished interest and pleasure in daily activities, weight problems (loss or gain), psychomotor agitation or retardation nearly every day, sleep problems (insomnia or hypersomnia), fatigue or loss of energy, concentration problems, feelings of worthlessness, and suicidal ideation. The diagnosis of MDD according to the American Psychiatric Association (DSM-IV-TR) criteria can be considered the assignment of people to the crisp set depressed (1) or not depressed (0) on the basis of the following membership assignment: If a person displays five or more of these symptoms for a period of at least two weeks, he or she is considered to be depressed, that is, to display MDD. This membership assignment scheme (not referred to as such in the DSM) is the topic of much discussion: Although most clinicians agree that these nine symptoms are of central importance, the exact criterion (5 or more during 2 weeks) immediately leads to numerous examples that defy intuition and clinical practice: people who either display a maximum of four symptoms for any period of time (even if it includes suicidal ideation) will not, according to these criteria, be considered depressed. Also, as all symptoms are created equal, we get an implicit rank-ordering of patients that does not align well with decisions of clinical practice or common sense. Consider the following example: Person A suffers from the following four, intuitively severe, MDD symptoms: depressed mood, diminished interest and pleasure in daily activities, feelings of worthlessness, and suicidal ideation. Now consider person B, who suffers from the following five symptoms: weight problems, psychomotor agitation, fatigue, sleep problems, and concentration problems. Strictly speaking, not only is person B more depressed than A, person A should not be considered depressed at all. Although we do not in any way imply that the latter symptoms are trivial or irrelevant, it seems a stretch to argue that all MDD symptoms are equal in terms of psychological impact. If this is something clinicians and academic psychologists would agree on, it is worth attempting to explicate and formalize this fact.

Several recent developments (e.g., Borsboom 2008; Cramer et al. 2010; Zachar and Kendler 2007) have focused on shortcomings of this classical approach and have considered a dynamical systems or causal modeling approach instead. Others have extended the conventional assessment of depression by means of IRT analysis (for an overview, see Reise and Waller 2009). It seems clear that the classic assessment scheme fails to line up with clinical practice and suffers from serious conceptual and psychometric problems. We propose that the application of fuzzy set theory to the psychological concept of depression provides a novel approach to the problem of MDD diagnosis and illustrates the benefits and flexibility of fuzzy set theoretical applications.

For the purpose of this illustration of the details of membership functions, we focus on Major Depressive Disorder (MDD) and its symptoms. The proposed framework can be extended to include larger networks of symptoms and disorders. The core is in line with conventional fuzzy set theory: Instead of considering an individual depressed or not depressed, we will consider any individual to occupy a position on a fuzzy set scale of depression that ranges from 0 (no depression symptoms) to 1 (all depression symptoms). Note that 0 does not necessarily imply happiness, but merely the absence of depression symptoms. To align with the requirement of duration, we will assume the symptoms as considered below are present for at least two weeks.

For the concept of depression, the fuzzy set membership values between 0 and 1 should be considered conceptually meaningful, as opposed to applications that consider fuzzy sets a quantification of uncertainty or measurement error. That is, a person who is assigned a value of 0.4 on a fuzzy set depression scale is in a certain psychologically and clinically meaningful state, which may yield predictive information about future psychopathology such as the extent to which certain types of therapy or intervention by means of medication will be successful.

In our example below, we will consider a hypothetical population of 10,000 members who display a representative selection of the MDD symptoms as described above. In the online appendix (see <http://mitpress.mit .edu/fuzzylogic>) we provide R code to simulate a representative population of subjects with realistic constellations of symptoms, and to implement three of the described membership functions. The probabilities of symptom patterns are based on work by Aggen, Neale, and Kendler (2005), but could also be adapted based on relevant empirical data. A given person may display any constellation of these nine symptoms, although they are not equally likely (a person who "only" suffers from sleep problems is much more likely than a person who "only" suffers from suicidal ideation, but none of the other symptoms). The following membership function implementations are examples, and may be applied to any dataset. In line with Smithson and Verkuilen (2006) and Verkuilen (2005), we will consider various ways in which we can assign membership values to individuals in this population, based on various membership function procedures. Conceptually, an individual can take on a value between 0 and 1, where 1 represents fully/very depressed, and 0 represents not depressed at all. We can translate the DSM-IV MDD diagnosis as the following (crisp) membership function: If a person displays five or more symptoms during two weeks, then that person is depressed (1); otherwise he or she is not depressed (0). For reasons mentioned above, this definition leads to undesirable consequences. We will now examine various perspectives that move away from the traditional, crisp set perspective to possible fuzzy membership functions that yield values between 0 and 1, based on differing membership functions.

6.4.1 Direct Assignment

Direct assignment is a simple and traditional implementation of fuzzy set theory. A group of expert clinicians rates a person on a depression scale between 0 and 1, based on, for instance, a diagnostic interview or the subjective assessment of the severity of symptoms. A severely depressed person may be assigned a 0.9, a person who displays some symptoms of depression may be assigned a 0.2, and a (control) person with no symptoms has a 0. Given these assignments and the symptoms people display (already known), we can use simple regression to deduce a weighting scheme for symptoms, such that the membership function's assignment corresponds most closely to the subjective ratings of the expert clinicians. The benefit of the estimates so derived is, first, that they reflect the *implicit* weighting scheme that clinicians apply. Second, it gives important diagnostic information about the error terms of symptoms: The regression yields information about the amount of information about MDD the presence of a symptom contains. For instance, it seems quite possible for a nondepressed person to have trouble sleeping, whereas a nondepressed person with suicidal ideation seems, at least intuitively, less likely. If true, this will yield larger confidence intervals for beta weights, which may represent important diagnostic information.

6.4.2   Indirect Scaling

With this method, instead of weighing overall severity of depression, experts can rate the relative severity of symptoms. Judging on the basis of criteria (such as the influence on daily life, the extent to which displaying a symptom is a mark of severe depression), experts such as psychiatrists can assign relative weights to the nine symptoms of depression on the basis of theoretical considerations, making sure the symptom weights sum to 1. For instance, lack of sleep is presumably weighted less severely than suicidal ideation. Together, the nine symptoms represent the full spectrum from 0 (absence of symptoms) to 1 (all symptoms). However, unlike the traditional DSM classification, not all symptoms are considered equal: If a person suffers from suicidal ideation and depressed mood, he or she will (presumably) be considered more depressed than a person who has problems sleeping and weight gain, although both persons display, or suffer from, two symptoms of depression. Doing so yields fuzzy set values between 0 and 1 for any subject depending on the number and severity of the symptoms they display.

6.4.3   Disorder Prevalence

One of the core benefits of using fuzzy set theory to model concepts is that it can better align with the manner in which (linguistic) concepts are used and interpreted. In fact, it is possible to utilize such interpretations as the basis of a membership function. One way to accommodate intuitions about psychological constructs into membership functions is to ensure that the distribution of values over a population fits with our commonsense perspective on the prevalence of the disorder (or psychological construct). For instance, whatever membership function we choose, if it yields membership values such that 80% of the population scores, say, higher than 0.9 (which would roughly align with the linguistic term "very depressed"), most would agree that this does not fit well with conventional intuition. This intuition can be formalized within the fuzzy set framework. It is possible to decide, by fiat, the approximate distribution of fuzzy set values for a population and deduce from this distribution the weights of symptoms in such a way that the desired distribution holds for the population under study. For instance, imagine that a group of experts decides that, for a meaningful and useful interpretation of fuzzy set values, the following distributional characteristics should hold: 50% of a population should score 0 (be completely MDD symptom free), 30% should score 0.3 or higher, 10% should score 0.7 or higher, and 1% should score 0.9 or higher. This can be represented as an approximate density function of fuzzy set values for a population. Given the multivariate distribution of symptoms, we can assign weights to each of these symptoms in such a way that the fuzzy set values so generated conform to the distribution decided on by a panel of experts. In this way, the fuzzy set values generated will conform to a natural interpretation understanding of the scale between 0 and 1. This strategy therefore may allow us to formalize and quantify natural intuitions concerning the prevalence of disorder severity in a population.

6.4.4 Benefits

The above are some examples of possible membership functions for MDD that formalize the common intuition that people can be in a psychological state somewhere between "not depressed at all" to "fully or severely depressed." There are several reasons to consider fuzzy set theoretical applications for psychological concepts such as MDD. Classifying people as either depressed or not depressed, with no shades of gray, does not align with clinical practice or common intuition, and limits the scientific study of the concept. Fuzzy set theory is much better in line with conventional thinking and therapeutic assessment, and its membership value criteria can be adjusted to allow the best fit. Although practitioners rightly argue that the DSM does not reflect actual clinical practice, it is still the authoritative source for clinical diagnosis. If what practitioners actually do is more subtle (and this seems likely), it is surely worth attempting to formalize these practices in models that can accommodate more sophisticated strategies.

Fuzzy set theory also has several benefits over other diagnostic tools that have been applied to psychiatric disorders, such as item response theory (IRT). (See Reise and Waller 2009 for an excellent overview.) First, IRT models have a latent variable scale that runs from minus to plus infinity. Although such scaling procedures are sensible for ability scales, for concepts such as MDD this is less appropriate. For instance, MDD is characterized by nine symptoms, which are either present or absent. This suggests (in addition to fuzzy boundaries) two natural endpoints: displaying no MDD symptoms (0) and displaying all symptoms (1). This is less restrictive than one might suppose, as the manifest properties of the data do not identify the latent space in an IRT model, so it is possible to have a model that makes exactly the same predictions as the Rasch model that generates scale values in [0,1] (Rossi, Wang, and Ramsey 2002). Second, given the nature of depression symptoms, IRT models of psychiatric disorders commonly encounter problems, such as the fact that the discrimination values of items are not distributed evenly over the ability scale, leading to problems in model fitting and item design. Reise and Waller (2009) note that common IRT models do not distinguish genuine absence of a trait from very low values.

Finally, fuzzy set membership has several interesting applications and extensions. We mention three such possibilities. First, by assigning fuzzy membership between 0 and 1, it is possible to assess fuzzy cardinality, that is, to sum partial values of a construct over a population. Within the classical DSM framework, this is not possible. To see why, consider two groups of individuals. In the first group, all individuals display four MDD symptoms over an extended period of time. In the other group, all members display no MDD symptoms at all. From a traditional perspective, both groups are considered "equally depressed." Thus, having a formalized quantification of degrees of depression gives the mathematical tools to study phenomena that may be too subtle to be measured by traditional means. Second, subtle temporal dynamics of psychiatric diagnoses such as seasonal affective disorder, the effect of (natural) disasters on populations, or the increase in depression due to economic adversity may be studied by fuzzy cardinality. That is, despite the fact that subtle changes in a population occur at a subthreshold level, it may be possible to study the change in (weighted) symptom distributions over time, and quantify such phenomena more accurately. Third, fuzzy set membership functions may allow one to model an archetypical feature of psychiatric diagnoses: the fact that symptoms of, for instance, MDD rarely appear alone. This phenomenon of co-occurring symptoms and psychopathology is commonly referred to as *comorbidity*. Fuzzy set membership assignments offers potentially valuable diagnostic information for comorbidity. For instance, a person might be diagnosed as having an MDD based on traditional DSM criteria, but may also display several symptoms of other disorders at a subthreshold level. These other, subthreshold symptoms (such as symptoms from generalized anxiety disorder) would formally not be considered in the clinical assessment of a person. This is especially troubling given the fact that comorbidity of different clinical disorders (or symptoms) is highly prevalent (Cramer et al. 2010). The phenomenon of subthreshold symptoms can be incorporated more naturally in fuzzy set theory, where the assessment of an individual can be made on the basis of fuzzy cardinality (i.e., the summation of partial memberships of various disorders). A weighted summation over the totality of symptoms may allow for more fine-grained assessment: A person who suffers from various symptoms that in isolation may not warrant a traditional diagnosis of, for instance, generalized anxiety disorder (GAD) can still be diagnosed based on appropriately weighted symptoms, which can be more accurately monitored over time than simple presence or absence of a disorder. Smithson and Verkuilen (2006) show some applications of fuzzy set theory for comorbidity, illustrating some commonalities between covariances and the sum and product operators for fuzzy union and intersection. They provide several examples that illustrate the comorbidity of dislike, disgust, and fear, and also several psychiatric symptoms in two samples of children, those referred to clinic or not.

These are but some of the possible extensions of the current proposition, namely, that fuzzy set theory allows for a tractable formalization of the intuition that phenomena of psychopathology are not clear and crisp, but a matter of degree, and should therefore be treated as such.

6.5 Discussion

Fuzzy set concepts enjoyed an initial surge of popularity in psychology in the 1970s, followed by a long period of skepticism. A more modern approach has been to avoid programmatic declarations and consider what problems could be solved using the concepts of fuzzy set theory. To appreciate this one first has to have an idea of what membership is and how "membership to a degree" is determined. Interpretations and methods can vary and are combined in many cases.

In this chapter, we have focused less on relationships between fuzzy sets (although obviously these are important) and more on properties internal to fuzzy sets. In particular, we have highlighted the notion of degree-vagueness and recognizable endpoints as essential in determining whether a fuzzy-set-based analysis is appropriate. We have focused on defining membership in a meaningful way. Three crucial elements in this respect are the interpretation of membership degree, the assignment method and the measurement level associated with this method, and the property of interest.

We have proposed several different interpretations; this makes sense, as any given case will depend on the context of the problem. More than one interpretation can be appropriate in some cases. The similarity and utility interpretations of membership degree seem to provide the most appealing view for social scientists. Assignment methods can also vary greatly and can be used in combination or in sequence in some cases. Indirect scaling such as paired comparison seems to best connect with existing methods, but other methods offer interesting new approaches for applied researchers. The measurement level associated with membership assignment is hard to determine. Often the best we can do is the ordinal level. In some cases, however, methods such as paired comparison or Rasch modeling can be used to at least investigate whether there is some indication of quantitative structure to the degree of membership. More work needs to be done on lesser-known representational structures for bounded empirical structures. Many of these structures are not amenable to standard measurement procedures, but they could prove useful in a fuzzy set context.

The application of fuzzy set theory to preference rating and decision making using the von Neumann–Morgenstern axioms and the diagnosis of depression shows that fuzzy set theory can serve as an important tool to further our understanding of complex psychological properties and processes. Undoubtedly, other areas could also benefit from the application of fuzzy set theory, especially areas where categorization problems are unsuccessfully approached with either continuous or categorical models, as in the depression example.

References

Ackerman, F. 1994. Roots and consequences of vagueness. *Philosophical Perspectives* 8:129–136.

Aggen, S. H., M. C. Neale, and K. S. Kendler. 2005. DSM criteria for major depression: Evaluating symptoms patterns using latent-trait item response models. *Psychological Medicine* 35:475–487.

Bilgiç, T., and I. B. Türkşen. 1999. Measurement of membership functions: Theoretical and empirical work. In *Fundamentals of Fuzzy Sets*, ed. D. Dubois and H. Prade, 195–232. Boston: Kluwer.

Böckenholt, U. 2004. Comparative judgements as an alternative to ratings: Identifying the scale origin. *Psychological Methods* 9:453–465.

Böckenholt, U. 2006. Thurstonian-based analysis: Past, present, and future utilities. *Psychometrika* 71:615–629.

Bond, T. G., and C. M. Fox. 2007. *Applying the Rasch model: Fundamental Measurement in the Human Sciences*. Hillsdale, NJ: Lawrence Erlbaum.

Borsboom, D. 2008. Psychometric perspectives on diagnostic systems. *Journal of Clinical Psychology* 64:1089–1108.

Brehm, J., and S. Gates. 1993. Donut shops or speed traps: Evaluating models of supervision on police behavior. *American Journal of Political Science* 37:555–581.

Campbell, N. R. 1920. *Physics: The Elements*. Cambridge: Cambridge University Press.

Cramer, A. O. J., L. J. Waldorp, H. L. J. van der Maas, and D. Borsboom. 2010. Comorbidity: A network perspective. *Behavioral and Brain Sciences* 33:137–150.

Crowther, C. S., W. H. Batchelder, and X. Hu. 1995. A measurement-theoretic analysis of the fuzzy logic model of perception. *Psychological Review* 102:396–408.

Embretson, S. E., and S. P. Reise. 2000. *Item response theory for psychologists*. Hillsdale, NJ: Lawrence Erlbaum.

Friedman, D., and D. W. Massaro. 1998. Understanding variability in binary and continuous choice. *Psychometric Bulletin & Review* 5:370–389.

Gaito, J. 1980. Measurement scales and statistics: Resurgence of an old misconception. *Psychological Bulletin* 87:564–567.

Hand, D. J. 2004. *Measurement theory and practice: The world through quantification*. New York: John Wiley.

Hardin, C., and M. H. Birnbaum. 1990. Malleability of "ratio" judgments of occupational prestige. *American Journal of Psychology* 103:1–20.

Healy, M. J. R. , and H. Goldstein. 1976. An approach to the scaling of categorized attributes. *Biometrika* 63:219–229.

Krantz, D. H., R. D. Luce, P. Suppes, and A. Tversky. 1971. *Foundations of Measurement*, vol. I. New York: Academic Press.

Lootsma, F. A. 1999. *Multi-criteria Decision Analysis via Ratio and Difference Judgement*. Boston: Kluwer.

Lord, F. M. 1953. On the statistical treatment of football numbers. *American Psychologist* 8:750–751.

Luce, R. D., and H. Raiffa. 1957. *Games and Decisions: Introduction and Critical Survey.* New York: John Wiley.

Michell, J. 1999. *Measurement in Psychology: A Critical History of a Methodological Concept.* New York: Cambridge University Press.

Perline, R., B. D. Wright, and H. Wainer. 1979. The Rasch model as additive conjoint measurement. *Applied Psychological Measurement* 3:237–255.

Ragin, C. 2000. *Fuzzy-Set Social Science.* Chicago: University of Chicago Press.

Reise, S. P., and N. G. Waller. 2009. Item response theory and clinical measurement. *Annual Review of Clinical Psychology* 5:27–48.

Reiss, A. J. 1971. *The Police and the Public.* New Haven, CT: Yale University Press.

Rossi, N., X. Wang, and J. O. Ramsey. 2002. Nonparametric item response estimates with the EM algorithm. *Journal of Educational and Behavioral Statistics* 27:291–317.

Saaty, T. L. 1977. A scaling method for priorities in hierarchical structures. *Journal of Mathematical Psychology* 15:234–281.

Sen, A. K. 1970. *Collective Choice and Social Welfare.* San Francisco: Holden-Day.

Shafir, E., and R. A. LeBoeuf. 2002. Rationality. *Annual Review of Psychology* 53: 491–517.

Smithson, M. 1987. *Fuzzy Set Analysis for Behavioral and Social Sciences.* New York: Springer.

Smithson, M. 2005. Fuzzy set inclusion: Linking fuzzy set methods with mainstream techniques. *Sociological Methods & Research* 33:431–461.

Smithson, M., and G. C. Oden. 1999. Fuzzy set theory and applications in psychology. In *Practical Applications of Fuzzy Technologies*, ed. H. Zimmermann, 557–585. Boston: Kluwer.

Smithson, M., and J. Verkuilen. 2006. *Fuzzy Set Theory: Applications in Social Sciences.* Thousand Oaks, CA: Sage.

Stevens, S. S. 1946. On the theory of scales of measurement. *Science* 103:677–680.

Takane, Y., and T. Shibayama. 1992. Structures in stimulus identification data. In *Probabilistic Multidimensional models of Perception and Cognition*, ed. F. Ashby, 335–362. Hillsdale, NJ: Lawrence Erlbaum.

Torgerson, W. S. 1958. *Theory and Methods of Scaling.* New York: John Wiley.

Townsend, J. T. 1992. On the proper scale for reaction time. In *Cognition, Information Processing, and Psychophysics: Basic Issues*, ed. H. Geissler, S. Link, and J. Townsend, 105–120. Hillsdale, NJ: Lawrence Erlbaum.

Townsend, J. T., and F. Ashby. 1984. Measurement scales and statistics: The misconception misconceived. *Psychological Bulletin* 96:394–401.

UNDP. 2009. *Human Development Report 2009*. New York: Palgrave Macmillan.

Verkuilen, J. 2005. Assigning membership in a fuzzy set analysis. *Sociological Methods & Research* 33:462–496.

Wakker, P. P. 2008. Explaining the characteristics of the power CRRA utility family. *Health Economics* 17:1329–1334.

Wallsten, T. S., D. V. Budescu, A. Rappoport, R. Zwick, and B. Forsythe. 1986. Measuring the vague meaning of probability terms. *Journal of Experimental Psychology* 115:348–365.

Wolfe, C. R., and V. F. Reyna. 2010. Semantic coherence and fallacies in estimating joint probabilities. *Journal of Behavioral Decision Making* 23:203–223.

Zachar, P., and K. S. Kendler. 2007. Psychiatric disorders: A conceptual taxonomy. *American Journal of Psychiatry* 164:557–565.

Zadeh, L. A. 1965. Fuzzy sets. *Information and Control* 8:338–353.

Zadeh, L. A. 1972. Fuzzy-set theoretical interpretation of linguistic hedges. *Journal of Cybernetics* 2:4–34.

Zand Scholten, A., and D. Borsboom. 2009. A reanalysis of Lord's statistical treatment of football numbers. *Journal of Mathematical Psychology* 53:69–75.

7 Formal Concept Analysis: Classical and Fuzzy

Radim Belohlavek

7.1   Introduction

7.1.1   What Is Formal Concept Analysis?

Formal concept analysis (FCA) is a method of data analysis that is becoming increasingly popular in various communities. FCA was initiated in a classic paper by Wille (1982), but the ideas behind FCA appeared earlier (Barbut and Monjardet 1970). FCA is based on a particular formalization of the notion of concept, inspired by the view of concepts in traditional logic (also known as Port-Royal logic; see Arnauld and Nicole 1996). In its basic form, the input data to be analyzed by FCA consist of a set of objects (such as patients), a set of attributes (such as "have fever" or "smoke"), and a binary relation specifying which objects have which attributes. The attributes are thus binary, but there exist extensions of FCA that make it possible to apply FCA to other types of attributes as well. The primary aim in FCA is to extract from the input data all relevant concepts (called *formal concepts*), along with the subconcept–superconcept hierarchy (called the *concept lattice*) and a fully informative set of particular attribute dependencies (called *attribute implications*). The output (formal concepts, concept lattice, attribute implications) is presented to a user (who may respecify his request and continue the analysis interactively) or is subject to further processing (if FCA is used as a data-preprocessing method). A formal concept is defined as a pair consisting of two sets: a set of objects to which the concept applies (the concept's *extent*) and a set of attributes that characterize the concept (the concept's *intent*);[1] an attribute implication is an expression $A \Rightarrow B$ (such as {drinks-alcohol, smokes} $\Rightarrow$ {heart-problems}), which means: If an object has all attributes in A then it has also all attributes in B (if a person drinks alcohol and smokes, then that person has heart problems). A distinct feature of FCA is the possibility to visualize formal concepts, the concept lattice, and attribute implications in a single diagram, called a *line diagram,* which is easily understood by users. Applications of FCA can be found in many areas of human affairs, including engineering, natural and social sciences, and mathematics (see, e.g., Carpineto and Romano 2004b for applications in information retrieval; Snelting and Tip 2000 for applications in object-oriented design; Ganapathy et al. 2007 for applications in security; Pfaltz 2006 for applications in software engineering; Zaki 2004 for how concept lattices can be used to mine nonredundant association rules; and Ganter and Wille 1999, Carpineto and Romano 2004a, for further applications and references). Note that papers on FCA and its applications can also be found in the literature on psychology, but these seem to be exceptions (Guénoche and Van Mechelen 1993; Storms and De Boeck 1997). Two monographs on FCA are available: Ganter and Wille (1999) focus on mathematical foundations, and Carpineto and Romano (2004a) focus on applications. Three international conferences are devoted to FCA: ICFCA (International Conference on Formal Concept Analysis), CLA (Concept Lattices and Their Applications), and ICCS (International Conference on Conceptual Structures). Papers on FCA can also be found in many journals and conference proceedings on mathematics, computer science, engineering, and various application areas.

7.1.2 Formal Concept Analysis and the Psychology of Concepts

Researchers in various areas use various notions of the term *concept*. The psychology of concepts plays a unique role among these areas in that it studies concepts and the cognitive processes that involve concepts per se (see chapter 2, this volume). That is, what is ultimately important for the psychology of concepts is the psychological plausibility of any particular theory of concepts, not the various possible applications of the theory. In other areas dealing with concepts, including FCA, the goal is to work out such a notion of the term *concept* that is suitable for a particular purpose. On the one hand, this notion has to be psychologically plausible, at least to some extent, because its user (domain expert, data analyst, etc.) needs to feel that he or she is working with a natural notion of the term. On the other hand, the notion has to be operational to serve the particular purpose at hand (it needs to be feasible from the point of view of computational complexity, possibly amenable to theoretical analysis, etc.). The demand for being operational usually outweighs the demand for being psychologically plausible. As a result, the notions of concept employed in various areas, including FCA, are likely to be considered overly simplistic and psychologically inadequate by psychologists.

In FCA, the purpose is to analyze data by revealing from the data human-like concepts and various other patterns involving human-like concepts. As is mentioned above, the notion of concept employed by FCA is inspired by Port-Royal logic. It has to be stressed that from the beginning, close attention has been paid to the fact that the notions and methods of FCA provide a sound formalization of the traditional logic of concepts

(Wille 2005). Therefore, FCA is not an ad hoc method, but rather a method based on solid foundations. As discussed in section 7.2, from the point of view of psychology, the concepts used in FCA can be seen as concepts in the sense of the classical theory of concepts (see chapter 2 of this volume or Murphy 2002). As a result, the objections raised against the classical theory of concepts can be raised against FCA as far as psychological plausibility is concerned. However, this does not mean that FCA is irrelevant to the psychology of concepts. I believe that interactive research between FCA and the psychology of concepts may lead to interesting results for both areas. I present some concrete proposals of possibly interesting research in section 7.4.

7.1.3 Chapter Preview
The main aims of this chapter are the following:

• to present FCA in a nontechnical manner, accessible to researchers in the psychology of concepts;

• to show how fuzzy logic in the narrow sense can be used to generalize FCA from its classical setting (i.e., the setting developed to handle yes-or-no attributes) to a fuzzy setting (i.e., the setting developed to handle fuzzy attributes);

• to demonstrate that in a fuzzy setting, new, nonclassical phenomena emerge that are relevant from a cognitive point of view; and

• to argue that an interaction between FCA and the psychology of concepts is natural and could be beneficial to both FCA and the psychology of concepts.

The chapter is organized as follows. Basic notions, results, and methods of classical FCA are presented in section 7.2. In section 7.3, I show how these components of classical FCA can be generalized to data with fuzzy attributes. The focus in this section is on explaining conceptually how fuzzy logic in the narrow sense is used in such a generalization and presenting the fundamental agenda of FCA for data with fuzzy attributes. Particular attention is given to a promising recent direction that is relevant to the psychological point of view, namely, the use of formal concepts for factor analysis. Limited space does not permit me to cover technical details; these can be found in some of the cited references. In section 7.4, I argue that interactive research between FCA and the psychology of concepts may yield interesting results, and I suggest some possible directions for future research. Section 7.5 gives a brief summary of the chapter.

7.2 Formal Concept Analysis: Yes-or-No Attributes

7.2.1 Formal Context and Formal Concepts

FCA assumes that there is a given finite set X of *objects*, a given finite set Y of yes-or-no *attributes*, and a binary relation I between X and Y. Therefore, $x \in X$ means that x is an object in X, $y \in Y$ means that y is an attribute in Y, and $(x,y) \in I$ means that object x is in relation I with attribute y. This latter fact, $(x,y) \in I$, is interpreted as saying that object x has attribute y (or attribute y applies to object x). The triplet (X,Y,I) consisting of such X, Y, and I is called a *formal context* and is one of the basic notions in FCA. A formal context represents the data to be analyzed and can be depicted by a table such as table 7.1. (For simplicity, this section includes only a small illustrative example. A real-world example is presented in section 7.3.) The formal context depicted in table 7.1 consists of a set of five objects $X=\{x_1, x_2, x_3, x_4, x_5\}$, a set of three attributes $Y=\{y_1, y_2, y_3\}$, and a binary relation I represented by 0s and 1s. If one prefers concrete objects and attributes, the objects may be thought of as a flea (represented by x_1), pig (x_2), bear (x_3), lion (x_4), rabbit (x_5), and the attributes may be thought of as "be-parasite" (y_1), "eats-flesh" (y_2), and "eats-herbs" (y_3). A table entry containing 1 indicates that the corresponding object has the corresponding attribute, and an entry of 0 indicates the opposite. For example, object x_2 has attribute y_2 (pigs eat flesh) as well as attribute y_3 (pigs eat herbs) but does not have y_1 (pigs are

Table 7.1
Example of formal context.

	y_1	y_2	y_3
x_1	1	0	0
x_2	0	1	1
x_3	0	1	1
x_4	0	1	0
x_5	0	0	1

not parasites). To express it in the above notation: $(x_2, y_2) \in I$, $(x_2, y_3) \in I$, and $(x_2, y_1) \notin I$.

As is mentioned in section 7.1, one of the aims in FCA is to identify and present to the user (a data analyst) all relevant concepts that are "hidden" in the data—that is, to reveal to the user all concepts that would be considered natural, human-like concepts supported by the data. To this end, FCA defines the notion of a formal concept, which can be seen as a formalization of the notion of concept of Port-Royal logic. Put verbally, a *formal concept* of a formal context (X,Y,I) is a pair (A,B) consisting of a set A of objects in X and a set B of attributes in Y satisfying the following condition: B is the set of all attributes shared by every object in A and A is the set of all objects to which every attribute in B applies. This condition can be expressed formally using so-called *concept-forming operators* $\uparrow$ and $\downarrow$, defined by

$$A^{\uparrow} = \{y \in Y : \text{for each } x \in A, (x,y) \in I\}, \tag{7.1}$$

$$B^{\downarrow} = \{x \in X : \text{for each } y \in B, (x,y \in I\}. \tag{7.2}$$

That is, $\uparrow$ can be applied to any subset A of objects in X and assigns to A the set $A^{\uparrow}$ of all attributes shared by every object in A; the operator $\downarrow$ can be applied to any subset B of attributes in Y and assigns to B the set $B^{\downarrow}$ of all attributes shared by every object in A. Then, a formal concept is a pair (A, B) satisfying $A^{\uparrow}=B$ and $B^{\downarrow}=A$. A is called the *extent* and B is called the *intent* of a formal concept (A, B). The extent is thought of as the set of objects to which the concept (A, B) applies; the intent is thought of as the set of attributes that characterize (A, B). The concept-forming operators form a Galois connection (Ore 1944) and have several natural properties that are important for further theoretical analysis and for the design of efficient algorithms. Perhaps the most important are: If $A_1 \subseteq A_2$ then $A_2^{\uparrow} \subseteq A_1^{\uparrow}$ (this is just the well-known property that the more objects there are, the fewer attributes they have in common), $A \subseteq A^{\uparrow\downarrow}$, $A^{\uparrow}=A^{\uparrow\downarrow\uparrow}$, and their dual counterparts: if $B_1 \subseteq B_2$ then $B_2^{\downarrow} \subseteq B_1^{\downarrow}$, $B \subseteq B^{\downarrow\uparrow}$, and $B^{\downarrow}=B^{\downarrow\uparrow\downarrow}$.

From the foregoing it is clear that *formal concepts can be seen as models of concepts of the classical theory of concepts*. That is, according to the classical theory, a concept is given by a collection of properties, and the concept applies to an object if and only if the object satisfies every property in the collection. A formal concept (A, B) can be thought of as such a concept: The properties are represented by the attributes in B, and A represents the set of all the objects to which the concept applies. Note, however, that *not every set B of attributes* (representing a collection of properties) *constitutes an intent* of a formal concept. It may happen that in a given formal context, an attribute y is not in B, but is possessed by every object that has all attributes in B. For example, think of integers as the objects and y as "be a multiple of 6," and B as consisting of "be a multiple of 2" and "be a multiple of 3." In such a case, B is not the intent of any formal concept and the least intent containing B is $B^{\downarrow\uparrow}$. It is a distinctive feature of FCA that only certain combinations of attributes define concepts. FCA assumes that these combinations will be considered important (relevant, interesting) by the user.

One can determine that for the formal context (X,Y,I) from table 7.1, $\{x_2, x_3\}^{\uparrow}=\{y_2, y_3\}$, $\{x_1\}^{\uparrow}=\{y_1\}$, $\{x_1, x_2\}^{\uparrow}=\varnothing$ (empty set), $\{y_2, y_3\}^{\downarrow}=\{x_2, x_3\}$, $\varnothing^{\downarrow}=\{x_1, x_2, x_3, x_4, x_5\}$, and so on. Using the interpretation described above, $\{x_2, x_3\}^{\uparrow}=\{y_2, y_3\}$ means that eating flesh (y_2) and eating herbs (y_3) are the common attributes of pigs (x_2) and bears (x_3). Thus, since $\{x_2, x_3\}^{\uparrow}=\{y_2, y_3\}$ and $\{y_2, y_3\}^{\downarrow}=\{x_2, x_3\}$, the pair $(\{x_2, x_3\},\{y_2, y_3\})$ is a formal concept of (X,Y,I). This formal concept can be interpreted as "omnivorous animals." Other formal concepts derived from the formal context in table 7.1 are: $(\{x_1\},\{y_1\})$ ("parasite"), $(\{x_2, x_3, x_4\},\{y_2\})$ ("carnivorous"), $(\{x_2, x_3, x_5\},\{y_3\})$ ("herbivorous"), and the boundary concepts $(\varnothing,\{y_1, y_2, y_3\})$ representing the empty concept, which does not apply to any object, and $(\{x_1, x_2, x_3, x_4\},\varnothing)$ representing the universal concept ("animal"), which applies to any object.

According to a useful geometric interpretation, formal concepts correspond to maximal rectangles in the input data table that are full of 1s (more precisely, they correspond to rectangles up to a permutation of rows and columns of the input data table). For example, the rectangles corresponding to formal concepts $(\{x_2, x_3\},\{y_2, y_3\})$, $(\{x_2, x_3, x_4\},\{y_2\})$, and $(\{x_2, x_3, x_5\},\{y_3\})$ are depicted by gray areas in the three parts of table 7.2.

7.2.2 Concept Lattice and the Basic Theorem

As shown in section 7.2.1, there (usually) exist several formal concepts in a given formal context (X,Y,I). The set of all formal concepts of (X,Y,I) along with a subconcept–superconcept hierarchy is called the *concept lattice* of (X,Y,I). Formally, the concept lattice is defined as follows. Denote the set of all formal concepts of a formal context (X,Y,I) by $\mathbf{B}(X,Y,I)$ ("**B**" comes from "Begriffsverband," the German word for "concept lattice"). That is:

$$\mathbf{B}(X,Y,I)=\{(A,B):A\subseteq X,B\subseteq Y,A^{\uparrow}=B,\text{ and }B^{\downarrow}=A\}. \qquad (7.3)$$

Table 7.2

Formal concepts as maximal rectangles.

	y_1	y_2	y_3
x_1	1	0	0
x_2	0	**1**	**1**
x_3	0	**1**	**1**
x_4	0	1	0
x_5	0	0	1

	y_1	y_2	y_3
x_1	1	0	0
x_2	0	**1**	1
x_3	0	**1**	1
x_4	0	**1**	0
x_5	0	0	1

	y_1	y_2	y_3
x_1	1	0	0
x_2	0	1	**1**
x_3	0	1	**1**
x_4	0	1	0
x_5	0	0	**1**

The *subconcept–superconcept hierarchy* of formal concepts is a partial order (i.e., a reflexive, antisymmetric, and transitive binary relation) $\leq$ on $\mathbf{B}(X,Y,I)$ defined by

$$\left(A_1,B_1\right)\leq\left(A_2,B_2\right) \text{ if and only if } A_1 \subseteq A_2 \text{ (or, equivalently, } B_2 \subseteq B_1). \quad (7.4)$$

If $(A_1,B_1) \leq (A_2,B_2)$, we say that (A_1,B_1) is a subconcept of (or, is more specific than) (A_2,B_2) and that (A_2,B_2) is a superconcept of (or, is more general than) (A_1,B_1). That is, (A_1,B_1) is a subconcept of (A_2,B_2) if the extent of (A_1,B_1) is contained in the extent of (A_2,B_2), or, in other words, (A_2,B_2) applies to every object to which (A_1,B_1) applies. An equivalent condition for $(A_1,B_1) \leq$ (A_2,B_2) is that the intent of (A_2,B_2) is contained in the intent of (A_1,B_1). The subconcept–superconcept hierarchy is familiar in everyday life. We say that the concept *dog* is a subconcept of the concept *mammal* because every particular dog is a mammal (i.e., every object in the extent of *dog* belongs to the extent of *mammal*), or equivalently, every attribute of mammals is also an attribute of dogs (i.e., every attribute in the intent of *mammal* belongs to the intent of *dog*).

One can see that for the formal concepts of the formal context in table 7.1, $(\{x_2, x_3\},\{y_2, y_3\})$ is a subconcept of $(\{x_2, x_3, x_4\},\{y_2\})$, as well as a subconcept of $(\{x_2, x_3, x_5\},\{y_3\})$; on the other hand, neither $(\{x_2, x_3\},\{y_2, y_3\})$ is a subconcept of $(\{x_1\},\{y_1\})$ nor is $(\{x_2, x_3, x_4\},\{y_2\})$ a subconcept of $(\{x_2, x_3, x_5\},\{y_3\})$.

The set of all formal concepts of (X,Y,I) equipped with the partial order $\leq$ defined by (7.4) is called the *concept lattice* of (X,Y,I) and is denoted by $\mathbf{B}(X,Y,I)$. Note that since there is no danger of confusion, the set of all formal concepts of (X,Y,I) and the concept lattice of (X,Y,I) are both denoted by the same symbol. From the user's point of view, the concept lattice represents a hierarchical structure of all natural concepts that were found in the input data. The concept lattice is the basic structure derived from the input data and appears in various forms in FCA as well as other methods of data analysis. Every concept lattice is mathematically a complete lattice (Ganter and Wille 1999). That is, for every set V of formal concepts from $\mathbf{B}(X,Y,I)$, there exist two formal concepts in $\mathbf{B}(X,Y,I)$: the infimum of V (the greatest lower bound, which is the most general concept that is a subconcept of every concept from V) and the supremum of V (the least upper bound, which is the most specific concept that is a superconcept of every concept from V). The structure of concept lattices is described by the so-called *basic theorem of concept lattices*, which was proven in a seminal paper by Wille (1982). The basic theorem states that every concept lattice is a complete lattice, describes the formulas for computing infima and suprema, and provides a technical condition regarding the isomorphism of complete lattices and concept lattices.

A concept lattice $\mathbf{B}(X,Y,I)$ may be visualized by means of its line diagram (also called a *Hasse diagram*). A line diagram consists of nodes connected by lines. The nodes and lines represent the formal concepts and the subconcept–superconcept hierarchy, respectively. A line going upward from node 1 to node 2 indicates that the formal concept corresponding to node

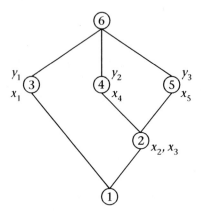

Figure 7.1
Line diagram of a concept lattice.

1 is a direct subconcept of the one corresponding to node 2. A line diagram of the concept lattice of the formal context from table 7.1 is presented in figure 7.1. The nodes that are labeled in the diagram with numbers 1, 2, ..., 6 represent the six formal concepts of the concept lattice as follows:

1. $(\emptyset, \{y_1, y_2, y_3\})$
2. $(\{x_2, x_3\}, \{y_2, y_3\})$
3. $(\{x_1\}, \{y_1\})$
4. $(\{x_2, x_3, x_4\}, \{y_2\})$
5. $(\{x_2, x_3, x_5\}, \{y_3\})$
6. $(\{x_1, x_2, x_3, x_4\}, \emptyset)$

The diagram uses a labeling that shows the extents and intents of the formal concepts represented by the nodes. That is, one can determine the extents and intents of the formal concepts solely from the diagram, without the need of a list specifying which nodes represent which formal concepts. In particular, the extent of a formal concept represented by a particular node consists of those x_i that can be reached by traveling downward from the node along the lines in the diagram. Similarly, the intent consists of those y_j that can be reached by traveling upward from the node. For example, consider node 4. Since x_2, x_3, and x_4 can be reached by traveling downward from the node, the extent of the formal concept represented by node 4 is $\{x_2, x_3, x_4\}$. In addition, since y_2 can be reached by traveling upward, the corresponding intent is $\{y_2\}$. This way one can directly see in the diagram that the formal concept represented by node 4 is $(\{x_2, x_3, x_4\}, \{y_2\})$. One can see in the same way that node 2 represents the formal concept $(\{x_2, x_3\}, \{y_2, y_3\})$. One can also see that $(\{x_2, x_3\}, \{y_2, y_3\})$ is a direct subconcept of $(\{x_2, x_3, x_4\}, \{y_2\})$ because node 2 is connected to node 4 from below. The empty concept and the universal concept are represented by the bottom and the top node, respectively.

7.2.3   Attribute Implications

In addition to the concept lattice, FCA makes it possible to extract from the input data particular attribute dependencies, called attribute implications, that exist in the input data. An *attribute implication* (over a set Y of attributes) is an expression $B_1 \Rightarrow B_2$ where B_1 and B_2 are sets of attributes in Y. An attribute implication $B_1 \Rightarrow B_2$ is considered true in a formal context (X, Y, I) if every object in X that has all attributes in B_1 has also all the attributes in B_2. Attribute implications represent quite natural dependencies, again quite familiar to us in ordinary life. For example, "people who smoke and drink alcohol have heart problems" is a verbal description of the attribute implication $\{\text{drinks-alcohol, smokes}\} \Rightarrow \{\text{heart-problems}\}$. In addition to the above definition of validity of attribute implications, which allows no exceptions, there exist more general definitions that do allow exceptions (e.g., $\{\text{drinks-alcohol, smokes}\} \Rightarrow \{\text{heart-problems}\}$ may be considered true even if it is not true for some number of persons). Because of space limitations here, I must skip this and other issues; the reader should see Carpineto and Romano 2004a and Ganter and Wille 1999 for further information and references.

The goal of FCA is to provide the user with information about all attribute dependencies that are true in the input data represented by a formal context (X, Y, I). However, listing all true attribute implications would probably overload the user because, as a rule, there are large numbers of them. Therefore, instead of listing all true attribute implications, FCA enables one to compute a smaller but still fully informative set of attribute implications, called a nonredundant base of attribute implications of (X, Y, I). The idea is the following. If a user knows that attribute implication $\{\text{drinks-alcohol, smokes}\} \Rightarrow \{\text{heart-problems}\}$ is true in the data, it must be the case that $\{\text{drinks-alcohol, smokes, is-married}\} \Rightarrow \{\text{heart-problems}\}$ is also true in the data. The latter implication is redundant because it follows semantically from the former. Formally, an attribute implication $B_1 \Rightarrow B_2$ follows semantically from a set T of attribute implications if $B_1 \Rightarrow B_2$ is true in every formal context in which each implication of T is true (i.e., $B_1 \Rightarrow B_2$ is true whenever all implications of T are true). Interestingly, there exists a simple set of syntactic deduction rules that completely describe semantic consequence in the following sense: $B_1 \Rightarrow B_2$ follows semantically from a set T of attribute implications if and only if $B_1 \Rightarrow B_2$ can be obtained by successive applications of the deduction rules to the implications of T and to the results of such applications. There is, therefore, a simple logic of attribute implication. The property just mentioned is referred to as the *completeness theorem* of the logic of attribute implications. Now, a nonredundant base of a formal context (X,Y,I) is a set T of attribute implications that satisfies the following properties:

(1) each implication of T is true in (X,Y,I),

(2) every implication that is true in (X,Y,I) follows semantically from T, and

(3) no implication can be removed from T without violating (2).

Note that (1) is an obvious requirement; (2) means that T carries the information about all true implications; and (3) asserts the minimality of T. Among the possibly many nonredundant bases, the so-called Guigues–Duquenne base (Guigues and Duquenne 1986) is the smallest one. It is important that efficient algorithms exist that enable us to compute from a given formal context a nonredundant base of attribute implications (Ganter and Wille 1999).

7.2.4 Further Issues

Because of limited space, many important issues relevant to FCA are omitted in this chapter. These include the FCA of so-called many-valued contexts (i.e., data with general attributes, such as nominal or ordinal); removing redundancy; various methods of construction and decomposition of formal contexts and the corresponding methods for concept lattices; measurement issues in FCA; and algorithmic issues and questions regarding computational complexity. Detailed information and further references on these issues can be found in Carpineto and Romano 2004a; Ganter and Wille 1999; and Wille 2005.

7.3   Formal Concept Analysis: Fuzzy Attributes

This section addresses the question of whether the methods of ordinary FCA can be generalized to data containing fuzzy attributes. Several approaches to such a generalization have been proposed, including the original approach taken by Burusco and Fuentes-Gonzales (1994). The approach in this section may be regarded as the mainstream approach. This approach was initiated by Pollandt (1997) and Belohlavek (1998) and was further investigated by many researchers. (Details and further information can be obtained, in, e.g., Belohlavek 1999, 2000, 2001, 2002, 2004; Belohlavek et al. 2010; Belohlavek and Vychodil 2005, 2006a; Ben Yahia and Jaoua 2001; Georgescu and Popescu 2004; Krajči 2003, 2005; Medina, Ojeda-Aciego, and Ruiz-Calviño 2009).

The section is organized as follows. Section 7.3.1 presents basic notions of FCA of data with fuzzy attributes. In section 7.3.2, I show that in the presence of fuzzy attributes, new phenomena arise that are important from a cognitive point of view. Section 7.3.3 presents a recent idea of how to use formal concepts for factor analysis of relational data. The reader is taken to be familiar with the basic ideas and concepts of fuzzy logic as explained in chapter 3.

7.3.1   Formal Contexts, Formal Concepts, Concept Lattices, and Attribute Implications in a Fuzzy Setting

The basic idea behind the generalization of FCA to data with fuzzy attributes is the following. Starting with the assumption that the input data contains fuzzy attributes, one needs to define the notions that properly generalize the corresponding notions of classical FCA, such as the notion of a formal concept, concept lattice, attribute implication, and so on. From the user's point of view, it is important that the classical notions have a simple and clear verbal description (see, e.g., the verbal description of the concept-forming operators following equations (7.1) and (7.2)). It is therefore desirable that the fuzzy counterparts of the classical notions have such a simple verbal description as well. One right way to proceed is to generalize according to the principles of fuzzy logic in the narrow sense (see chapter 3, section 3.6). This in turn means that one uses formal logical formulas that are behind the classical notions and evaluates the formulas according the rules of semantics of fuzzy logic in the narrow sense. As is shown later in this section, this approach results in intuitively natural notions, such as the notion of a formal fuzzy concept whose extent and intent are both fuzzy sets, that is, a formal notion of a concept with fuzzy boundaries. The problems faced when developing such a generalization are of two kinds. The first consists of technical problems of how to generalize the various classical notions (the generalization is in this case a nontrivial process from the mathematical point of view). The second consists of conceptual problems regarding the right way to generalize the various notions (this is also nontrivial since there are usually several possible ways to generalize any given classical notion).

One straightforward way to generalize the notion of a formal context is the following. A *formal fuzzy context* is a triplet (X,Y,I) where X and Y are finite sets of objects and attributes, respectively, and I is a binary fuzzy relation between X and Y. For $x \in X$ and $y \in Y$, the degree $I(x,y)$ to which x is related to y is interpreted as the degree to which object x has attribute y (or, the degree to which attribute y applies to object x). A formal fuzzy context may be represented by a table in a similar manner as the ordinary formal context. The only difference is that the table entries of an ordinary context contain only 0s and 1s, whereas in case of a formal fuzzy context, the entries contain elements from a given scale L of truth degrees, such as 0.3.

It is often convenient to visualize a formal fuzzy concept by an array with entries containing shades of gray representing truth degrees (the darker the shade, the higher the truth degree; white and black represent 0 and 1, respectively). An example of such an array is shown in figure 7.2. The

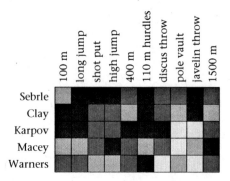

Figure 7.2
Formal fuzzy context (truth degrees represented by degrees of shading).

array represents performances of the top five athletes in the 2004 Olympic Decathlon. The objects correspond to the five athletes, Sebrle (winner), Clay, Karpov, Macey, and Warners; the attributes correspond to the ten disciplines of the decathlon. The array entries represent truth degrees expressing whether the performance of a particular athlete was good in that particular discipline. For example, the black entry of the array for Clay and 100m indicates Clay's excellent performance in the 100 meter sprint, whereas the light entry of the array for Sebrle and 100m indicates Sebrle's weak performance in the same discipline. For simplicity, only the array is presented, rather than the actual scores of the athletes. (The details can be found in Belohlavek and Vychodil 2009b.) Note that the actual scores were transformed to a five-element scale of truth degrees and that the five truth degrees are represented by five shades of gray, from white representing 0 to black representing 1.

One important issue in a fuzzy setting is the choice of the appropriate structure of truth degrees, that is, the choice of a set of truth degrees and truth functions of logical connectives, to have a general framework covering important particular cases that one might want to use in practice (finite or infinite sets of truth degrees, etc.). For the purpose of this chapter, we assume that the set L of truth degrees is the real unit interval $[0,1]$ or a finite equidistant subchain of $[0,1]$, that is, $L = \{0, 1/n, ..., n-1/n, 1\}$ for an appropriate n. Moreover, L is assumed to be equipped with a t-norm i (as a truth function of conjunction) and its residuum r defined by equation (3.28) (as a truth function of implication). In the rest of this section, L, i, and r denote such a set of truth degrees, and the truth functions of conjunction and implication, respectively. Also, it is assumed that $I(x,y) \in L$, that is, the degrees assigned to objects by attributes are in L. The sets of all fuzzy sets in X and Y are denoted by L^X and L^Y, respectively.

Given a formal fuzzy context (X,Y,I), the concept-forming operators are functions $\uparrow : L^X \to L^Y$ and $\downarrow : L^Y \to L^X$ (i.e., $\uparrow$ assigns fuzzy sets of attributes to fuzzy sets of objects, and $\downarrow$ assigns fuzzy sets of objects to fuzzy sets of attributes) defined for all $x \in X$ and $y \in Y$ by the formulas

$$A^{\uparrow}(y) = \min_{x \in X} r(A(x), I(x,y)), \qquad (7.5)$$

$$B^{\downarrow}(x) = \min_{y \in Y} r(B(y), I(x,y)). \qquad (7.6)$$

Let us look in detail at the meaning of the truth degree $A^{\uparrow}(y)$ defined by equation (7.5). Using the principles of fuzzy logic in the narrow sense (see chapter 3, section 3.6), one can see that $A^{\uparrow}(y)$ is the truth degree of the proposition "for every object $x \in X$, if x is in A then x has y." Indeed, r is the truth function of implication, and since L is a chain and X is finite, the universal quantifier "for every object $x \in X$" is evaluated using $\min_{x \in X}$ according to equation (3.30). Analogously, $B^{\downarrow}(x)$ defined by equation (7.6) is the truth degree of "for every attribute $y \in Y$, if y is in B then x has y." This shows that the concept-forming operators defined by equations (7.5) and (7.6) generalize the ordinary operators defined by equations (7.1) and (7.2). It is important to note that even though degrees are involved, the resulting degrees $A^{\uparrow}(y)$ and $B^{\downarrow}(x)$ have a clear meaning as described by the above propositions. In a sense, everything is as in the classical case except that the truth degrees are not restricted to the values of 0 and 1. Formally, the concept-forming operators form a fuzzy Galois connection and have several useful properties (Belohlavek 1999).

Using the definition of concept-forming operators, the definitions of further notions of FCA in a fuzzy setting are straightforward. A *formal fuzzy concept* of a formal fuzzy context (X,Y,I) is a pair (A,B) of fuzzy sets A (a fuzzy set of objects) and B (a fuzzy set of attributes) satisfying $A^{\uparrow}=B$ and $B^{\downarrow}=A$. As in the ordinary case, A is called the *extent* and B is called the *intent* of (A,B). The extent and intent of a formal fuzzy concept have essentially the same meaning as in the ordinary case; the only difference is that to every object, the extent assigns a degree $A(x)$ to which the concept applies to x, and to every attribute y, the intent specifies a degree $B(y)$ to which y is a characteristic attribute of the concept. Intuitively, this is quite natural because the extensions and intensions of typical fuzzy concepts are fuzzy (think of the concept *light-blue ball*; this concept applies to various balls to various degrees, i.e., its extension is fuzzy; the attribute be-blue is characteristic of this concept to a high degree but this degree is smaller than 1, i.e., its intension is fuzzy).

As mentioned in section 7.2.1, ordinary formal concepts can be thought of as maximal rectangles that are full of 1s in the input data table. The situation with formal fuzzy concepts is similar: Formal fuzzy concepts correspond to particular rectangular patterns in the input data (Belohlavek 1999). As an illustrative example, one particular formal fuzzy concept of the formal fuzzy context from figure 7.2 is shown in figure 7.3. The pattern can be read as follows: If the entry in the pattern is dark, both the corresponding object (athlete) and attribute (discipline) belong to the extent

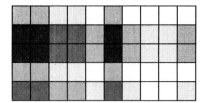

Figure 7.3
Rectangular pattern representing a formal fuzzy concept.

and the intent of the formal concept to a high degree. Therefore, from figure 7.3 we can see that the objects with a high degree in the extent are Clay and Karpov and that the disciplines with a high degree in the intent are 100m, long jump, and 110m hurdles. These three attributes are thus highly characteristic of the formal fuzzy concept. The formal concept can therefore be termed "speed" (speed is required for a good performance in all three disciplines). Note that both Clay and Karpov, to whom this concept applies the best, are known for their excellent speed.

As in the ordinary case, the set of all formal fuzzy concepts in a given formal fuzzy context (X,Y,I) is denoted by $\mathbf{B}(X,Y,I)$. A *subconcept–superconcept hierarchy* on formal fuzzy concepts is defined by

$$\left(A_1, B_1\right) \le \left(A_2, B_2\right) \text{ if and only if } A_1 \subseteq A_2 \text{ (or, equivalently, } B_2 \subseteq B_1). \quad (7.7)$$

Note that (7.7) is almost the same as (7.4). The difference is that in (7.7), A_1, A_2, B_1, and B_2 are fuzzy sets and $\subseteq$ is the inclusion of fuzzy sets (see chapter 3, section 3.3), that is, $A_1 \subseteq A_2$ means that $A_1(x) < A_2(x)$ for every $x \in X$. Here again, $\le$ is a partial order and the set $\mathbf{B}(X,Y,I)$ of all formal fuzzy concepts equipped with $\le$ forms a complete lattice, called the *fuzzy concept lattice* of (X,Y,I). The structure of fuzzy concept lattices is described by the basic theorem of fuzzy concept lattices (Belohlavek 2002), which generalizes the basic theorem of ordinary concept lattices (Wille 1982). As explained in section 3.6.3, inclusion of fuzzy sets is a graded notion. In general, one may consider the degree to which a fuzzy set A_1 is included in a fuzzy set A_2, and this degree is defined by equation (3.32). It seems therefore natural to consider the structure of $\mathbf{B}(X,Y,I)$ to be equipped with a fuzzy order that defines the degrees to which a given formal fuzzy concept is a subconcept of another one. This problem is addressed by Belohlavek (2004), who presents a version of the basic theorem of concept lattices for this case.

Attribute implications of data with fuzzy attributes represent another issue that has been investigated in several papers (see Belohlavek and Vychodil 2006a for an overview with a detailed exposition of the technical notions). It is beyond the scope of this chapter to present this topic in detail; I will present only an outline of the main issues. A *fuzzy attribute implication* is an expression $B_1 \Rightarrow B_2$ where B_1 and B_2 are fuzzy sets of attributes. Briefly, the degrees in B_1 and B_2 can be seen as thresholds in that the truth of $B_1 \Rightarrow B_2$ for data with fuzzy attributes means that every object that has all the attributes at least to the degrees prescribed by B_1 also has all the attributes to the degrees given by B_2. Whereas an ordinary attribute implication is either true of false for a given dataset, a fuzzy attribute implication is true to a certain degree. The other notions regarding attribute implications of data with fuzzy attributes are graded as well. For instance, in general there is a degree to which a given attribute implication $B_1 \Rightarrow B_2$ follows semantically from a given set T of attribute implications. The completeness theorem, which holds true in the fuzzy setting and generalizes the corresponding classical theorem, then says that the degree to which $B_1 \Rightarrow B_2$ follows semantically from T equals the degree to which $B_1 \Rightarrow B_2$ is provable from T (degree of provability is a standard notion in fuzzy logic in the narrow sense and will not be discussed here). Belohlavek and Vychodil (2006a) discuss further issues regarding attribute implications, such as the important question of how a nonredundant base can be appropriately defined and computed.

7.3.2 Nonclassical Issues

When fuzzy logic replaces classical logic, new phenomena and problems arise, which are degenerate in the classical case. In this section, I mention two such nonclassical issues in FCA of data with fuzzy attributes.

The first one is studied by Belohlavek (2001) and relates to the general question of the relationship between "fuzzy notions" and "ordinary notions." In particular, the problem is whether the fuzzy concept lattice of a formal fuzzy concept (X,Y,I) can be regarded as an ordinary concept lattice (of some ordinary formal context). Can a formal fuzzy context (X,Y,I) be transformed into an ordinary formal context (X^*,Y^*,I^*) in such a way that the fuzzy concept lattice $\mathbf{B}(X,Y,I)$ be isomorphic (possibly via some natural isomorphism) to the ordinary concept lattice $\mathbf{B}(X^*,Y^*,I^*)$? A "yes" answer to this question could make it possible to obtain properties of fuzzy concept lattices by a "translation" from established properties of ordinary concept lattices. In addition, a positive answer would make it possible to compute fuzzy concept lattices by using algorithms for ordinary concept lattices. Belohlavek (2001) answers this question in the affirmative. The required transformation can be described as follows: X^* and Y^* are the Cartesian products $X{\times}L$ and $Y{\times}L$, respectively, and I^* is defined by

$$((x,a),(y,b)) \in I^* \text{ if and only if } i(a,b) \leq I(x,y)$$

for every object x, attribute y, and truth degrees a and b (note that i is the truth function of conjunction). The corresponding theorem makes it indeed possible to translate some results from the classical setting to a fuzzy setting. However, it is much slower to compute a fuzzy concept lattice using the algorithms for ordinary concept lattices than to use the special algorithms designed particularly for fuzzy concept lattices (Belohlavek et al. 2010).

The second nonclassical issue presented here stems from the following question. Can we utilize similarity of concepts to construct, instead of a possibly large fuzzy concept lattice, its approximation in which we identify concepts that are sufficiently similar? This question is studied by Belohlavek (2000) and Belohlavek et al. (2007). These papers show that with a particular definition of similarity of formal fuzzy concepts, one can form classes of formal concepts pairwise similar to degree at least a (the degree prescribed by the user) in such a way that the structure of the classes itself becomes a complete lattice and the new lattice is a factor lattice of the original fuzzy concept lattice. The factor lattice can thus be seen as an approximation of the original fuzzy concept lattice "modulo similarity." The factor lattice contains fewer formal concepts than the original and is thus easier to comprehend. Interestingly, the factor lattice can be computed directly from the input data without the need to compute the original fuzzy concept lattice (the speedup is significant and is inversely proportional to the similarity threshold a).

7.3.3 Factor Analysis of Relational Data with Formal Concepts as Factors

The aim of this section is to explain how formal concepts can be used for the purpose of factor analysis of data with fuzzy attributes. Belohlavek and Vychodil (2009b) provide details; a particular case of data with yes-or-no attributes is investigated by Belohlavek and Vychodil (2010). The general aim of factor analysis (Bartholomew and Knott 1999) is to describe directly observable variables in terms of a possibly small number of other variables called factors. The factors are usually interpreted as some general categories of which directly observable variables are particular observations. The goal in factor analysis is to retrieve the factors from directly observable variables. The observable variables are given in the form of a matrix (table) with entries containing the values of the observable variables (matrix columns) on particular objects (matrix rows). For example, the matrix may represent test scores that people (objects) achieve in particular tests (attributes). The factors in this case might be variables representing some general cognitive abilities such as the ability to think abstractly.

Classical factor analysis assumes that the values of variables are real numbers and uses the methods of linear algebra and statistics. Such methods have been shown to have several drawbacks when applied to data with yes-or-no attributes (most importantly, the factors are difficult to interpret). As a result, several other methods have been proposed for the purpose of factor analysis of binary data (see, e.g., Belohlavek and Vychodil 2010 for discussion and references). One idea is to replace the ordinary matrix product used in the classical factor analysis with a different type of matrix product such as the Boolean matrix product or its extension, the sup-t-norm product, mentioned below. The resulting factor analysis model is then easy to interpret and the factors revealed have clear meaning, as illustrated below.

Let I be an $n{\times}m$ matrix with rows and columns corresponding to objects and attributes, respectively, and entries $I(x,y)$ corresponding to truth degrees on a scale L. Let $I(x,y)$ be interpreted as the degree to which object x has attribute y. Clearly, if $L = \{0,1\}$, I is just a binary matrix. Note that I may be viewed as representing a formal fuzzy context with $X = \{1,...,m\}$ and $Y = \{1,...,n\}$ being its sets of objects and attributes, respectively. Denote such formal fuzzy context by (X,Y,I). That is, I denotes both the matrix and the corresponding fuzzy relation between X and Y. Since there exists a one-to-one correspondence between $n{\times}m$ matrices with truth degrees and fuzzy relations between sets $\{1,...,m\}$ and $\{1,...,n\}$, there is no danger of confusion when using I to denote both the matrix and the corresponding relation. Our aim is to decompose matrix I into a particular matrix product,

$$I = A \circ B, \qquad\qquad (7.8)$$

of an $n \times k$ matrix A and a $k \times m$ matrix B in such a way that the number k is the smallest possible among all such decompositions. That is, k represents the number of factors in the model, and the aim is to have a model with as few factors as possible. The entries of matrices A and B are again truth degrees from L and are interpreted the following way: $A(x,l)$ is the degree to which factor l applies to object x; $B(l,y)$ is the degree to which attribute y is a particular manifestation of factor l. The product $\circ$ in (7.8) is defined by the formula

$$(A \circ B)(x,y) = \max_{l=1,\ldots,k} i(A(x,l), B(l,y)) \tag{7.9}$$

for all $x = 1,\ldots,m$, and $y = 1,\ldots,n$. In equation (7.9), i is a truth function of conjunction (section 7.3.1). Given the interpretation of $A(x,l)$ and $B(l,y)$ and using the basic principles of fuzzy logic in the narrow sense (section 3.6) one can see that $(A \circ B)(x,y)$ can be interpreted as the truth degree of the proposition:

There exists factor l such that l applies to x and y is a particular manifestation of l.

That is, finding a decomposition (7.8) of I is equivalent to describing the relationship between objects and attributes by means two relationships, a relationship between objects and factors and a relationship between factors and attributes. In particular, the degree to which an object has an attribute is equal to the degree to which it is true that there is a factor that applies to the object and of which the attribute is a particular manifestation. This is the basic meaning of the factor analysis model given by (7.8).

A crucial question is: How can we find good decomposition, that is, a small set of factors to decompose a given matrix I? Interestingly, as proved by Belohlavek and Vychodil (2009b), we can use formal fuzzy concepts from $\mathbf{B}(X,Y,I)$ (i.e., the fuzzy concept lattice corresponding to I) as factors. Moreover, such factors are optimal in the sense that the best decompositions can be achieved by using formal concepts as factors. That is, if k is the least number of factors (arbitrary ones, i.e., not necessarily formal concepts) such that a given I may be decomposed using these factors, then there exist a decomposition of I into a product of an $n \times k$ matrix A and a $k \times m$ matrix B such that the k factors in this decomposition are formal concepts from $\mathbf{B}(X,Y,I)$. Employing formal concepts $(C_1,D_1), \ldots, (C_k,D_k)$ as factors means that the degrees in the first column of A (first row of B) are just the degrees

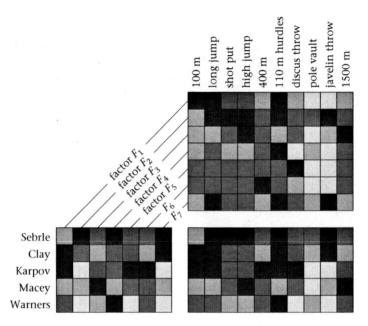

Figure 7.4
Decomposition of matrix I using formal fuzzy concepts as factors.

from C_1 (from D_1), that is, $A(x,1) = C_1(x)$ and $B(1,y) = D_1(y)$, and so on up to the kth column of A and row of B. That is, the columns of A and rows of B are extents and intents of formal concepts, respectively. Belohlavek and Vychodil (2009b) describe an algorithm for computing decompositions that uses formal concepts as factors. Next, I describe illustrative example of factor analysis (see Belohlavek and Vychodil 2009b for details).

Consider the matrix I corresponding to the formal fuzzy context in figure 7.2. A decomposition of $I = A \circ B$ with seven factors, shown in figure 7.4, was found by using an algorithm developed by Belohlavek and Vychodil (2009b). Matrix I is the one in the bottom right corner; A and B are the ones labeled by athletes' names and disciplines. As described above, factor 1 corresponds to a formal fuzzy concept of I whose extent and intent are represented by the first column of A and the first row of B. Similarly, the extent and intent of the formal fuzzy concept corresponding to factor 2 are represented by the second column of A and the second row of B, and so on. The rectangular patterns representing the formal fuzzy concepts corresponding to factors 1, …, 7 are shown in figure 7.5. Let us now consider

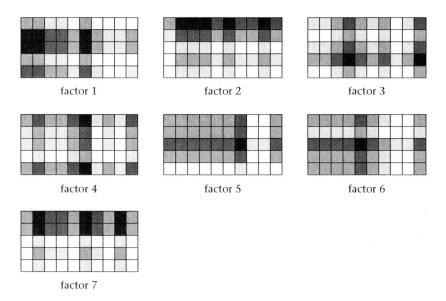

factor 1   factor 2   factor 3

factor 4   factor 5   factor 6

factor 7

Figure 7.5
Rectangular patterns representing seven factors (formal fuzzy concepts) of the decathlon data.

how the factors can be interpreted. The formal fuzzy concept corresponding to factor 1 is the one depicted in figure 7.3, and from the above discussion we know that it can be interpreted as "speed." This factor covers most of the input data and can thus be regarded as the most important one (see Belohlavek and Vychodil 2009b for details). From the rectangular pattern in figure 7.5 corresponding to factor 2, as well as from the second column and the second row of matrices A and B in figure 7.4, we can see that the athlete to whom this factor applies the most (i.e., who belongs to the extent of the formal fuzzy concept to degree 1) is Sebrle and that the most characteristic attributes of this factor are long jump, shot put, high jump, 110m hurdles, and javelin (they belong to the extent of the formal fuzzy concept to degree 1). This factor can be termed "explosiveness." Factor 3 applies most to Macey, and its characteristic attributes are high jump and 1500m. This factor is typical for lighter, not very muscular, athletes. With a height of 6 feet, 5 inches and weight of 215 pounds, Macey is evidently among that type of decathletes. One can interpret the other factors similarly. However, as discussed by Belohlavek and Vychodil (2009b), factors 4, 5, 6, and

7 can be disregarded in practice, because factors 1, 2, and 3 alone enable us to reconstruct the input data with sufficient precision.

7.4   Possible Research Directions

One can expect that cooperation between researchers in FCA and the psychology of concepts will lead to interesting results for both areas. The following are some reasons supporting this expectation:

• As mentioned in sections 7.1.2 and 7.2, the concepts used in FCA can be seen as concepts in the sense of classical theory of concepts (see chapter 2 of this volume, or Murphy 2002). The classical theory, like every existing theory of concepts, has its drawbacks. As Murphy (2002, 488) puts it, "there is no clear, dominant winner" when comparing the existing theories of concepts. Nevertheless, even though the class of concepts described by the classical theory is limited, it is important and appealing. One may expect that various phenomena of general interest in the psychology of concepts appear in a clearer form and can be studied in a greater depth both experimentally and theoretically on this particular class of concepts.

• FCA provides advanced formal methods for representation, analysis, and processing of concepts described by the classical theory. A good formalization of a particular domain usually makes it possible to advance in studying the domain. Even though the benefit of formalization should not be overestimated, it can be expected that the employment of FCA methods in the psychology of concepts will help to advance the study of concepts, particularly those described by the classical theory.

• Concepts in the classical theory are usually thought of as yes-or-no concepts (a concept either applies or does not apply to a particular object). This is a consequence of the assumption of the classical theory that a concept is given by a finite collection of yes-or-no attributes and that a concept applies to an object if and only if each of the attributes applies to the object. (Note that the possibility to include fuzzy concepts by allowing fuzzy attributes is sometimes mentioned but without further details regarding, e.g., how the conjunction of fuzzy attributes is to be handled; see chapter 2 of this volume.) The generalization of FCA to a setting of fuzzy attributes presented in section 7.3 demonstrates that it is possible to have a sound and formally advanced treatment of the approach to concepts proposed by the classical theory that includes fuzzy attributes. To employ the generalized FCA model in the psychology of concepts thus seems an interesting direction both from the point of view of the classical theory of concepts and from the point of view of the research on fuzzy concepts (concepts with graded boundaries).

• The various issues and results in the psychology of concepts might enhance the current state of FCA, add new aspects to the methodology of FCA, and help to solve some of the problems faced in FCA. From a more general viewpoint, the FCA's model of concepts is used, explicitly or implicitly, in various areas of computer science. For some of these areas, particularly when a user engages in, for example, Internet search, psychological aspects are highly relevant. On the one hand, it seems natural to employ the body of knowledge established by the psychology of concepts to make progress in these areas. On the other hand, experiments that are abundant in those areas could provide interesting empirical data for the psychology of concepts.

In the rest of this section, examples of possible research problems that involve both FCA and the psychology of concepts are outlined.

Relevant formal concepts and the problem of large number of formal concepts
As explained in sections 7.1 and 7.2, one of the outputs of FCA is the concept lattice of the input data, that is, a set of all formal concepts of the input data ordered by the subconcept–superconcept relation. The concept lattice is supposed to present to the user all potentially interesting concepts and their hierarchy, which may be hidden in the data. One of the problems faced by FCA is the fact that even for middle-size data, the number of formal concepts is usually quite large. It is thus difficult for the user to comprehend the entire concept lattice. Classical FCA offers several methods to handle large concept lattices (Ganter and Wille 1999). A different approach to the problem of a large number of formal concepts was proposed and studied in a number of papers (see, e.g., Belohlavek and Vychodil 2006b 2009a). The basic idea in this approach is to utilize a user's background knowledge and present to the user only those formal concepts that are relevant according to that background knowledge. Clearly, there are many possible kinds of background knowledge that a user may possess and hence many possible ways to formalize the notion of "relevant formal concept."

One such way, which proved to be useful in applying FCA to extracting taxa (identified with formal concepts) from paleobiological data (Belohlavek, Košťák, and Osička 2010) is presented by Belohlavek and Vychodil (2009a). The intuition behind this approach is that when forming concepts, people consider some attributes to be more important than others. For example, when someone is categorizing books, he is likely to consider attributes that describe whether a book is hardbound or paperback less important than attributes describing the book's topic, such as mathematics, psychology, or law, as well as attributes describing the type of a book, such as textbook or research monograph. In terms of FCA, the data from which one may want to extract natural concepts about books (such as the concept *textbooks on mathematics*) consists of a formal context describing books as objects and their attributes (hardbound, paperback, mathematics, . . . , textbook, . . . , etc.). In ordinary FCA, the user's additional (or background) knowledge regarding the relative importance of attributes is not taken into account; the only information taken into account is the formal context. A practical consequence is that among the extracted formal concepts would be formal concepts such as *hardbound books* that would likely be considered not relevant (not natural). When the background knowledge is properly formalized and taken into account, formal concepts that are not compatible with the background knowledge are not extracted from the data and thus are not presented to the user. For example, Belohlavek and Vychodil (2009a) formalize the relative importance of attributes using so-called attribute-dependency formulas, and a formal concept is considered compatible with the background knowledge if it satisfies all the attribute-dependency formulas prescribed by the user. Although this approach and the notions involved (background knowledge, relevant concepts) have psychological relevance, they are based on an intuitive idea that has never been tested by psychological experiments. Appropriate psychological experiments and, in general, considering the problem from the point of view of the psychology of concepts could result in useful methods for FCA and also new findings in the psychology of concepts.

Basic level of concepts

The existence of a basic level of concepts (Murphy 2002, chapter 7) is an important phenomenon studied by the psychology of concepts. The essence of the principle is that even though a given object belongs to several concepts in a conceptual hierarchy, some of them more general than others, people tend to use concepts from their "basic level of concepts." The concepts from the basic level are neither too general nor too specific. For example, when seeing a particular dog named Jerry (object), people usually say "Jerry is a dog" rather than "Jerry is a mammal" or "Jerry is a poodle." In this case, *dog* is a concept from the basic level whereas *mammal* and *poodle* are not (*mammal* is too general, *poodle* is too specific). Hierarchies of concepts (concept lattices, in FCA terms) are of primary importance in FCA; FCA provides numerous results regarding various properties of concept lattices (Ganter and Wille 1999). An investigation of the phenomenon of basic level of concepts utilizing the framework of FCA seems a promising direction of research, the results of which may add to the existing results on the basic level, particularly to the results on quantitative characterization of the basic level (see Murphy 2002, chapter 7 and references). In addition to that, from the point of view of the problem described in the previous paragraph, the concepts of the basic level can be thought of as the relevant ones that are to be presented to a user. The studies on the basic level could therefore help researchers make progress in solving the problem of the large number of formal concepts described above. Two related problems are how to identify an appropriate basic level in a concept lattice and how to efficiently compute the formal concepts from this level.

Choice of fuzzy logic connectives and the scale of truth degrees

One of the problems fundamentally important for applications of fuzzy logic in general is the problem of the choice of fuzzy logic connectives. This problem, discussed in chapter 6 of this volume, has to be addressed from the point of view of the measurement theory of mathematical psychology. In the particular case of FCA of data with fuzzy attributes, one related problem is the following. Given a formal fuzzy context, what truth function i of conjunction and the corresponding truth function r of implication should we choose (recall that i and r are related by residuation expressed by eq. (3.28))? These truth functions are employed in the definition of a formal fuzzy concept as well as in the definition of other notions in FCA. As a consequence, the resulting concept lattice and other information provided by FCA depend on these fuzzy logic connectives. Up to now, almost no research has been done on this topic. One exception is Belohlavek (2005), who shows that if Gödel operations are used (see chapter 3, section 3.6.2,

this volume), the fuzzy concept lattice depends only on the relative ordering of the truth degrees in the table representing a formal fuzzy context,
not on the absolute values of the truth degrees (i.e., only ordinal information of the input data is relevant; see Belohlavek 2005 for details). Further
research in this direction is important not only for FCA and the classical
theory of concepts, but for applications of fuzzy logic in general. In this
regard, research on considerations of measurement theory for fuzzy logic
reported in chapter 6 provides important hints for this direction.

Factor analysis in psychology

Factor analysis is one of the most important mathematical techniques used
in psychology. In fact, factor analysis itself as well as its various extensions
originated in psychological research. The method presented in section 7.3.3
provides an alternative to the existing factor analysis methods. Notice that
this method is conceptually compatible with the general idea common
to existing factor analysis methods: to extract a possibly small number of
new variables (factors) from data that describe directly observable variables.
From a technical point of view, however, the method is different. Whereas
the existing methods of factor analysis are, by and large, based on statistics
and are relatively difficult to understand by nonstatisticians, the method
described in section 7.3.3 is based on the calculus of fuzzy relations. It can
be argued that this is one reason that the factor model in section 7.3.3
is relatively easy to understand and the interpretation of factors straightforward. The verbal description of the model (i.e., that an object has an attribute if and only if there exists a factor that applies to the object and such
that the attribute is one of its manifestations, or characteristics) accurately
materializes the basic idea behind factor analysis. A comparison, both theoretical and experimental, of the model described in section 7.3.3 with existing models of factor analysis, and in particular the suitability to analyze
psychological data, is an interesting topic for further research.

7.5 Summary

This chapter presents a simple (and somewhat incomplete) introduction
to formal concept analysis (FCA). The chapter describes the aims of FCA
and the role of concepts in FCA, and also presents an overview of basic
notions, methods, and results of FCA for data with yes-or-no attributes and
a generalization of FCA for data with fuzzy attributes. After discussing the

relationship between FCA and the psychology of concepts, I have argued that a interactive research between these two areas is likely to be beneficial for both of them. Finally, I have suggested several specific problems for prospective research involving both these areas.

Note

1. The extent and intent are simple mathematical models of the extension and intension of a concept.

References

Arnauld, A., and P. Nicole. 1996. *Logic, or The Art of Thinking.* Cambridge: Cambridge University Press. (Originally published in French, *La logique, ou l'art de penser,* 1662.)

Barbut, M., and B. Monjardet. 1970. *Ordre et classification. Algébre et combinatoire.* Paris: Collection Hachette Université, Librairie Hachette.

Bartholomew, D. J., and M. Knott. 1999. *Latent Variable Models and Factor Analysis,* 2nd ed. London: E. Arnold.

Belohlavek, R. 1998. Fuzzy concepts and conceptual structures: induced similarities. In *Proceedings of 1998 Joint Conference on Information Sciences,* vol. I, 179–182, Durham, NC: Association of Intelligent Machinery.

Belohlavek, R. 1999. Fuzzy Galois connections. *Mathematical Logic Quarterly* 45: 497–504.

Belohlavek, R. 2000. Similarity relations in concept lattices. *Journal of Logic and Computation* 10:823–845.

Belohlavek, R. 2001. Reduction and a simple proof of characterization of fuzzy concept lattices. *Fundamenta Informaticae* 46:277–285.

Belohlavek, R. 2002. *Fuzzy Relational Systems: Foundations and Principles.* New York: Kluwer.

Belohlavek, R. 2004. Concept lattices and order in fuzzy logic. *Annals of Pure and Applied Logic* 128:277–298.

Belohlavek, R. 2005. Invariance to scaling in formal concept analysis of data tables with fuzzy attributes. In *Proceedings of the 8th Joint Conference on Information Sciences,* 86–89. Salt Lake City, UT.

Belohlavek, R., B. De Baets, J. Outrata, and V. Vychodil. 2010. Computing the lattice of all fixpoints of a fuzzy closure operator. *IEEE Transactions on Fuzzy Systems* 18:546–557.

Belohlavek, R., J. Dvorak, and J. Outrata. 2007. Fast factorization by similarity in formal concept analysis of data with fuzzy attributes. *Journal of Computer and System Sciences* 73:1012–1022.

Belohlavek, R., M. Košťák, and P. Osička. 2010. Reconstruction of belemnite evolution using formal concept analysis. In *Proceedings of the 20th European Meeting on Cybernetics and Systems Research*, ed. R. Trappl, 32–38. Vienna: Austrian Society for Cybernetic Studies.

Belohlavek, R., and V. Vychodil. 2005. What is a fuzzy concept lattice? In *Proceedings of 3rd Intern. Conf. on Concept Lattices and Their Applications*, 34–45. Olomouc, Czech Republic: Palacky University.

Belohlavek, R., and V. Vychodil. 2006a. Attribute implications in a fuzzy setting. *Lecture Notes in Artificial Intelligence* 3874:45–60.

Belohlavek, R., and V. Vychodil. 2006b. Formal concept analysis with constraints by closure operators. In *Proceedings of the 14th International Conference on Conceptual Structures*, ed. H. Scharfe, P. Hitzler and P. Ohrstrom, 131–143. Berlin: Springer.

Belohlavek, R., and V. Vychodil. 2009a. Formal concept analysis with background knowledge: attribute priorities. *IEEE Transactions on Systems, Man, and Cybernetics (Part C)* 39:399–409.

Belohlavek, R., and V. Vychodil. 2009b. Factor analysis of incidence data via novel decomposition of matrices. *Lecture Notes in Artificial Intelligence* 5548:83–97.

Belohlavek, R., and V. Vychodil. 2010. Discovery of optimal factors in binary data via a novel method of matrix decomposition. *Journal of Computer and System Sciences* 76:3–20.

Ben Yahia, S., and A. Jaoua. 2001. Discovering knowledge from fuzzy concept lattice. In *Data Mining and Computational Intelligence*, ed. A. Kandel, M. Last, and H. Bunke, 167–190. Berlin: Physica-Verlag.

Burusco, A., and R. Fuentes-Gonzales. 1994. The study of the L-fuzzy concept lattice. *Mathware & Soft Computing* 3:209–218.

Carpineto, C., and G. Romano. 2004a. *Concept Data Analysis: Theory and Applications*. Chichester: John Wiley.

Carpineto, C., and G. Romano. 2004b. Exploiting the potential of concept lattices for information retrieval with CREDO. *Journal of Universal Computer Science* 10:985–1013.

Ganapathy, V., D. King, T. Jaeger, and S. Jha. 2007. Mining security-sensitive operations in legacy code using concept analysis. In *Proceedings of the 29th International Conference on Software Engineering*, 458–467. Los Alamitos, CA: IEEE Computer Society.

Ganter, B., and R. Wille. 1999. *Formal Concept Analysis: Mathematical Foundations.* Berlin: Springer-Verlag.

Georgescu, G., and A. Popescu. 2004. Non-dual fuzzy connections. *Archive for Mathematical Logic* 43:1009–1039.

Guénoche, A., and I. Van Mechelen. 1993. Galois approach to the induction of concepts. In *Categories and Concepts*, ed. I. Van Mechelen, et al., 287–308. San Diego, CA: Academic Press.

Guigues, J.-L., and V. Duquenne. 1986. Familles minimales d'implications informatives resultant d'un tableau de donne'es binaires. *Mathematiques et Sciences Humaines* 95:5–18.

Krajči, S. 2003. Cluster based efficient generation of fuzzy concepts. *Neural Network World* 5:521–530.

Krajči, S. 2005. A generalized concept lattice. *Logic Journal of IGPL* 13:543–550.

Medina, J., M. Ojeda-Aciego, and J. Ruiz-Calviño. 2009. Formal concept analysis via multi-adjoint concept lattices. *Fuzzy Sets and Systems* 160:130–144.

Murphy, G. L. 2002. *The Big Book of Concepts*. Cambridge, MA: MIT Press.

Ore, O. 1944. Galois connections. *Transactions of the American Mathematical Society* 55:493–513.

Pfaltz, J. L. 2006. Using concept lattices to uncover causal dependencies in software. In *Proceedings of the 4th International Conference on Formal Concept Analysis*, ed. R. Missaoui and J. Schmid, 233–247. Berlin: Springer.

Pollandt, S. 1997. *Fuzzy Begriffe*. Berlin: Springer-Verlag.

Snelting, G., and F. Tip. 2000. Understanding class hierarchies using concept analysis. *ACM Transactions on Programming Languages and Systems* 22:540–582.

Storms, G., and P. De Boeck. 1997. Formal models for intra-categorical structure that can be used for data analysis. In *Knowledge, Concepts, and Categories*, ed. K. Lamberts and D. Shanks, 439–459. Cambridge, MA: MIT Press.

Wille, R. 1982. Restructuring lattice theory: an approach based on hierarchies of concepts. In *Ordered Sets*, ed. I. Rival, 445–470. Boston: Kluwer.

Wille, R. 2005. Formal concept analysis as mathematical theory of concepts and concept hierarchies. In *Formal Concept Analysis: Foundations and Applications, State-of-the-Art Survey*, ed. B. Ganter, G. Stumme, and R. Wille, 1–33. Berlin: Springer.

Zaki, M. J. 2004. Mining non-redundant association rules. *Data Mining and Knowledge Discovery* 9:223–248.

8   Conceptual Combinations and Fuzzy Logic

James A. Hampton

8.1   What Are Conceptual Combinations?

Suppose that an intelligent system has two concepts *A* and *B*. A *conceptual combination* will then be a third concept that is the result of combining *A* and *B* according to some principle. Some examples will make this clearer. If *A* is the concept of the action of *frying* and *B* is the concept of the class of objects called *pan*, the two concepts could be combined in order to generate the complex concept *frying pan*. The ability of humans to combine concepts is a vital part of our creativity. We can take concepts that have never been combined before and try them out together. So by recombining *frying pan* and *washing machine*, we could easily generate *frying machine* and *washing pan*. Sometimes such novel combinations will appear meaningless, but often enough new ideas will be formed.

Conceptual combination is not confined to the combination of actions and objects. In fact, many concepts are freely combinable with others. However, there must clearly be constraints on which combinations will make much sense. Concepts have to be the *right kind of thing* in order to combine successfully. Chomsky's famous sentence example of "colorless green ideas sleep furiously" contains conceptual combinations that are all quite problematic. Can an idea have a color? Can something be both colorless and green at the same time? Can an idea sleep, and is it possible for anything to sleep in a furious way?

8.2   Intersective and Nonintersective Combinations

To bring some clarity to this general idea of combining concepts, we need to distinguish between different kinds of conceptual combination. It is sensible to distinguish those combinations that appear to have some recognizable *logical* form from those that rely on a wider range of heuristic processes to derive an interpretation. Intersective combinations are those that (at least at first blush) appear to correspond to set intersection of the categories designated by the meanings of the two words. Often, adjective+noun phrases will take this form, as in "green shirt" or "friendly neighbor." A green shirt is green and it is a shirt. A friendly neighbor is both friendly and a neighbor. In terms of set membership, someone is a member of the set of all friendly neighbors if and only if he or she is a member of the set of all friendly people and also a member of the set of all neighbors. Conversely, noun+noun phrases combining two noun categories often fail to be intersective. A bottle opener is not both a bottle and an opener, and a traffic cop is not both traffic and a cop. Note that even though the role of the first word can vary widely, the second word in the combination plays a more or less fixed role. It points to a given class of things. Traffic cops are cops, bottle openers are openers, and so forth. In linguistic terminology, the second noun is the *head noun*, while the first plays the role of *modifier*, qualifying the meaning of the head by restricting it to a subclass. So a traffic cop is the subtype of cop who manages road traffic.

From these examples, we can broadly generalize that a conceptual combination involves taking the second word (the head), and modifying or restricting its meaning in some way. Intersective modification will involve finding the intersection of the classes that are named by the two words, while nonintersective modification involves the discovery of the implicit link that explains just how the modifier works to modify the head noun meaning. Often enough, a nonintersective combination will still denote a subtype of the head noun category, such as a type of cop who directs traffic, or a type of opener designed for opening bottles. The difference is that the semantic relation needed to make the connection (e.g., "directs" or "designed for") must be generated by the hearer before the meaning of the whole can be understood.

8.2.1 Nonintersective Combination

Nonintersective conceptual combination has been widely studied. Building on work in linguistics (Gleitman and Gleitman 1970; Levi 1978), psychologists (Cohen and Murphy 1984; Gagné and Shoben 1997; Rips 1995; Wisniewski 1997) have developed an account of the common ways in which such combinations are interpreted. It would appear that there is a set of around 6–10 fundamental semantic/thematic relations, which can be employed in either direction in order to generate interpretations. Thus the combination *AB* could be interpreted in different cases as

USE: *B* used for *A* (*cooking gas*), *B* that uses *A* (*gas cooking*);

MATERIAL: *B* made of *A* (*clay brick*), *B* used to make *A* (*brick clay*);

LOCATION: *B* in which *A* is found (*deer mountain*), *B* found in *A* (*mountain deer*);

CONTAINMENT: *B* contained in *A* (*pot noodle*), *B* in which *A* is contained (*noodle pot*);

and so forth. Other thematic relations include CAUSE, HAS, MAKES, and ABOUT.

These basic relations are reminiscent of the relations used in case grammars (Fillmore 1968). In modern Romance languages they are encoded with specific prepositions such as French *á*, *de*, *pour*, *dans*, *sur*, and *en*. Thus a *tasse de thé* in French is a cup of tea, while a *tasse à thé* is a teacup.

In addition to these interpretations based on thematic relations, people also employ other heuristic strategies to arrive at interpretations. One, discovered by Wisniewski (1997), is to find a salient property of the modifier and to use that to modify the head noun. For example, a "zebra mussel" is a mussel that has stripes like a zebra. Wisniewski calls this process *property mapping*, and it involves a different strategy from that of finding a thematic relation. In particular, as Estes and Glucksberg (2000) demonstrate, a property mapping requires that the modifier noun has a highly salient property (such as the stripes of a zebra) and that this salient property corresponds to a variable dimension of the head noun (in this case the surface appearance of the mussel shell). Otherwise, the property mapping interpretation is unlikely to be available as a sensible meaning for the phrase.

In sum, the process of combining concepts can involve a wide range of knowledge structures, and can lead to interpretations that will defy the application of any given logical formalism. There is plenty of scope for ambiguity (a *criminal lawyer* may be a lawyer who represents defendants accused of crimes, or may be a lawyer who is him- or herself a criminal) and creative extensions of word meaning (*couch potato* leading to *web potato*), all of which should warn the logician that this is territory not best traversed with the meager representational formulas of logic, of whatever kind. As Murphy (1988, 2002) is at pains to point out, general conceptual combination is one of those problems in cognitive science/artificial intelligence, like nonmonotonic reasoning, that cannot be solved without an open-ended access to world knowledge.

8.2.2 Intersective Combination: Adjectival Modification

In the case of adjectival modification, the problems of laying out a logical structure governing conceptual combination are at first sight more easily solved, in that many adjective-noun combinations are intersective, as defined above. The semantics of the combination is just a matter of finding the set intersection of the two categories denoted by the two words. A *green shirt* is green and it is a shirt.

The appearance of simplicity is, however, misleading, as there are still major difficulties to be overcome. The first is that many adjectives change their meaning as a function of the noun that they are modifying. Murphy (1990) demonstrated this with a number of adjectives such as "open" or "fresh." An open door, an open face, an open question, an open view, and an open golf championship all use very different senses of the word. Interestingly, they all still retain a common sense, suggesting that this is not a simple matter of lexical ambiguity (as with words like "palm" or "bank"). Rather, the adjectival concept has become specialized, adapting a very abstract schematic idea (lack of boundaries, freedom of access) to the very different conceptual domains of a person's friendly expression, an unanswered question, and a competition with no entry restrictions. Such expressions do not always translate well between languages, either, indicating that to a greater or lesser degree they rely on the language-speaker learning the individual expressions as idioms. As Lakoff (1987) has pointed out, many extensions of the use of words can be justified post hoc, without having a predictive model of where extensions will occur. This fact is to be expected, given that languages evolve much like biological species, taking adaptive turns based on sequences of random shifts in usage within a population of speakers. Biology cannot predict that there should be creatures like zebras in Africa, but given that fact, the theory of evolution can provide a story of how they got there.

Another example of the polysemy of adjectives is the case of evaluative adjectives. Kamp and Partee (1995) point out that from "John is a good violinist" one can infer "John is a violinist," but not "John is good." The sense of "good" here is tied to the concept of violinist and cannot be treated independently.

A second problem for the logic of adjectival combinations is that even within a given narrow domain, the noun may still determine the applicability of the adjective. The words "big" and "small" can refer to a range of domains (minds, ideas, mistakes), but suppose we just restrict ourselves to physical size. Even then we have to know something about the normal range of size for the noun category in order to decide if an object is big or small. A large ant is much smaller than a small cat. Color terms such as "red" will similarly take different expected typical values when applied to different nouns such as "hair," "wine," "face," or "car." Once again the meaning of the adjective has to be taken *within the context* of the noun. A "large ant" is an ant that is large *for an ant*. To evaluate the truth of the statement "that is a large *x*," we need to have knowledge of the distribution of sizes for the class of all *x*, and adapt the truth conditions accordingly.

A final problem (for now!) consists of so-called privative adjectives. Adjectives may include within them the power to change the truth-value assigned to category membership in the noun category. A flawed proof is not a proof, in the sense that it does not prove anything. Other privatives are words such as "former," "fake," "pretend," "putative," "seeming," and "alleged." Nor does the adjective itself have to be privative for this change to occur. A chocolate egg, a plastic flower, and a wooden horse are none of them things of the right kind to be called respectively eggs, flowers, and horses. It seems that our use of language allows us to take the name of a concept and extend it to refer to things that have the same appearance. A chocolate egg is an egg because it has the right shape. In fact language use includes a wide variety of ways in which meanings get extended. Words are often used figuratively or metaphorically. Capturing conceptual combinations with fuzzy logic will require a very strict means of identifying when such extended uses are being employed. Unfortunately, as with everything else, the question of when a meaning has been extended has no precise answer, so that the applicability of fuzzy logic to a segment of language may itself be a matter of degree.

8.3   Compositionality

The relevance of all of this to a book on fuzzy logic relates to the notion of compositionality. In a series of papers, Fodor and Lepore (2002) have argued for the importance of compositionality as a fundamental assumption in the representational theory of mind. Briefly, the principle of compositionality says that the meaning of a complex phrase should be based on the meaning of its components, the syntax of the language by which they are combined, and *nothing else*. Much has been written on compositionality and on ways in which the principle can be explicated (Werning, Hintzen, and Machery 2011). It should be clear from the foregoing discussion that one cannot reasonably expect to find compositional concept combination in much of everyday language. The adherent to the principle will therefore have to rely on a lot of additional linguistic/pragmatic theory of how the underlying compositional logic of a complex phrase can be derived from its noncompositional surface form (Recanati 2004). Even then, the challenge of providing a compositional semantics for natural language is daunting.

Putting aside these problems for now, let us consider the treatment of truth conditions for complex phrases that are apparently compositional, and hence suitable for a logical treatment.

8.3.1   Intersective Combination: Restrictive Relative Clause Constructions

In a series of empirical studies (Hampton 1987, 1988b, 1997) I investigated how people combine concepts when they are placed in an explicitly intersective linguistic form. A restrictive relative clause, such as "a sport that is also a game," is unambiguous in referring to the subset of recreational activities that are both sports and games. If we accept this interpretation, then we would expect the logical relation of conjunction to underlie the meaning of the combined phrase. In that case, (a) people should treat the phrase symmetrically ("a sport that is also a game" should apply to the same set of activities as "a game that is also a sport"), and (b) people should only consider the phrase to apply to an activity if they also agree that the activity is a sport and that it is a game.

Hampton (1988b) reported a number of studies using six different conjunctive combinations of this kind (others included "a tool that is also a weapon" and "a machine that is also a vehicle"). Participants in the studies were given a list of potential category members (e.g., tennis, archery, chess, trampolining, sky-diving, crosswords) and made three sets of category judgments. First they decided if they were sports, then if they were games, and then finally if they were "sports that are games." Responses were given on a scale from −3 to +3, where a positive number indicated a "yes" decision with increasing confidence from +1 to +3, and a negative number indicated a "no" decision in the same way. A zero could be used in case the item was exactly on the borderline of the category, and the item could be left blank if it was unknown.

The data were analyzed as follows. First, mean judgments were calculated for each item for each of the three category judgments (the constituents A and B, and their conjunction As that are B). Regression analysis was applied to these means to identify the strength of a linear relation between degree of belonging to the conjunction and degree of belonging to each constituent. Across three experiments, the fit of the regression function was extremely good, providing a positive interaction term was included. Multiple R (the correlation between predicted and observed values of membership for the conjunction) averaged around 0.97, where a value of 1 means a perfect match. R squared of 0.94 indicated that 94% of the variance in conjunctive membership across items could be explained in terms of items' membership for the conjunct categories. The success of the model suggests that a fuzzy logic function could be used to successfully predict membership degree in a relative clause conjunction from membership in the two conjuncts. The function was *not*, however, one of those usually associated with the intersection of fuzzy sets. The model used a function that was based on the product of the two conjunct memberships, but rescaled so that a hypothetical item that was on the borderline for each conjunct would also be on the borderline for the conjunction. Given that an item that was very clearly not in one of the conjuncts was clearly not in the conjunction, while items that were very typical of both conjunctions were very typical of the conjunction, a geometric mean (the square root of the product of the two conjunct memberships) may be the best approximation to the empirical function.

Further studies (Hampton 1997) confirmed this pattern of data, using different participants to provide the ratings for each category. In addition, combinations involving negated relative clauses were used (e.g., "games that are not sports"), which had the effect of reversing the sign of the negated conjunct in the empirical function, so that the negated conjunct and the interaction term both had negative regression weights. For these later studies, regression analysis applied to frequencies of positive responses (as opposed to mean scale ratings) produced the same pattern of results.

It would seem, then, that a fuzzy logic function based on a geometric average, with suitable scaling, would provide a good model for the way in which people form this kind of conceptual combination. It is interesting that the function was anchored at the borderlines of each concept. Effectively one can suppose that the 0.5 point on the membership scale (which in the present case was the point where 50% of participants agreed that the item belonged) corresponds to a point of complete "quandary," to use Wright's (2001) term. This is the point where people are most likely to be in a perfect state of indecision about the categorization of the item. The result of the experiment suggested the following principle for the logic of such states:

When a person is in a quandary about whether x should be in category A and also in a quandary about whether x should be in category B, then they are also in a quandary about whether x is in the conjunction of A and B.

This principle is intuitively plausible, corresponding to the propagation of a state of quandary about each conjunct to a state of quandary about the conjunction. (It would also apply to being in a quandary about the disjunction of the two categories—see below). The fuzzy logical averaging function then has the following consequences:

(a) *Overextension*: An item that is somewhat above 0.5 for A but somewhat below 0.5 for B may still correspond to the state of quandary (0.5) for the conjunction AB. Hence the likelihood of an item's being placed in the conjunction will be *greater* than the likelihood of its being placed in category B. This overextension of conjunctive membership is a direct consequence of the principle and of the use of an averaging function (see chapter 3, section 3.4). The overextension has been found in a number of studies (Hampton 1988b, 1997; Storms et al. 1993, 1996, 1999; Storms, Ruts, and Vandenbroucke 1998).

(b) *Compensation*: An item's good degree of membership in one conjunct can compensate for its poor degree of membership for the other, in determining membership in the conjunction. It is as if in choosing a home one had two necessary requirements—a location within one hour's commute of work, and a minimum of 80 square meters of floor space. This conjunctive requirement determines the set of acceptable homes as the intersection of the two sets defined by each criterion. The averaging conjunctive rule allows that if one found a place that was only 30 minutes from work, one might still consider it acceptable, even though the floor space was only 70 square meters (Chater, Lyon, and Myers 1990).

8.3.2   Overextension and Compensation

Overextension can be readily handled within fuzzy logic by the adoption of a suitable function such as the geometric average. One puzzle is why the function should not be closer to one of the standard functions for conjunction, such as the minimum rule or the product rule. A standard constraint on fuzzy logics for categorization is that membership in a conjunction cannot be greater than membership in a conjunct (see chapter 3, section 3.4). The truth of *two* statements together cannot be greater than the truth of each one considered individually. Yet overextension clearly violates this constraint. The logician may not be too concerned. It may be considered sufficient to have shown empirically that membership in the conjunction can be accurately modeled with a fuzzy logic function of one kind or another. However, this obviously leaves a lot to be explained. In particular, why do we have the strong sense that the phrase "*A* that is a *B*" should be the overlap of *A*s and *B*s, and should be a subset of *A*s, when in practice this is not how we categorize items within the complex set? This question suggests a worrying disconnect between the apparent (even transparent) logical form of an expression and the categorization behavior that it invokes.

Compensation—the second consequence of an averaging function—can be even more of a problem. According to prototype theory (Hampton 1979, 1995; Rosch and Mervis 1975) degree of membership in a category can be most easily explained in terms of the similarity of an item to the prototype or idealized representation of the category's central tendency. Thus, tennis is considered a sport because in terms of the properties that characterize typical sports (physical, skilled, involves exertion, competitive, has championships, has stars) it ticks all the boxes. Other activities may be marginal to the category because while they have some properties they lack others (for example, scuba diving is normally noncompetitive although it does involve skill and some physical exertion). Within the psychology of concepts, prototype theory has been superseded in a number of ways, but some form of property-based similarity remains the only account of why there are differences in typicality and why there are marginal members of categories. It is true that some have argued that borderline cases are owing to ignorance of the world, rather than semantic indeterminacy (e.g., Williamson 1994; Bonini et al. 1998). However, there remains very little psychological evidence that this provides a general account of the problems of vagueness of meaning in language.

The difficulty for fuzzy logic lies in the fact that the similarity of items to the prototype of a category can continue to increase beyond the point at which membership in the category has reached a maximum. Osherson and Smith (1997) used this fact as a critique of the prototype account of graded membership. Typicality (as similarity to a prototype is usually termed) cannot be simply identified with grades of membership, since the former can differ among items that all have full membership in the category. A robin is a more typical bird than a penguin (having the requisite features characteristic of birds in general), but both robins and penguins are fully birds, as judged by the 100% endorsement of the statements "A robin/penguin is a bird." Thus the continuous truth-value assigned to the statement "a penguin is a bird" must be 1, if the person doing the assigning has a firm belief that a penguin is definitely a bird. I argued (Hampton 2007) that this is not after all a problem for prototypes and graded membership, since typicality and graded membership should be treated as two functions based on the same underlying similarity measure. Typicality is a monotonically rising function of similarity, whereas membership is a nondecreasing function of similarity that starts at 0, starts to rise at a certain point k_1, and then reaches a ceiling of 1 at a further point k_2, where k_1 and k_2 are above the minimum and below the maximum values that similarity can take.

Why should this represent a problem for fuzzy logic accounts of conjunction? The difficulty comes when an increase in the typicality of items with respect to category A continues to affect membership in the conjunction AB, even when membership of the items in A is already at the maximum of 1. Consider two stimuli that are identical in shape, being composed of a figure halfway between a capital A and a capital H. The vertical lines at the side of the H have been bent in at the top so that they could be taken to be an A or an H, and in fact when people have to choose, they are 50% likely to say one or the other. Now let both figures be colored red, so that everyone agrees 100% that they are both red. If asked if they are examples of a "red H," they should therefore be inclined to agree around 50% of the time. Being red is unproblematic—everyone says they are red—so the only question relevant to their membership in the conjunction is whether they look more like an H or more like an A. Being identical in shape, there should be no difference in the degree of agreement. So far so good. Now let us suppose that the first figure, Stimulus 1, is a very bright prototypical red, while Stimulus 2 is a rather pale watery red with a slight hint of purple. So while both are 100% red in terms of the membership function, they are not equally typical.

In another study (Hampton 1996) looking at this issue, I found that membership in the conjunction could be affected by differences in typicality, even when the point had been reached where membership was no longer in doubt. Typicality of a clear red could compensate for lack of match in the angle of the letter verticals. For fuzzy logic the challenge is to decide just how to define the membership function $c_A(x)$ in terms of the underlying similarity to prototypes. There are two possibilities, neither of which is without problems. If $c_A(x)$ is mapped to probabilities of category membership, then it will capture differences in the amount of disagreement and inconsistency in membership decisions. As a measure of "truth" it is intuitively most plausible to map $c_A(x)$ in this way. The function reaches a value of 1 at the point at which everyone assents to the truth of the state-ment, and a value of 0 at the point where no one assents to it. But then it is not possible to capture differences in typicality within the measure, since typicality continues to increase after the point at which $c_A(x)$ reaches a maximum (and continues to decrease after the point at which it reaches a minimum). Alternatively, $c_A(x)$ could be mapped to the typicality/similarity of an item. But then there would be the unintuitive result that although everyone accepts that x is an A, yet its membership in A is only (say) 0.9.

The phenomenon of compensation argues for the second mapping, since differences in typicality for one category once membership has reached a maximum *do* have an effect on degrees of membership in the conjunction of that category with another.

8.3.3   Disjunction

Further studies (Hampton 1988a, 1997) looked at other logical connectives as they are applied to natural language categories. Hampton (1988a) looked at how judgments of category membership in two categories were related to judgments in their disjunction. Unlike conjunctions, disjunctions can be formed without there being any overlap between the two categories in question. For example, one could form the disjunction "birds or trucks," and in such a case it is plausible (although there is no empirical data on this question) to propose that the maximum rule would apply unproblem-atically. After all, anything that is at all close to being a bird is not going to have any chance of being a truck, and vice versa, so the two membership functions can simply be summed. A maximum rule and a sum will give the same values for the disjunction of A and B in the case that $c_A(x) \cdot c_B(x) = 0$ for all x, which for birds and trucks seems very probable. The more interesting case arises when the disjunction is formed of two categories that are seman-tically related and fall within the same domain, so that $c_A(x) \cdot c_B(x) > 0$, for some item x. Hampton (1988a) measured degrees of membership in two categories A, B and their disjunction $A \vee B$, using a selection of eight pairs of categories, and showed that a regression function of the form

$$c_{A \vee B} = p c_A + q c_B - r c_A c_B, \tag{8.1}$$

where p, q, and r are positive constants, could do a fair job of predicting disjunctive membership, with multiple R varying from 0.95 to 0.99 in a within-subjects design and 0.86 to 0.97 in a between-subjects design.

In terms of the probability of an item's belonging in the disjunction, given that it was judged to be in one of the disjuncts, there was a tendency for people to underextend. Just as people overextended conjunctions, they underextended the disjunctions. For example, 90% of a participant group thought that a refrigerator was a "house furnishing," and 70% of a different group that it was "furniture," but of a third group only 58% agreed that it was either one or the other. Unlike conjunctions, where the borderline of each conjunct appeared to anchor the borderline for the conjunction (the point of quandary), for disjunctions, an item that was borderline for both disjuncts tended to be excluded from the disjunction. In fact, a function closely fitting the disjunctive borderline was defined (for mean membership values on a scale from −3 to 0 to +3) by the equation

$$c_A + c_B = -2. \tag{8.2}$$

Thus, to achieve a borderline membership in the disjunction an item had to have a summed value in the two disjunctions greater than some constant value. Items that were good members (+3) in one of the disjuncts were guaranteed to belong. But items that were only atypical members (+1) were only borderline to the disjunction if they were very poor members (−3) of the other disjunct.

The challenge for any type of logic, fuzzy or otherwise, is that the disjunction operation appears to violate the constraints of classical logic. More people believe that the refrigerator is a "house furnishing" than believe that it is either a "house furnishing" or "furniture." The principle of disjunction introduction that says that if A is true then A or B is also true does not apply to these judgments.

Underextension was not the only problematic result in this study. Where a pair of categories divide a larger domain, such as "fruits and vegetables," the judgments of disjunctive membership go the other way, exceeding the constraints of the maximum and *even* the sum rule. For example, across the three groups of participants no one in the first group ever judged a mushroom to be a fruit, 50% of the second judged it to be a vegetable, while 90% of the third group judged it to be either a fruit or a vegetable. So given that no one apparently believes that a mushroom is a fruit, why is it more likely to be in the disjunction "fruits or vegetables" than in the class "vegetables" alone?

8.3.4 Negation

A further study (Hampton 1997) looked at the function of negation within restricted relative clause constructions. Negative concepts have sometimes been cited as examples of concepts that have no prototype (e.g., Connolly et al. 2007). Although it is easy to determine the membership of a class such as "not a fruit," it seems that this determination does not involve similarity to some prototypical nonfruit. We therefore have to assume (along with fuzzy logic) that negation is part of the set of syntactic operations that can be applied to given positively defined concepts. In the context of conceptual combinations, however, negation can play a role in determining the attributes of a given concept. For example, "nonalcoholic beverage" and "nonsmoking bar" are easily understood, and could even permit degrees of set membership; many nonalcoholic beers state that they contain less than 1% alcohol, which would make them less clear members of the category of nonalcoholic beverage than, say, lemonade or orange juice.

Hampton (1997) investigated the relation between membership of items in two constituent categories such as "sports" and "games," and then membership either in the conjunction (sports that are also games) or a conjunction with negated relative clause (sports that are not games). Different groups were used to make each of the judgments. Judgments were made on a seven-point rating scale, in which a positive number (+1 to +3) was used to indicate that an item was in the category (with increasing typicality), and a negative number (−1 to −3) indicated that it was not in the category (with increasing unrelatedness). Data were analyzed both in terms of mean scale ratings, and also in terms of the proportion of positive (versus negative) ratings given. For regression functions predicting either mean rated degree of category membership, or proportion of positive categorization responses, the results were consistent with Hampton (1988b). The negated conjunctions were predictable by a multiplicative function of the two constituent membership values, but with membership in the second category taking a negative weight. One notable difference from the earlier results (Hampton 1988b) was the occurrence of many more cases where an item was in the (negated) conjunction but not in the corresponding conjuncts. For example, a tree house was considered to be a "dwelling" by 74% of one group, to be "not a building" by 20% of the second group, but to be a "dwelling that is not a building" by 100% of a third group. There was considerable overlap between the sets As that are B and As that are not B. When the probability of an item's being in one was added to the probability of its being in the other, theoretically the sum should be the probability of its being in set A, according to

$$c_{A \wedge B}(x) + c_{A \wedge \neg B}(x) = c_A(x). \tag{8.3}$$

In practice, the sum could reach values well above 1.0, indicating that equation (8.3) does not constrain judgments of membership in these categories. The actual value of the sum in (8.3) was predicted by a weighted average of $c_A(x)$ and the distance of $c_B(x)$ from a probability of 0.5.

8.4   Conceptual Combination: The Need for an Intensional Approach

By this point it should be apparent that truth-functional approaches to conceptual combination based on extensional measures of category membership find it very difficult to account for the actual data on how people combine concepts. It is not so much a matter of finding the *right* fuzzy logic function to define conjunction, disjunction, or negation. Rather, the function depends on the semantic contents or intensions of the concepts in question. Several papers in the psychological literature responded to the challenge of Osherson and Smith's (1981, 1982) papers by making the same point. Thus, Cohen and Murphy (1984), Hampton (1987), and Smith and Osherson (1984) all came to the conclusion that the effect of forming a conjunction of two concepts A and B will vary depending on the relation between the intensions of the two concepts, and how they interact.

By an intension I mean the set of descriptive properties that are held to be generally true of a class and thus provide a means of determining whether some novel item belongs in the class or not. Concepts have both extensions and intensions. For a concept like *triangle*, the extension is the set of all plane figures that fall under the term "triangle." Extensions are used for quantificational logic and most truth-functional semantic systems. Hence the interpretation of a green shirt as the intersection of green things and shirts uses the extensions of each of the terms and forms the set of items that fall in both extensions. Intensions are of more interest to psychologists, since they reflect the way in which we represent the concept internally. Frege (to whom we owe much of this way of seeing things) pointed out that two concepts could have the same reference or extension (denote or refer to the same set of objects in the world) and yet have different senses or intensions. If a *triangle* is a closed plane figure with three angles, and a *trilateral* is a closed plane figure with three sides, the two concepts refer to the same set of mathematical objects, since (as should be obvious) every triangle has three sides, and every trilateral has three angles. But intensionally they are different, since it is possible for John (whose knowledge of geometry is very slight) to know that the angles in a triangle sum to 180°, but not to know that the angles in a trilateral sum to 180°. To explain how we combine natural concepts into conjunctions and disjunctions, it is necessary to look closely at the intensional information that represents each concept, and how the intension of one concept interacts with that of the other. We cannot even get close to an account of the logic of natural categories by looking at the extensions alone.

8.4.1   Contradictions and Fallacies

One of the key reasons for looking for an intensional model to explain conceptual combinations is the widespread occurrence of apparently contradictory or fallacious reasoning involving concepts. We have seen above how people consistently place items in the conjunction of two sets, while at the same time denying that the item is in one of the conjuncts. And people are reluctant to allow that an item is in the disjunction of two sets even though they will allow it in one of the disjuncts. Other similar effects have been reported in the literature, and all point to the fact that the human conceptual system is not based on a firm grounding in logic (classical or otherwise) but instead has a different design with different purposes. I will briefly give some examples of these nonlogical effects, starting with a study of my own (Hampton 1982). Participants were asked to judge whether categorizations of the kind "*A* is a kind of *B*" were true or false. The study showed that this form of categorization may be intransitive. People said that clocks and chairs were furniture, and that Big Ben was a clock and a car-seat was a chair, but that Big Ben and car-seats were *not* furniture. A well-reported effect of the same kind is Tversky and Kahneman's (1983) conjunction fallacy. Just as people overextend conjunctive concepts, so they judge subjective probabilities in a way that overestimates the likelihood of conjunctive events. In this case people were told about Linda, who was a radical when in college, and then went on to judge it more likely that she was a feminist bank teller than simply a bank teller.

Similar nonlogical effects have been reported by Sloman in studies of category-based inductive reasoning. In the premise specificity effect, people consider that an argument such as

All apples are diocogenous; therefore all McIntosh apples are

is stronger than

All fruits are diocogenous; therefore all McIntosh apples are,

even though both arguments are perfectly strong (given people's knowledge that McIntosh apples are apples, and that apples are fruit). They preferred an argument with a more specific premise. A similar effect was seen in the conclusion of an argument, with more typical conclusions being preferred. For example,

All animals have property X; therefore all mammals do

was considered a stronger argument than

All animals have property X; therefore all reptiles do.

Finally, Jönsson and Hampton (2006) reported an intensional equivalent of the Tversky and Kahneman fallacy, which they termed the inverse conjunction fallacy. People were inclined to consider it more likely to be true that *All lambs are friendly* than that *All dirty lambs are friendly*, paying no heed to the inclusion relation between lambs and dirty lambs.

8.4.2 An Intensional Theory of Concepts

From the earliest theories, psychologists have sought to model concepts in terms of their intensions. It makes intuitive sense to propose that people represent a class of things in the world by representing their typical characteristic properties. However, this has not been the standard approach taken by logic, where the focus has been on the sets of objects in the world and the relations between those sets. Thus, semantic theories in linguistics and philosophy have concentrated on describing the relation between statements in a language and the conditions of the world that would make those statements true or false (or in the case of fuzzy logic, true to some degree). Given a set of statements and their associated truth-values, the task of logic is to determine how truth is preserved as statements are combined with various syntactic operators. Psychological data, however, show that one cannot treat the truth of statements in a content-independent way.

For example, when two related categories are combined in a disjunction, Hampton (1988a) showed that the function relating a disjunct's degrees of truth to truth of the disjunction varies across different pairs. While *hobbies or games* tended to be underextended (*beer drinking* was considered a hobby, but not to be in the category "hobbies or games"), *fruits or vegetables* was overextended, with *mushroom* and *coconut* being near perfect members of the disjunction, although only partial members of one disjunct and not members at all of the other. To account for this dependence of the functions on the contents of the particular concepts being combined requires that they not be treated as logical atoms, but that the interaction of their intensions be considered.

Hampton (1988b) provided a detailed account of how one might combine concepts into conjunctions, using the intensions of each concept as the starting point. Classically a conjunction of extensions can be formed by taking a set union of the intensions. For example, to pick out the class of green shirts, one has to take all the defining properties of green things and all the defining properties of shirts and form their set union, so that green shirts have the defining properties of both classes. Hampton's composite prototype model (CPM) takes the same approach as a starting point, but with the proviso that the properties in question are not *defining* in the classical sense of being necessary and constitutive of the class, but are instead *prototypical*. In fact the properties vary, from some that may be highly central and universally present in the class (e.g., *fish have gills*) to those that are almost incidental to the kind (e.g., *fish are eaten with French fries*). It is hypothesized that attributes have an "importance" that will reflect the degree to which they affect the similarity of an item to the concept prototype. Differences in attribute importance arise from statistical frequency of co-occurrence, and from the degree to which attributes are embedded in causal dependencies with other attributes. Thus, an attribute will be important if it has high predictive validity (most category members have the attribute, and most items with the attribute are category members), and if it is the cause or the effect of other attributes in the concept prototype.

The model for constructing a conjunction follows a number of steps (see Hampton 1988b, 1991 for details). In the model, properties are called "attributes":

(a)   All attributes of each concept are recruited into a composite prototype representation for the conjunction, with an importance based on their average importance for the two conjuncts.

(b)   Where an attribute has very low importance, it is dropped from the representation.

(c)   Where an attribute is of very high importance for one conjunct, the attribute will have very high importance for the conjunction.

(d)   Where an attribute of one concept is inconsistent with an attribute of the other concept, then a means of resolving the conflict is found, usually by dropping one or other of the attributes.

(e)   New "emergent" attributes may find their way into the conjunction, either from accessing world knowledge (e.g., that pet fish live in tanks), or from attempts to improve the coherence of the new attribute set (e.g., that a blind lawyer is highly motivated—see Kunda, Miller, and Claire 1990).

This model is based on empirical studies of how attributes are inherited in conjunctions with or without negation and in disjunctions (Hampton 1987, 1988a, 1997). While importance for a conjunction was well approximated by an arithmetic average of the two constituent importances, it was also found to be subject to constraints, such that necessary attributes remain necessary, and impossible attributes remain impossible. One function that satisfies these constraints is defined by the formula

$$I(i, A \cap B) = \frac{I(i,A) \cdot I(i,B)}{I(i,A) \cdot I(i,B) + (1 - I(i,A)) \cdot (1 - I(i,B))}, \tag{8.4}$$

where $I(i, A)$ denotes the importance of attribute i for concept A. Clearly, $I(i, A \cap A) = 1$ when $I(i, A) = 1$ or $I(i, B) = 1$ and neither $I(i, A) = 0$ nor $I(i, B) = 0$. Similarly, $I(i, A \cap B) = 0$ when $I(i, A) = 0$ or $I(i, B) = 0$. Note also that if an attribute is necessary for one concept ($I(i, A) = 1$), but impossible for the other concept ($I(i, B) = 0$), then $I(i, A \cap B)$ is undefined, being zero divided by zero. Such a case would correspond to a conjunction with no members, the empty set.

8.4.3   Explaining the Data

Intensional models such as Hampton's CPM provide a good account of the different nonlogical effects reported in the literature. Overextension of conjunctions occurs because in forming a composite prototype, typical attributes of each concept may be lost through the process of conflict resolution. A typical pet is warm, cuddly, and affectionate, while a typical fish lives in a river, lake, or ocean and is caught for food. Put these two concepts together and the result is a creature that is neither warm and affectionate, nor ocean-living and eaten. The more central attributes of each concept have eliminated some of the less central attributes of the other concept, leaving a typical pet fish as a cold, slimy water-living creature that lives in the home, and has a name and an owner who cares for it and feeds it. Naturally enough, it is then very possible for some items (such as a guppy or goldfish) to be a much better fit to this new composite concept than they are to either of the original conjoined concepts. A guppy is not a typical fish, or a typical pet, but it *is* a typical pet fish. Hampton's (1988b) discovery that not only are some items more *typical* of a conjunction than of each conjunct, but that they are also *more likely to belong* in the conjunctive class, provides a strong endorsement of this account of concept combination.

There are, of course, intensional logics. They share with psychological intensional models the idea that concepts are concerned not just with the actual current world but also with the set of possible worlds. Modal notions of necessity and possibility are a part of intensional logic, just as they are a crucial element in psychological accounts of concept combination. For example, for the composite prototype of a pet fish to be formed, it is not sufficient just to average out the importance of attributes for each component; issues of compatibility, necessity, and possibility also need to be addressed. Human thought is certainly not constrained to the here and now or even to the actual. Our intensional concepts can be combined in ever more creative and imaginative ways to create fictional worlds of infinite possibility.

8.5 Fuzzy Logic and Conceptual Combinations

In the course of this chapter I have tried to lay out some of the complexities of the way in which concepts can be combined in everyday thought and language. On one hand, a continuous-valued logic will be of key importance for understanding the psychological data, since there are indefinitely many situations in which the statements we wish to make are neither completely true nor completely false (see chapter 9). On the other hand, a truth-functional approach that seeks to find the "logical rules" by which the applicability or extension of complex concepts is determined by the extension of their parts and the syntax of their combination is unlikely to provide an answer to more than a very restricted range of human cognition. My approach has always been to collect empirical data first, and then to theorize in a way that attempts to account for those data. This approach has led to some surprising discoveries. Ways of speaking that appear to have a certain logical form turn out to work differently from the way we had supposed. But the approach has also led to some fruitful theorizing that has brought together a range of phenomena under the general heading of "intuitive reasoning," to use Tversky and Kahneman's phrase.

References

Bonini, N., D. N. Osherson, R. Viale, and T. Williamson. 1998. On the psychology of vague predicates. *Mind & Language* 14:377–393.

Chater, N., K. Lyon, and T. Myers. 1990. Why are conjunctive concepts overextended? *Journal of Experimental Psychology. Learning, Memory, and Cognition* 16: 497–508.

Cohen, B., and G. L. Murphy. 1984. Models of concepts. *Cognitive Science* 8:27–58.

Connolly, A., J. A. Fodor, L. R. Gleitman, and H. Gleitman. 2007. Why stereotypes don't even make good defaults. *Cognition* 103:1–22.

Estes, Z., and S. Glucksberg. 2000. Interactive property attribution in concept combination. *Memory & Cognition* 28:28–34.

Fillmore, C. J. 1968. The Case for Case. In *Universals in Linguistic Theory*, ed. E. Bach and R. T. Harms, 1–88. New York: Holt, Rinehart & Winston.

Fodor, J. A., and E. Lepore. 2002. *The Compositionality Papers*. Oxford: Clarendon Press.

Gagné, C. L., and E. J. Shoben. 1997. Influence of thematic relations on the comprehension of Modifier-Noun combinations. *Journal of Experimental Psychology: Learning, Memory, and Cognition* 23:71–87.

Gleitman, L. R., and H. Gleitman. 1970. *Phrase and Paraphrase*. New York: Academic Press.

Hampton, J. A. 1979. Polymorphous concepts in semantic memory. *Journal of Verbal Learning and Verbal Behavior* 18:441–461.

Hampton, J. A. 1982. A demonstration of intransitivity in natural categories. *Cognition* 12:151–164.

Hampton, J. A. 1987. Inheritance of attributes in natural concept conjunctions. *Memory & Cognition* 15:55–71.

Hampton, J. A. 1988a. Disjunction of natural concepts. *Memory & Cognition* 16: 579–591.

Hampton, J. A. 1988b. Overextension of conjunctive concepts: Evidence for a unitary model of concept typicality and class inclusion. *Journal of Experimental Psychology: Learning, Memory, and Cognition* 14:12–32.

Hampton, J. A. 1991. The combination of prototype concepts. In *The Psychology of Word Meanings*, ed. P. J. Schwanenflugel, 91–116. Hillsdale, NJ: Erlbaum.

Hampton, J. A. 1995. Testing prototype theory of concepts. *Journal of Memory and Language* 34:686–708.

Hampton, J. A. 1996. Conjunctions of visually based categories: Overextension and compensation. *Journal of Experimental Psychology. Learning, Memory, and Cognition* 22:378–396.

Hampton, J. A. 1997. Conceptual combination: conjunction and negation of natural concepts. *Memory & Cognition* 25:888–909.

Hampton, J. A. 2007. Typicality, graded membership, and vagueness. *Cognitive Science* 31:355–383.

Jönsson, M. L., and J. A. Hampton. 2006. The inverse conjunction fallacy. *Journal of Memory and Language* 55:317–334.

Kamp, H., and B. Partee. 1995. Prototype theory and compositionality. *Cognition* 57:129–191.

Kunda, Z., D. T. Miller, and T. Claire. 1990. Combining social concepts: The role of causal reasoning. *Cognitive Science* 14:551–578.

Lakoff, G. 1987. *Women, Fire, and Dangerous Things*. Chicago: University of Chicago Press.

Levi, J. 1978. *The Syntax and Semantics of Complex Nominals*. New York: Academic Press.

Murphy, G. L. 1988. Comprehending complex concepts. *Cognitive Science* 12: 529–562.

Murphy, G. L. 1990. Noun phrase interpretation and conceptual combination. *Journal of Memory and Language* 29:259–288.

Murphy, G. L. 2002. *The Big Book of Concepts*. Cambridge, MA: MIT Press.

Osherson, D. N., and E. E. Smith. 1981. On the adequacy of prototype theory as a theory of concepts. *Cognition* 11:35–58.

Osherson, D. N., and E. E. Smith. 1982. Gradedness and conceptual conjunction. *Cognition* 12:299–318.

Osherson, D. N., and E. E. Smith. 1997. On typicality and vagueness. *Cognition* 64:189–206.

Recanati, F. 2004. *Literal Meaning*. Cambridge: Cambridge University Press.

Rips, L. J. 1995. The current status of research on concept combination. *Mind & Language* 10:72–104.

Rosch, E. R., and C. B. Mervis. 1975. Family resemblances: Studies in the internal structure of categories. *Cognitive Psychology* 7:573–605.

Smith, E. E., and D. N. Osherson. 1984. Conceptual combination with prototype concepts. *Cognitive Science* 8:337–361.

Storms, G., P. De Boeck, I. van Mechelen, and D. Geeraerts. 1993. Dominance and non-commutativity effects on concept conjunctions: Extensional or intensional basis? *Memory & Cognition* 21:752–762.

Storms, G., P. De Boeck, I. van Mechelen, and W. Ruts. 1996. The dominance effect in concept conjunctions: Generality and interaction aspects. *Journal of Experimental Psychology: Learning, Memory, and Cognition* 22:1–15.

Storms, G., W. Ruts, and A. Vandenbroucke. 1998. Dominance, overextensions, and the conjunction effect in different syntactic phrasings of concept conjunctions. *European Journal of Cognitive Psychology* 10:337–372.

Storms, G., P. De Boeck, J. A. Hampton, and I. van Mechelen. 1999. Predicting conjunction typicalities by component typicalities. *Psychonomic Bulletin & Review* 4:677–684.

Tversky, A., and D. Kahneman. 1983. Extensional versus intuitive reasoning: The conjunction fallacy in probability judgment. *Psychological Review* 90:293–315.

Werning, M., W. Hintzen, and E. Machery, eds. 2011. *Oxford Handbook of Compositionality*. Oxford: Oxford University Press.

Williamson, T. 1994. *Vagueness*. London: Routledge.

Wisniewski, E. J. 1997. When concepts combine. *Psychonomic Bulletin & Review* 4: 167–183.

Wright, C. 2001. On being in a quandary: Relativism, vagueness, logical revisionism. *Mind* 110:45–98.

9   Concepts and Natural Language

James A. Hampton

9.1   Concept, Word, and Object

In this chapter, I am concerned with a particular kind of concept. The term "concept" can be used for a wide variety of mental and cultural entities. We can talk about the concept of art, the concept of a mathematical function like addition, the concept of democracy, or the concept of a space-time continuum. In fact it can be argued that the history of all human intellectual endeavor, with the possible exception of the arts, is the history of the development of concepts. One particular domain in which concepts play a crucial role is that of enabling us to communicate our ideas via language, and it is this type of "lexical" concept that is the focus of this chapter. In the first section I describe the close association between language and concepts, and in the second section I present three ways in which the content of a concept can be determined or individuated. I then turn in section 3 to the issue of vagueness in meaning and the relevance of fuzzy logic approaches.

As a starting assumption, we can think of lexical concepts as the meanings of single words (or idiomatic phrases) in a given language. Hence, if in English we have the words "apple" and "sauce," we assume that each of these words names an underlying concept—respectively, *apple* and *sauce*. When we wish to communicate to another person a fact, or a question or a comment, then we do so by composing a thought and then expressing it in our language. Our companion then hears the expression that we have uttered and uses it, together with the context in which it was uttered, to arrive at an understanding of what our intention was in making the utterance (Clark 1992). Much of everyday discourse is an elaborate ritual of asking after each other's health, joking around, commenting on news items that we believe the other would be interested in, raising questions about future events, and so forth. It is very important to recognize that a great deal of linguistic behavior is not about the assertion of true beliefs. However, an equally important function of language is that it *does* allow the expression and assertion of beliefs, and it is when language is used in this way that questions of logic and truth arise. Our present interest in the concepts that correspond to the meanings of nouns, verbs, adjectives, and so on is thus going to derive from the question of how we can construct truth-bearing propositions from language. These propositions can then be asserted, denied, entertained, assumed, or generally allow us to be in a mental state that involves having a "propositional attitude" toward a given proposition.

It is fair to assume that language and thinking have evolved in close parallel in the evolution of human cognition. Our ability to think particular thoughts and to communicate them to others has led to the structure of propositional thought closely mirroring that of language. In other words, the meaning of a sentence such as "John likes ice cream" can be "translated" into a conceptual representation as something like

$$Likes \text{ (John, ice cream)},$$

where *Likes* is a two-place function that takes as arguments an agent (John) and a patient (ice cream) and maps these onto truth-values. For example, all the pairs (x,y) corresponding to someone (x) who likes something (y) will have a value of True for this function. Pairs in which someone does not like something would return a value of False.

This "language of thought" hypothesis was made explicit by Fodor (1975) in his book of that title. Fodor used the term "mentalese" for the hypothetical internal language in which our thoughts are expressed. It can be argued that concepts are finer grained than words (Sperber and Wilson 1998). We have a single word "apple" that serves to name a concept that includes a whole range of individual varieties of apples, which an individual may wish to differentiate with different conceptual tokens. But generally speaking, as soon as a need arises to make conceptual distinctions, then words will appear in the language to allow those distinctions to be expressed and communicated. Others hearing those words will seek to discover their meanings, and in this way language and concepts develop and evolve in tandem.

9.2 Three Meanings of "Concept"

Concepts correspond to the building blocks or atoms from which we can construct thoughts with propositional contents. But where do these concepts come from, and how is their individual content determined? Three answers need to be distinguished: the objective, the intersubjective, and the subjective. Let us consider each in turn.

9.2.1 Objective Concepts and Externalist Theories of Meaning
If our use of language is to be more than "just talk," then the words that we use need to label concepts that actually refer to real classes of things in the world. The first place to look for the determination of conceptual content is therefore the objective world. Philosophers such as Kant proposed that we must be born with certain conceptual capacities in order to be able to

make any sense of the world at all (for a more recent development of this argument, see Keil 1981). It would in fact be very odd if in the evolution of the human brain there was not a survival advantage for individuals whose brains are able to conceptualize the experienced world in ways that correspond to the reality of the world out there. The ability to detect cause and effect, to monitor the passage of time, to "parse" a visual scene into a set of individual objects standing in relation to each other in a three-dimensional space, are all examples of this type of innate conceptual ability.

Locating conceptual contents in the external "real" world gives us a so-called externalist account of the content of concepts, a position commonly defended in philosophy (e.g., Fodor 1998; Rey 1983). Arguments for this position were offered independently by Putnam (1975) and Kripke (1980). To take one example, Putnam asked us to imagine that our planet has a twin in which the colorless, tasteless liquid that covers two-thirds of the planet and freezes to make ice and snow does not have the chemical formula H_2O, but instead XYZ. People on the two planets, he argued, would have identical mind and brain states, since their experience, their naming behavior, and everything else about them would be identical. But whereas "water" on earth *means* H_2O, on twin earth the equivalent word *means* XYZ. Hence, the meaning of our everyday conceptual terms is determined not by what they lead us to think, but by what they *actually* refer to or denote in the outside world.

The externalist theory of meaning provides a solid foundation for the semantics of natural language, since the semanticist can focus on finding the logical relations that relate simple terms in the language, and their combinations, to classes and relations in the external world. A person can use language in order to express ideas, but it is possible that the person can be *wrong*, not just in the propositions that they express, but in their usage of the words and their meanings. Externalism thus also provides an account of the so-called problem of error, or how it is possible for someone to have a false belief about the contents of a concept. As externalists point out, if we define the content of a concept in terms of the content of a mental state (i.e., a psychological view of contents), then the concept means just whatever the person has in his or her head to represent that concept at the time. If you and I have different information representing the meaning of a word like "war" then the externalist would argue that we could never be said to disagree about any statement concerning war. Whenever you assert a statement about war that I would deny, then that could be just a sign that we have different concepts—we are talking at cross-purposes.

Surveying the range of words and meanings that we use, we can discern certain domains in which externalist accounts of meaning work well. Words that relate to the natural world (e.g., the names of animal and plant species) tend to have different psychological properties from those that relate to the human-made world. These differences are particularly marked in regard to the focus of this book, namely, partial truth and borderline category membership. For example, Estes (2004) investigated borderline cases of semantic categories, like tomatoes and olives as fruits. He measured the degree to which people see borderline cases of conceptual categories as having *partial* degrees of membership, as opposed to having *uncertain* membership. In the first case, a person might be quite certain that the tomato is only partly entitled to belong in the fruit category. So membership in the category can be a matter of degree (as in the fundamental axiom of fuzzy logic). On the other hand, another person may be quite certain that a tomato has to be either a fruit or not a fruit, it is just that he or she is uncertain which it is. Estes (2004, Experiment 2) accordingly asked people first to judge whether an item was a clear member, partial member, or clear nonmember of a category, and then to rate on a 10-point scale how confident they were in their decision. He found that judgments of artifact kinds, like clothing, furniture, ships, or weapons, were more likely to use the partial response, and also more likely to be rated with greater confidence than were judgments of biological kinds. Within each domain there was, however, a negative correlation, with items with more partial responses also having lower confidence ratings. Other studies have also found consistent differences between the natural kind or biological domain and the domain of artifacts (Diesendruck and Gelman 1999; Hampton 1998; Kalish 1995).

The externalist view of conceptual content may therefore work best for so-called natural kinds—types of things that existed in the external world before any people came along.

9.2.2 Intersubjectivity and the Social World

While many biological kinds happily exist without the intervention of humans,[1] there are many other lexical concepts that refer to kinds of things that are more or less entirely cultural artifacts. How the "correct" meaning of a term is then determined becomes a more complex matter. In many cases societies create "nominal kinds" in which the meaning of terms is stipulated by a public *dictat*. As parliaments or congresses pass laws, they create legal language, which needs to be as clear and as precise as is possible. Hence the concepts that are central to such laws will usually be given some more or less explicit definition. To find someone guilty of driving a car while under the influence of alcohol, the law doesn't concern itself with the vagueness and fuzziness of the concept of "under the influence of" and instead goes for a simple test of the concentration of alcohol within the blood. Fuzziness at the borderline can be handled by issuing warnings to those with up to 10% excess, and prosecuting those where the concentration is sufficiently high to allow no doubt concerning the accuracy of the test result. For a modern society to function efficiently, a lot of common or everyday concepts have to be given stipulative definitions, be it in terms of the legal limits for late-term abortions, the age at which it is safe for children to drink alcohol, or the age at which a person should be entitled to free bus travel. Vague intuitive concepts are replaced by rules that compromise between capturing the vaguely defined intuition in a rather insensitive way and being easily understood and easily enforced.

It appears, then, that many of our concepts are defined for us as a result of explicit conventions adopted by people with the political power to make such decisions. The process is recursive and adaptive. As public attitudes to homosexuality have changed over the last fifty years, so there has been pressure to redefine other social concepts including family, parenthood, and marriage.

Social forces on concepts also operate at a much less explicit level in the way that everyday word meanings evolve and adapt to changing social circumstances. Many lexical concepts, like *furniture* or *game* or *phone*, have neither an objectively determined content to be found in the world nor a nominally stipulated content derived from explicit convention. Instead there is a dynamic equilibrium among different language users that keeps the meanings stable over the short term, but allows them to drift and adapt in the longer term. This equilibrium leads naturally to fuzziness in the application of a term, since at any particular point in time the usage will have a natural variability within the population. Furthermore, to remain calibrated with others, an individual's usage has to remain flexible and adaptable, consequently giving rise to inconsistent and variable categorization or naming behavior.

9.2.3   The Individual and Word Meanings

The third way in which one can try to determine the content of concepts is at the individual level. This approach puts the "owner" of the concepts first. It asks: What is it to have a particular concept?

How do you know what the word "game" means? Your knowledge of its meaning could be characterized in two ways. You have experience of other speakers referring to a certain class of activities as games (e.g., chess, tennis, poker), and you have noticed that whenever you have used the word to refer to members of that class, you have been easily understood and no one has corrected you. So there is a common understanding between you and other speakers on the *appropriate use* of the term. Note that this kind of conceptual knowledge is primarily extensional. It involves knowing the usual things that the term refers to. It need have relatively little intensional content, since I may just have learned the things that are called "game" as a list of items, without any further understanding of what they might have in common or what the basis is for calling anything a game.

The second way to characterize your knowledge of the word's meaning is in terms of the concept's *intension*, the information that the concept carries about the likely properties of members of the concept's extension. You may not have actually come across many occasions on which the word is used to refer to other concepts, but you may have come across the word "game" in the context of discussions about the importance of different attributes of games—how playing games develops a sense of fair play and justice, how games are often competitive but allow aggression to be displayed in a harmless way without causing personal affront to others. In other words, you may know a lot about the role that games play in social settings and in people's lives, without actually knowing too much about which activities actually count as games. Having this intensional information is also the basis for using the word in creative and metaphorical extensions as in "God is playing a game with us," or "I was dealt a poor hand in the game of life."

So the two aspects, the extension and the intension, are both represented to a greater or lesser degree in individuals who possess a particular concept. Having a full representation of both aspects means that not only could you generate a list of examples of games, but you could also tell me what are the common characteristics, purposes, and social functions of games. These two aspects of concepts have been captured in the laboratory through models of concept learning that focus on either the learning of exemplars (Nosofsky 1988) or of intensional prototypes or schemas (Ahn et al. 2000; Hampton 2006). Both models have means for classifying novel cases in the category. Exemplar models rely on a notion of similarity. A new activity would be classed as a game if it had more similarity to other games than it did to members of other contrasting categories. Intensional models would determine how closely the new activity matched the expected attributes of a game, including the relational links between attributes, before the subject decides if the degree of match was sufficient. In both cases, then, membership in a category has the potential to be partial or borderline.

In the determination of word meaning, both extensional and intensional learning will involve a similar interchange with other language users and other sources of cultural information. To remain a successfully functioning member of a linguistic community, speaking a common dialect of a language, an individual has to calibrate her use of words to the usage of the other members of the community (in just the same way as different regional accents arise through mutual calibration within interacting speech communities.)

9.2.4   Extensional Knowledge May Not Depend on Intensions

In the preceding section, I suggested that people may have both extensional and intensional understanding of a term such as "game." As described earlier, there are good arguments that for at least some domains of concept, the intension (as defined here) may not be relied on to determine the extension. These domains are those in which we have some notion that there are real classes in the external world that exist independently of human cognition. Biological species are an example, as are chemical elements and compounds. Following Putnam's and Kripke's arguments about external determination of conceptual content, there have been psychological studies that confirm that in these cases people consider their own concepts to be possibly incorrect. If asked whether a particular object is made of gold, most people would have to admit that they don't actually know what *makes* something gold rather than something else. There just is this stuff called gold, and chemists have figured out what it is, what properties it has, why it has the properties that it does, and how you can test something to see if it is made of gold, and if so what purity, and so on. As a fully signed-up well-educated member of your language community, you are ready to admit that there are domains of common words in your vocabulary that you don't actually know the meaning of, at least in the sense of providing any of the above information with any confidence. This prospect has been captured in the theory of psychological essentialism (Medin and Ortony 1989). The theory makes two proposals. First, it claims that we believe that some conceptual kinds have an "essence" that makes them the kind of thing they are. Gold is stuff with some kind of atomic essence, and tigers are creatures with some kind of genetic essence. The second proposal is that we often lack information about what the essence may be. So our conceptual representation of the concept contains an empty placeholder—a promissory note that says that there is someone we could go to who can tell us the answer (an idea that Putnam referred to as the "linguistic division of labor"[2]). A corollary of the proposal is that people should be willing to defer to those who do know the answer. They should be prepared to change their concept in the face of properly qualified expert opinion to the contrary.

A set of studies by Braisby (2001, 2004) examined the idea that people should defer to experts. In one study (Braisby 2001, Study 2), people were told that a number of foodstuffs (apple, potato, salmon, and chicken) had been genetically modified, introducing either 0% or 50% of genetic material from another species either in the same superordinate category (e.g., another fish for salmon) or from a different superordinate (e.g., a mammal for salmon). They were also told that according to biologists the food was (or was not) still (say) salmon. Participants tended to defer to the expert opinion around 75% of the time, suggesting that the majority of people are willing to accept expert opinion. Willingness to defer, however, was reduced when the genetic modification was more extreme (using material from an unrelated animal or plant), with only 63% now agreeing with expert opinion that the stuff was still of the same kind. (The design was such that 50% agreement would indicate no effect of deference to the expert.)

In a control study, Braisby (2001, Study 3) changed the source of the "expert" opinion from biologists to other shoppers. In this case there was still significant deference, but the shift dropped to about 60% average compliance with the opinion of other shoppers.

Another study that tested for beliefs in essences was run by Kalish (1995). In one of his reported studies, Kalish posed the following kind of question. Suppose there are two people who are visiting the zoo. They see a creature in a cage, but there is no information available about what kind of creature it is. They discuss what kind of creature they are looking at, and they disagree. Is there a matter of fact that will decide who (if either) is correct, or is it possible for both of them to be right? Kalish used a variety of examples from both biological and artifact categories, and also included clear cases where it should be obvious that the answer is a matter of fact (e.g., mathematical cases) and others where it should be clearly a matter of opinion (e.g., whether a B+ constitutes a "good grade"). Kalish found that people were more inclined to consider a biological kind to be a matter of fact, and an artifact kind to be a matter of opinion. Like those found by Braisby (2001), however, the results were not overwhelmingly strongly in favor of essentialism. There was still a substantial minority of people who considered that even questions of biological categorization could be a matter of subjective opinion.

9.2.5   Relating Extensions and Intensions

I have suggested that full possession of a given lexical concept is likely to involve knowledge of both the extensional class to which the term refers, and the intensional information of what belonging in the class entails in terms of characteristic attributes and causal structures. An intriguing result by Malt and others (1999) has shown that in certain domains the link between extension and intension may be surprisingly weak. A common assumption, for example Gärdenfors (2000), is that the referential use of different language terms in a given domain should map onto the intensional similarity structure of the domain. That is, if a set of objects is laid out in terms of the similarity of one to another so as to form a "similarity space" with proximity between items proportionate to their similarity, then the set of terms with the same name should form a convex region of that space. Concept terms should label sets of things that are similar to one another and that are different from things with other labels. Malt and others (1999) took photographs of a set of 60 different containers, including cups, mugs, cans, pots, juice boxes, lunch boxes, and the like. Participants came from three different language groups, speaking English, Spanish, and Chinese. When they rated the pairwise similarity of the containers by different criteria of similarity, there was good consensus across languages in terms of which pairs were similar. However, when it came to giving a name to each container, the three languages divided up the 60 containers in very different ways. While the correlation of overall similarity judgments across languages was above 0.90, the correlation in naming categories was between 0.35 and 0.55. Malt and Sloman (2007) and Sloman and Malt (2003) argue that naming behavior is subject to other historical/linguistic factors so that the way in which a thing is named does not give a direct path to its conceptual content. Support for this idea can also be found in folk-taxonomy for biological kinds where early misclassifications have been resistant to correction. Thus, poison oak is not an oak, and poison ivy is not an ivy.

9.3   Vagueness and Meaning

Having laid out a brief account of how language and concepts interrelate, I turn in this section to issues of vagueness and truth in natural language concepts. There are many theories of vagueness in the philosophical literature. The interested reader is referred to the collection of papers with an excellent introductory overview by Keefe and Smith (1997), and the highly readable book by van Deemter (2010). Broadly speaking, vagueness arises when the applicability of a concept to the world is not precisely determined. Much of the philosophical discussion has focused around the issue of the logic of Sorites series. The Sorites paradox (from the Greek for "heap") concerns the applicability of the word "heap" to a quantity of sand. If one starts with a heap of sand, can the removal of a single grain change the heap into a "non-heap"? If the answer is "no," then you remove the grain, and then ask the question again. Paradoxically, it seems that removing a single grain cannot change the categorization of the pile, whereas removing many grains can. Discussion of the best logical treatment of this problem is ongoing, and continuous-valued logics are one of the currently favored types of model (Smith 2008), although others find them problematic (Keefe 2000). I do not attempt to review this large literature. Instead I try to show how the different means through which the content of concepts is determined can lead to different problems of vagueness in language use.

9.3.1   Vagueness in Real-World Categories

It might be argued (indeed it has been argued) that the world itself cannot be vague. If you believe in the reality of the world (as most of us do), then you can believe that there are atoms, composed of elementary particles, and that these atoms move and cohere together to create the world. There is nothing else but this. Apart from the niceties of Heisenberg's uncertainty principle, we don't need to worry about the world of things and stuff being imprecise or vague. But now consider the idea of properties. Are properties real in the same way that stuff is real? Or are properties a creation of our minds that we use for describing and explaining the behavior of atomic stuff? A deep question (Mellor and Oliver 1997)! The question is important because there are many important terms even in a scientific description of the world that lack precise definitions and so are open to problems of vagueness. The concept of *species* in biology has been central in the development of the theory of evolution, in the development of taxonomic classification and an understanding of the relation of one type of organism to another. Yet, the concept has no precise definition (Mayr 1982). Neighboring species of trees, for example, can form hybrids of differing degrees of viability and fertility, so that the question of whether one particular organism is of a given species may become a matter of degree.

More generally, however, concepts that take their contents from the external world are much less likely to be vague than those that derive from social norms or from individual mental contents. Science is our theory of the external world, and scientific concepts are developed in order to improve the precision of scientific descriptions and enable the construction of better theories. When we are uncertain about the truth of statements that are expressed in precise language, then we are in a position of *epistemological* uncertainty. When the weather forecasters say that there is a 50% chance of rain tomorrow, they mean something quite precise, in fact something like the following. The forecasters have taken the current dynamic and static properties of the weather as it is now, and linked it to a set of situations in the past that have similar properties in all relevant respects. Within that set, 50% of the situations went on to a situation in which it rained the next day.

Vagueness for concepts with external content is therefore most likely to arise from epistemological uncertainty rather than from vagueness in the concepts themselves.

9.3.2 Vagueness in Nominal Categories

Vagueness for our second kind of concept determination is also likely to be restricted. When society needs to reduce vagueness, then explicitly stipulated meanings are provided, which will be designed to show as little vagueness as possible. A vaguely expressed law will inevitably result in lengthy and costly litigation.

9.3.3 Vagueness in Everyday Language

Probably the most common source of vagueness, and hence of partial truth, comes from the way in which language relates to the world. As we saw in the previous section, most of our vocabulary is the result of a process of mutual coordination among the users of the language. It shifts with the changes in culture and across different generations, and for the most part there is no particular reason why anyone should need to stipulate a precise meaning. According to Dunbar (1996), language evolved as an advanced form of social bonding, similar to the grooming behavior of other primate species. Word meanings only need to be as precise as is necessary to achieve successful communication, and if the primary function of conversation is in any case not to communicate facts but to share a warm social experience, then it is not surprising that there has been little pressure on word meanings to be more precise.

There are also good reasons (or good adaptive pressures) for retaining vagueness in language terms. The world is a very complex and constantly changing place. Word meanings have to be imprecise so that we can still achieve reference in the face of things for which we have no word that fits well.

Vagueness in meaning is closely associated in psychology with the prototype theory of concepts (see chapter 4). According to Hampton (2006), there are four aspects of concepts that lead to them being considered as prototypes, two based on extensions and two based on intensions.

On the extensional side are the phenomena of borderline cases and of typicality. The things to which a term refers (its extension) form a fuzzy set, with some cases that are not clearly in or out of the category. This fuzziness can be measured empirically by asking a group of people to judge whether the term applies (a measure of vagueness suggested by Black 1937). McCloskey and Glucksberg (1978) provided additional evidence by asking the same group to remake the judgments a few weeks later. Borderline cases, where people disagreed, were also likely to be the same cases where people gave responses on the second occasion that were inconsistent with their original judgments. Being a borderline case is therefore not just a matter of lack of consensus, but also of individual uncertainty. We will call this aspect of categorization "graded membership" to indicate that belonging in the extension is not all-or-none but graded. Typicality is a related phenomenon, first identified by Rosch and Mervis (1975). Even if we just consider the set of items for which everyone agrees that a term applies, there may still be differences in how *typical* or *representative* the item is of that category. Penguins and robins are both given 100% endorsement as birds, but at the same time most people agree that robins are more typical as birds than penguins are.

Typicality and graded membership look very similar, and in early work on the problem of prototypes they were often confounded, leading to criticisms of the whole approach (Osherson and Smith 1981, 1982, 1997). It makes more sense to keep the ideas separate since the two measures have different ranges (Hampton 2007). According to prototype theory, both typicality and graded membership reflect how close an item is to the central tendency or prototype of the fuzzy class. However, whereas typicality is a continuously increasing function of similarity to the prototype, graded membership remains at 0 until the borderline region is reached, then rises continuously to 1, where it then remains constant as typicality continues to increase. The problems of how to use fuzzy logic to reflect both typicality and graded membership are discussed in chapter 8 of this volume. Strictly, since logic is concerned with truth, the truth-value of a statement should be mapped to its graded membership. However, certain phenomena (such as compensation within concept conjunctions) require that typicality can also influence truth-values.

Turning to the intensions of lexical concepts, the standard way to measure or access these is to interview participants about the attributes or features that they consider to be part of the meaning of the term. In other words, individuals are invited to reflect on the meanings of their words. Their answers are then listed out as a set of descriptive properties. For birds, this list might include "has wings," "flies," "has feathers," and "has two legs." The properties that are listed by more than a few participants are then assembled into a list, which (at least for Hampton 1995b, 2006) constitutes the prototype of the category. Note that I take the notion of a prototype to be intensional—a set of correlated features or attributes—and not extensional (such as the best or maximally typical exemplar). The reason here is that some concepts may not match anything in the world very well. They can be used to refer, but they have no typical examples. (Tongue-in-cheek examples would be "Gourmet English cooking recipes," or "cool university professors." The best real-life example falls short of the most typical example that could be imagined in a different possible world. Hence the need for an intensional basis for prototypes.)

What about intensions leads to the prediction of vagueness? First, it can often happen that the set of properties generated in this way does not provide a set of defining features that can be used to identify the reference or extension of the concept. As Wittgenstein (1953) noted, the members of a class identified with a natural language term may share "family resemblances" but have no common element definition. There is no set of features F such that their conjunction provides a necessary and sufficient definition of the class. As a corollary of this result, we find that people generate many properties in the concept intension that are just "characteristic" of the set. They describe what a typical member of the class would be like. Hence, the properties of birds that they fly and sing are not true of all birds. Flying is not necessary for being a bird, and nor is it sufficient (many insects and some mammals also fly). To explain the lack of conjunctive definitions, and the failure of people to differentiate features that are necessary for membership (birds are the only two-legged creatures with feathers) from features that are just generic to the class (birds generally fly), prototype theory proposes that we represent the meaning of a concept of this kind by representing what is common or typical about the class to which the word refers.

9.4   Some Cases of Vagueness in Language

In this section, I explore a number of cases of vagueness in the use and meaning of language terms. In each case the fact that the relation of language to the world is vague invites the logician to use some variety of fuzzy logic to describe the truth of statements involving these terms.

9.4.1   Adjectives

The most commonly debated form of vagueness in the philosophical literature is that which relates to simple scalar adjectives such as "tall" or "bald." As he grows, Joe's height increases from, say 5 feet (152 cm) to 6 feet (183 cm), so the "truth" of the statement "Joe is tall" increases from 0

(It is definitely false that Joe is tall) to 1 (It is definitely true that Joe is tall). Since the underlying reality that is being described is a continuous scale of height, with interval and ratio-scaling properties, the problem of vagueness arises in deciding how this continuous variable should be converted to a binary truth-value of "tall or not tall."

Briefly, several options have been proposed, with three main varieties:

(a)   The *epistemological approach* (Williamson 1994) stipulates that there is in fact a precise height at which it is correct to say that someone is tall. This height could depend on numerous contextual factors, so it is beyond our cognitive capacities to discover it. Vagueness in whether it is correct to call Joe tall is therefore of the same kind as uncertainty about whether it is correct to say that the population of London at this precise moment in time is greater than 7.5 million. There is arguably a fact of the matter about the population of London, but so many individual cases would need to be resolved (people in the process of being born and dying, people in temporary residences but planning to remain, people who have moved out but still have their addresses, etc.) that it is practically impossible to know the answer precisely.

(b)   The *supervaluation approach* proposes that there is a range of heights for which "*x* is tall" is neither true nor false (in the related *subvaluation approach*, it is both true and false). On any given occasion on which the term is used, however, the term can be made precise by choosing a particular cut-off point—for example, over 5 feet 10 inches is tall, and under or equal to 5 feet 10 inches is not tall. Statements employing vague terms can then be definitely true if they are true on every possible way of making the term precise (this is to be "super-true"). Hence a statement like

> Either Joe is tall or he is not tall

is necessarily true, and a statement like

> Joe is both tall and not tall

is necessarily false, in spite of the vagueness of "tall."

This approach handles this kind of sentence well, at least if one shares the common intuition about the necessary truth and falsity of the two statements. Some empirical studies, however, suggest that people may sometimes entertain contradictory statements as being true. In experiments

performed by Alxatib and Pelletier (2010), participants had to make judgments about a line-up of men set against height markers on a wall. For each
of the five men, they had to judge whether the following four statements
were "true," "false," or "can't tell":

a. No. 1 is tall
b. No. 1 is not tall
c. No. 1 is tall and not tall
d. No. 1 is neither tall nor not tall

For cases of borderline tallness, participants were quite willing to judge
that (c) was correct. Some 54% saw it as true, and of these a substantial
number also thought that (d) was true for the same individual. The intuition that (c) must always be false was not shared by all the students who
took part in the study. (The results were, however, consistent with a simple
fuzzy logic account using the minimum function for conjunction: someone
who is 0.5 tall will also be 0.5 "not tall," and the conjunction of these will
also be true to degree 0.5.)

(c)   The third option is to use a continuous-valued truth function, so that
as the likelihood of someone x being called tall increases (as her height
increases), so does the truth of the statement "x is tall." As outlined in earlier chapters, fuzzy logic has a wide and powerful array of tools for handling
this type of case. I list just a couple of the common objections, from Keefe
(2000).

First, when combining the truth of two propositions, the *relation*
between the propositions has to be included; they cannot be treated as
always independent. Thus, the truth of the statement

Ken is tall and Joe is not bald

could be captured by a minimum rule, since the two statements are
independent.

However, if Joe is known to be one inch taller than Ken, then the
statement

Ken is tall and Joe is not tall

should (arguably) always be false, since it would be irrational to say that the
taller man is not tall, but that the shorter man is.

Thus, even though the truth of the components may be equivalent (Joe is not bald = Joe is not tall), the outcome is affected by the lack of independence.

Second, fuzzy logic assigns to each proposition a precise degree of truth. So "Joe is tall" may be true to degree 0.7. But this use of the full power of the real numbers is inappropriate for capturing the genuine vagueness of language. Not only is it vague as to whether Joe is tall, but it is also vague as to just how vague it is! Fuzzy logicians can respond by assigning a fuzzy interval to be the truth-value of a statement, but the interval itself would need to have fuzzy limits if the vagueness of vagueness is to be fully captured.

Talk of the vagueness of vagueness is obviously quite mind-bending, but the issue of so-called higher-order vagueness is a critical problem for logical treatments of vagueness. There is no evidence that statements can be neatly divided into those that are definitely true, those that are definitely false, and the rest. In fact there is evidence to the contrary. Although the following study used noun categories rather than adjectives, it is likely that the results will generalize to any semantic decisions about concepts.

Hampton (2008) describes a study that examined whether people know when things are vague and when they are not. Two groups of participants were given a set of borderline cases to categorize, such as whether an olive is a fruit or whether sociology is a science. One group had to make a clear categorization True or False, so if they were uncertain they had to make a guess. The second group was allowed to use three responses. They were instructed that if they were 100% certain about the answer they should respond with Definitely True or Definitely False. In all other cases they should respond with Unsure. They were encouraged to use the latter category whenever they were not completely clear in their minds about the answer. The list included clear cases to enable them to use all three responses freely. The critical test came when the same individuals returned two weeks later and performed the test again, under exactly the same conditions. Now the performance of the first group with just two options should reflect the vagueness in the categorization task. If the truth of a statement like "Olives are fruit" is vague, then there is a good chance that a person would be inconsistent in the two responses that he or she gave. This, after all, was the result that McCloskey and Glucksberg (1978) reported, as described previously. The second group, however, had the advantage of being able to place any inconveniently tricky statements into the Unsure response category. They should therefore be able to respond much more consistently to the categorization task, using their three response categories in the same way on each occasion.

In fact, across several experiments using this methodology, I found no evidence at all that the group with three response options would be more consistent in their responding than the group with only two. The three-response group's data were analyzed by averaging the likelihood of changing one's mind about a Definitely True and the likelihood of changing one's mind about a Definitely False response. This average came out as exactly the same as the likelihood that someone in the two-response group would simply change a True to a False or vice versa.

It would appear, then, that logical treatments of vagueness have to be careful about not introducing sharp or precise values at any stage.

9.4.2 Vagueness in Noun Categories

A great deal of the psychological work on vagueness/fuzziness in language has focused on noun categories (Hampton 1998; McCloskey and Glucksberg 1978; Rosch and Mervis 1975). As detailed above, categories such as fruit, fish, furniture, or sport provide an excellent set of materials with which to test the nature of vagueness in concepts. The advantage is that each category contains somewhere between 30 and 100 different category "members." People can be interrogated about what things they would place in the category, they can judge how typical those things are, they can provide ratings of whether each of the putative members possesses each of the intensional properties of the category, and so forth. In a large-scale data-collection exercise by De Deyne and others (2008), a large dataset has been collected including a wide range of psychological measures for a reasonably large sample of different semantic categories. This dataset, which can be freely downloaded from their website at Leuven University (see http://ppw.kuleuven.be/concat) has started to provide valuable tests of different quantitative models of variability in categorization (and hence fuzziness of semantic sets).

Why should noun categories be vague? We can identify the following possible sources of vagueness in a semantic category such as *fruit*, as seen in the levels of disagreement, within-rater inconsistency, and/or expressed lack of confidence in a categorization decision about an item such as *tomato*.

(a)   Different beliefs exist within the population. Perhaps 60% of people firmly believe that a tomato is a fruit, and 40% firmly deny it. Fuzziness then only exists at the group level, and we would expect disagreement, but no inconsistency and no lack of confidence. This difference in belief could either reflect a difference in what people think a fruit needs to be, or a difference in what people believe about the properties of tomatoes, or both.

(b)   Some people may feel *ignorant* of the facts about either tomatoes or fruits, or both. In that case they may hazard a guess, and we should find all three indicators of vagueness.

(c)   Categorization may be sensitive to the context or the perspective in which the judgment is made. What counts as a sport for TV sports channels may differ from what counts as a sport for an elementary school sports event. If the categorization task provides no context for the decision, then different contexts may be imagined by different people, and we should find both disagreement and inconsistency.

(d)   Categorization may be inherently probabilistic. When judging whether a tomato is a fruit, people generate a prototype for fruit, based on memories, knowledge and whatever contextual influences may be in play. They then generate a similar representation for tomatoes. Finally they compare the one with the other, and determine an asymmetric similarity function of the tomato concept to the fruit concept. (For a suggestion of how the asymmetric similarity could work, see Hampton 1995a). This degree of similarity will contain random noise owing to the attributes that have been retrieved and the weights that have been attached to them. The similarity is then compared to a threshold value (also subject to random variation) and a positive decision results if the similarity is greater than the threshold.

The fact that people are inconsistent in categorization argues that differences in belief are not the only source of vagueness. A study by Hampton, Dubois, and Yeh (2006) suggests that the context may not be that critical either. In this study, participants categorized lists of items in eight different categories. Four different groups were used (only three were reported in the published article). One had no context—they simply decided if the items (like tomato) belonged in the categories (like fruit). A second group was given "linguistic" instructions. They had to imagine that we were interested in how speakers of U.S. English used these words; did they think that as a speaker themselves they would spontaneously refer to the item (tomato) using the category name (fruit)? A third group had the task set in a more technical legalistic setting. They were told to imagine that they were advising a governmental agency in setting up the basis for tax and import regulations concerning different classes of products. In this case, should the tomato count as a fruit or not? Finally, a fourth group was set a pragmatic version of the task. They were asked to place things in the fruit category in the context of a search engine. Thus if they thought people would expect to find "tomato" listed under the search term "fruit," they should include it in the category.

In spite of our attempt to produce widely different categorization contexts, the results were almost entirely negative. Context had only a few, category-specific effects. For example, in one context people were invited to place items in the furniture category for the purposes of an inventory database for a department store. This context generated some shifts from the standard no-context control, which reflected people's knowledge of how items are displayed in department stores (for example, refrigerators are found with electrical goods and not with furniture). Overall, however, providing a context had zero effect on either reducing disagreement, reducing inconsistency, or reducing the high correlation between probability of categorization and context-free ratings of the typicality of items in the categories.

It is most likely, then, that the major source of vagueness in semantic categorization comes from the final source listed above. Deciding on category membership is an inherently probabilistic process, subject to random processes in the collection and assessment of the evidence involved.

9.4.3   A Model of Vagueness in Semantic Categorization

Verheyen, Hampton, and Storms (2010) provide a formalization of a quantitative probabilistic model for capturing the fuzzy nature of categorization. It assumes that categorization is a probabilistic process in which each individual assesses the similarity of any item relative to his or her own individual threshold for making a categorization response. Formally, the model uses the Rasch model developed in the domain of psychometrics (Rasch

1960). The probability of a positive categorization of item i in Category A by participant p, $P(A,i,p)$, is given by

$$P(A,i,p) = \frac{e^{\alpha(\beta_i - \theta_p)}}{1 + e^{\alpha(\beta_i - \theta_p)}}. \tag{9.1}$$

The function defined by equation (9.1) increases from 0 to 1 as the difference between β_i and θ_p becomes more positive. The β_i parameter represents the position of item i on a scale that measures similarity to the category prototype. The parameter θ_p is the threshold for participant p. Thus, as an item's similarity exceeds the person's threshold to a greater extent, so the probability of making a positive response also increases.

The model was fit to data from 250 participants who each made yes/no categorization judgments on lists of 24 items for each of 8 categories, some 48,000 data points. The fit of the model was good, and it was shown to correctly estimate the degree of nonmodal responding across the scale (the amount of disagreement among participants), as well as the degree of inconsistency observed in previous studies. Most impressively, the estimates of the β_i parameters for particular items correlated at around 0.95 with an independent measure of the typicality of those items for the category. A further result was to show that an individual's threshold parameter θ_p showed consistency across categories. Correlations were fairly low, but were significantly greater than zero, indicating that some individuals tend toward a liberal view and some a conservative view when categorizing across a range of categories (Gardner 1953).

We also examined whether the parameter α in equation 9.1 needed to be allowed to vary from item to item, or whether a single value could be used. This parameter is a measure of the degree of vagueness or fuzziness in an item's categorization. As it increases, so the slope of the S-shaped curve relating probability of categorization to similarity becomes steeper. Hence, high values of α indicate a sharply defined item-category decision, and low values a vaguely defined (more probabilistic) item and category. We found that different values were required for different categories, but that overall the best model used a constant α for all items *within* the same category.

The value of this model for studies of fuzziness in categorization is that it can incorporate differences in individuals, differences among items, and differences between categories or category domains. It therefore provides a general methodology for testing important hypotheses about the source and nature of variability and fuzziness in human categorization.

9.5   Final Remarks

The meanings of the substantive words in human languages are almost always vague. I have reviewed how within a language there are different kinds of words that owe their contents respectively to the external world, to experts in a society, or to individuals who form part of a group of language users. The kind of vagueness that is found is accordingly dependent on its source. I have reviewed the difference between knowledge of a concept's extension and knowledge of its intension, and the existence of cases where the two appear to be only weakly coordinated. Finally, I have argued that the major source of vagueness in language is the fact that people's conceptual contents are determined through a dynamic process of keeping themselves calibrated with other language users. This process generates a certain optimal level of vagueness that allows successful communication while providing the flexibility for meanings to adapt as the social and physical world around us changes.

Notes

1. Exceptions are the biological kinds that we have created through selective breeding, which include almost all our plant and animal foods, much of the contents of gardens and parks, and, of course, animals like cats and dogs and race horses.

2. For some questions it may be that we believe that the answer will be provided by experts at some point in the future.

References

Ahn, W. K., N. S. Kim, M. E. Lassaline, and M. J. Dennis. 2000. Causal status as a determinant of feature centrality. *Cognitive Psychology* 41:361–416.

Alxatib, S., and F. J. Pelletier. 2011. The psychology of vagueness: Borderline cases and contradictions. *Mind and Cognition* 26:287–326.

Black, M. 1937. Vagueness: An exercise in logical analysis. *Philosophy of Science* 4:427–455.

Braisby, N. R. 2004. Deference and essentialism in the categorization of chemical kinds. In *Proceedings of the 25th Annual Conference of the Cognitive Science Society*, ed. R. Alterman and D. Kirsch, 174–179. Mahwah, NJ: Lawrence Erlbaum.

Braisby, N. R. 2001. Deference in categorisation: Evidence for essentialism? In *Proceedings of the 23rd Annual Conference of the Cognitive Science Society*, ed. J. D. Moore and K. Stenning, 150–155. Mahwah, NJ: Lawrence Erlbaum.

Clark, H. H. 1992. *Arenas of Language Use.* Chicago: Chicago University Press.

De Deyne, S., S. Verheyen, E. Ameel, W. Vanpaemel, M. Dry, W. Voorspoels, and G. Storms. 2008. Exemplar by feature applicability matrices and other Dutch normative data for semantic concepts. *Behavior Research Methods* 40:1030–1048.

Diesendruck, G., and S. A. Gelman. 1999. Domain differences in absolute judgments of category membership: Evidence for an essentialist account of categorization. *Psychonomic Bulletin & Review* 6:338–346.

Dunbar, R. 1996. *Grooming, Gossip, and the Evolution of Language.* London: Faber & Faber.

Estes, Z. 2004. Confidence and gradedness in semantic categorization: Definitely somewhat artifactual, maybe absolutely natural. *Psychonomic Bulletin & Review* 11:1041–1047.

Fodor, J. A. 1975. *The Language of Thought.* New York: Crowell.

Fodor, J. A. 1998. *Concepts: Where Cognitive Science Went Wrong.* Oxford: Clarendon Press.

Gärdenfors, P. 2000. *Conceptual Spaces.* Cambridge, MA: MIT Press.

Gardner, R. W. 1953. Cognitive styles in categorizing behavior. *Journal of Personality* 22:214–233.

Hampton, J. A. 1995a. Similarity-based categorization: The development of prototype theory. *Psychologica Belgica* 35:103–125.

Hampton, J. A. 1995b. Testing prototype theory of concepts. *Journal of Memory and Language* 34:686–708.

Hampton, J. A. 1998. Similarity-based categorization and fuzziness of natural categories. *Cognition* 65:137–165.

Hampton, J. A. 2006. Concepts as prototypes. In *The Psychology of Learning and Motivation: Advances in Research and Theory*, vol. 46, ed. B. H. Ross, 79–113. Amsterdam: Elsevier.

Hampton, J. A. 2007. Typicality, graded membership, and vagueness. *Cognitive Science* 31:355–383.

Hampton, J. A. 2008. The Rumsfeld Effect: The unknown unknown. Paper presented at the Annual Convention of the Psychonomic Society, Chicago, November.

Hampton, J. A., D. Dubois, and W. Yeh. 2006. The effects of pragmatic context on classification in natural categories. *Memory & Cognition* 34:1431–1443.

Kalish, C. W. 1995. Essentialism and graded membership in animal and artifact categories. *Memory & Cognition* 23:335–353.

Keefe, R. 2000. *Theories of Vagueness.* Cambridge: Cambridge University Press.

Keefe, R., and P. Smith. 1997. Theories of vagueness. In *Vagueness: A Reader,* ed. R. Keefe and P. Smith, 1–57. Cambridge, MA: MIT Press.

Keil, F. C. 1981. Constraints on knowledge and cognitive development. *Psychological Review* 88:197–227.

Kripke, S. 1980. *Naming and Necessity.* Cambridge, MA: Harvard University Press.

Malt, B. C., and S. A. Sloman. 2007. Artifact categorization: the good, the bad, and the ugly. In *Creations of the Mind: Theories of Artifacts and Their Representation,* ed. E. Margolis and S. Laurence, 85–123. Oxford: Oxford University Press.

Malt, B. C., S. A. Sloman, S. Gennari, M. Shi, and Y. Wang. 1999. Knowing versus naming: Similarity and the linguistic categorization of artifacts. *Journal of Memory and Language* 40:230–262.

Mayr, E. 1982. *The Growth of Biological Thought: Diversity, Evolution, and Inheritance.* Cambridge, MA: Harvard University Press.

McCloskey, M., and S. Glucksberg. 1978. Natural categories: Well-defined or fuzzy sets? *Memory & Cognition* 6:462–472.

Medin, D. L., and A. Ortony. 1989. Psychological essentialism. In *Similarity and Analogical Reasoning,* ed. S. Vosniadou and A. Ortony, 179–195. Cambridge: Cambridge University Press.

Mellor, D. H., and A. Oliver, eds. 1997. *Properties.* Oxford: Oxford University Press.

Nosofsky, R. M. 1988. Exemplar-based accounts of relations between classification, recognition, and typicality. *Journal of Experimental Psychology: Learning, Memory, and Cognition* 14:700–708.

Osherson, D. N., and E. E. Smith. 1981. On the adequacy of prototype theory as a theory of concepts. *Cognition* 11:35–58.

Osherson, D. N., and E. E. Smith. 1982. Gradeness and conceptual conjunction. *Cognition* 12:299–318.

Osherson, D. N., and E. E. Smith. 1997. On typicality and vagueness. *Cognition* 64:189–206.

Putnam, H. 1975. The meaning of "meaning." In H. Putnam, *Mind, Language, and Reality: Philosophical Papers*, vol. 2, 215–271. Cambridge: Cambridge University Press.

Rey, G. 1983. Concepts and stereotypes. *Cognition* 15:237–262.

Rasch, G. 1960. *Probabilistic Models for Some Intelligence and Attainment Tests*. Copenhagen: Danish Institute for Educational Research.

Rosch, E. R., and C. B. Mervis. 1975. Family resemblances: Studies in the internal structure of categories. *Cognitive Psychology* 7:573–605.

Sloman, S. A., and B. C. Malt. 2003. Artifacts are not ascribed essences, nor are they treated as belonging to kinds. In *Conceptual Representation*, ed. H. E. Moss and J. A. Hampton, 563–582. Hove: Psychology Press.

Smith, N. J. J. 2008. *Vagueness and Degrees of Truth*. Oxford: Oxford University Press.

Sperber, D., and D. Wilson. 1998. The mapping between the mental and the public lexicon. In *Thought and Language*, ed. P. Carruthers and J. Boucher, 184–200. Cambridge: Cambridge University Press.

van Deemter, K. 2010. *Not Exactly: In Praise of Vagueness*. Oxford: Oxford University Press.

Verheyen, S., J. A. Hampton, and G. Storms. 2010.. A probabilistic threshold model: Analyzing semantic categorization data with the Rasch model. *Acta Psychologica* 135 (2):216–225.

Williamson, T. 1994. *Vagueness*. London: Routledge.

Wittgenstein, L. 1953. *Philosophical Investigations*. New York: Macmillan.

10 Epilogue

Radim Belohlavek and George J. Klir

10.1 Theories of Concepts and Mathematical Theories

This book is about the prospective role of fuzzy logic in the psychology of concepts. As discussed in detail in chapter 5, fuzzy logic was rejected in the psychology of concepts in the early 1980s, based on arguments presented in a single paper (Osherson and Smith 1981). Although all the presented arguments were later exposed as fallacious (see chapter 5, this volume; Zadeh 1982; Fuhrmann 1988b; Belohlavek et al. 2002, 2009), they have continued to be uncritically accepted as valid within the psychology of concepts. As a consequence, advances in fuzzy logic have been completely ignored in this branch of psychology, contrary to many other areas of human affairs (see chapter 3, section 3.8), and researchers have lost interest in exploring applications of fuzzy logic in the psychology of concepts. It is fairly obvious that this peculiar and unfortunate situation can be overcome only by wholehearted cooperation between psychologists of concepts and fuzzy logicians, liberated form the baggage of erroneous arguments that have delayed progress for some three decades. This book is an attempt to stimulate such cooperation.

As we have seen, the psychology of concepts is a scientific discipline whose aim is to study concepts from the psychological point of view. It contains various theories of concepts, which are surveyed in chapter 2. Fuzzy logic is a mathematical discipline that, in its narrow sense, consists of various formal systems of special fuzzy logics, each defined by suitable axioms (section 3.6.2). Theories of concepts are scientific theories, whereas systems of fuzzy logics are mathematical theories.

There are some fundamental differences between scientific theories and mathematical theories. Each scientific theory deals with phenomena of some specific experimental domain. It serves to elicit consequences, which can then be used for making predictions but also for testing the theory. It always carries the connotation of a hypothesis regarding the phenomena, regardless of how well it is established. This means that it is always open to refutation or revision in the face of new experimental evidence.

Contrary to scientific theories, mathematical theories deal with abstract phenomena and are completely independent of any experimental domain. They are concerned with proofs rather than experiments. As a consequence, they are closed to refutation by any experimental evidence. However, each mathematical theory is required to be sound (every provable statement must be true) and possibly also complete (every true statement must be provable) in order to be acceptable.

In spite of these profound differences between scientific and mathematical theories, fuzzy logic (a mathematical theory) has often been viewed and criticized as a theory of concepts (a scientific theory), as discussed in section 5.4.1. This is, of course, completely wrong. As a mathematical theory, fuzzy logic has no fixed interpretation. However, it is open to many interpretations, so it can be used for building models in various areas of science, including the psychology of concepts. It is of course up to the psychologist who builds a particular model based on fuzzy logic how to interpret the truth degrees. For example, degrees of membership in fuzzy sets have no a priori interpretation in fuzzy logic. On the other hand, the various notions of degrees studied in the psychology of concepts, such as degrees of typicality, degrees of membership, degrees of goodness of example, or degrees of similarity, have a psychological meaning and can be studied by appropriate experiments. Likewise, the various operations on fuzzy sets, such as intersections or unions of fuzzy sets, have no a priori interpretation in fuzzy logic, whereas the operations of conceptual combinations studied in the psychology of concepts have a psychological meaning.

In summary, the construction of a particular model based on fuzzy logic in a given application domain (such as a model for decision making in economics, a model of sedimentation in geology, or a model of some particular combination in the psychology of concepts) and the interpretation of truth degrees, and other notions of fuzzy logic in terms of notions of the application domain, are up to the domain experts (economists, geologists, or psychologists of concepts). As a rule, various models may be constructed; whether they are good or bad is a question to be resolved experimentally. Constructing good models usually requires substantial knowledge of both the application domain and the mathematical theory employed. This is why cooperation between psychologists of concepts and fuzzy logicians is so important. Such cooperation is likely to produce various challenges for both areas, which we discuss in the following two sections.

10.2   Challenges for Fuzzy Logic from the Psychology of Concepts

As any mathematical theory, fuzzy logic is open to including new traits if desirable. In fact, fuzzy logic in its current state is the outcome of the gradual expansion of its traits. For example, the scope of fuzzy logic operations has considerably expanded in fuzzy logic since its beginnings (section 3.4). New types of aggregation operations were added to fuzzy logic and formally studied whenever the existing ones were found insufficient for dealing with applications of fuzzy logic in various application domains. That is, the scope of considered fuzzy logic operations has gradually expanded in fuzzy logic via challenges from various prospective application domains; these have been positive contributions to the further development of fuzzy logic.

For fuzzy logic to be useful for representing and manipulating concepts, it is almost certain that new operations will have to be introduced into fuzzy logic. This is a simple consequence of the many psychological experiments that show how people manipulate concepts in numerous complex ways. The new operations may be truth-functional (section 3.6.1), such as the various aggregation operations introduced in section 3.4, but may even be more general, as suggested by psychological evidence on the intensional nature of concepts (section 8.4). As far as prospective new aggregation operations are concerned, for example, it is fortunate that there is now an impressive inventory of aggregation operations, some of which might be suitable to add to the repertoire of fuzzy logic operations for the purpose of formalizing conceptual combinations. Moreover, theoretical study of aggregation operations is a rapidly growing area of mathematics (Grabisch et al. 2009).

It is important to understand that adding new operations or other notions to fuzzy logic is perfectly consistent with the further development of fuzzy logic as a mathematical theory. Therefore, applying fuzzy logic to the psychology of concepts should not be understood as necessarily applying it in its current state of development, but rather as a complex process during which fuzzy logic itself will evolve. Clearly, this process can be begun and maintained only by challenges posed to fuzzy logicians by cooperating psychologists.

Although some challenges to fuzzy logic from the psychology of concepts are presented in this book, especially in chapters 4, 8, and 9, many more are likely to emerge from cooperation between researchers from the two areas.

10.3   Challenges for the Psychology of Concepts from Fuzzy Logic

It is obvious that researchers in fuzzy logic should be able to pose challenges to their cooperating colleagues in the psychology of concepts as well. For example, some well-developed formal theories subsumed under fuzzy logic, such as those introduced in section 3.6.2, may be suggested to psychologists as simple models to be used for performing experiments regarding various psychological phenomena. Each individual experiment alone is likely to be insufficient for understanding a complex psychological phenomenon of interest. However, it is reasonable to expect that results from multiple experiments of this kind, all based on distinct formal theories, will provide us with a new way of looking at the phenomenon, and that, in turn, will likely help us to clarify the various issues involved in formalizing the psychological phenomenon at issue.

Various other types of experiments, suggestive on mathematical grounds, may be proposed by fuzzy logicians to their cooperating colleagues in psychology, but it will always be up to the latter to evaluate their psychological significance. It seems likely that some particularly interesting ideas for experiments and other challenges to psychologists of concepts will emerge from the fuzzified formal concept analysis introduced in chapter 7.

It seems appropriate to mention at this point that an attempt to establish a fruitful cooperation between researchers in the area of fuzzy logic and those in the psychology of concepts was made some decades ago by a Hungarian scholar, Giörgy Fuhrmann. He published several papers (Fuhrmann 1988a,b,c, 1990, 1991), which demonstrated that he was proficient in both fuzzy logic and the psychology of concepts. He proposed a modified notion of a fuzzy set, more appropriate for representing the structure of concept categories. It is unfortunate that this potentially important idea and its proposed utility in representing and dealing with concepts have gone virtually unnoticed by researchers working in the areas of fuzzy logic as well as the psychology of concepts. We hope that this book will stimulate interest in examining Fuhrmann's ideas in an interactive way by researchers from both areas.

10.4   Psychology of Concepts and Fuzzy Logic: Conditions for Effective Research Cooperation

As discussed in chapter 4, convincing experimental evidence has established that most concepts have a graded structure. Results of the first experiments revealing the graded structure of concepts were published almost forty years ago. Fuzzy logic, whose primary aim is to provide mathematical tools to model reasoning that involves grades, emerged more than forty-five years ago. Yet whether and to what extent fuzzy logic can be useful in the psychology of concepts remains an open question.

The best way of addressing this challenging question is to involve researchers from both these areas in a cooperative fashion. There is no doubt that the prospective cooperation between fuzzy logicians and psychologists of concepts, if successful, will offer rich opportunities for progress in both areas. However, to develop a successful cooperation between mathematicians and scientists is not simple. It requires that the researchers in either area be genuinely interested in acquiring substantial knowledge in the other area. The acquired knowledge need not be complete, but it must be sufficient for effective communication with colleagues in the other area. Fuzzy logicians need not learn the various skills required for conducting relevant psychological experiments, but they have to be able to understand the content and significance of psychological experiments, criticize them, and possibly suggest some new experiments. Psychologists need not learn skills involved in theorem proving, but they have to be able to understand the psychological significance of relevant notions and theorems and possibly suggest some desirable new notions and directions for developments in fuzzy logic.

Without a genuine mutual interest, communication between psychologists and fuzzy logicians is likely to result in only a superficial exchange of ideas. However, the various issues in the psychology of concepts, as presented in this book, as well as the potential for further developments in fuzzy logic suggest that there is room for a truly collaborative research that will go well beyond such a superficial exchange. We hope that this book will help to stimulate such research, from which the psychology of concepts as well as fuzzy logic are likely to benefit, and which may possibly lead to important discoveries.

References

Belohlavek, R., G. J. Klir, H. W. Lewis, III, and E. Way. 2002. On the capability of fuzzy set theory to represent concepts. *International Journal of General Systems* 31 (6):569–585.

Belohlavek, R., G. J. Klir, H. W. Lewis, III, and E. Way. 2009. Concepts and fuzzy sets: Misunderstandings, misconceptions, and oversights. *International Journal of Approximate Reasoning* 51 (1):23–34.

Fuhrmann, G. 1988a. "Prototypes" and "fuzziness" in the logic of concepts. *Synthese* 75:317–347.

Fuhrmann, G. 1988b. Fuzziness of concepts and concepts of fuzziness. *Synthese* 75:349–372.

Fuhrmann, G. 1988c. M-fuzziness in brain/mind modeling. In *Fuzzy Sets in Psychology*, ed. T. Zétényi, 155–202. Amsterdam: North Holland.

Fuhrmann, G. 1990. Note on the generality of fuzzy sets. *Information Sciences* 51:143–152.

Fuhrmann, G. 1991. Note on the integration of prototype theory and fuzzy set theory. *Synthese* 86:1–27.

Grabisch, M., J.-L. Marichal, R. Mesiar, and E. Pap. 2009. *Aggregation Functions*. Cambridge: Cambridge University Press.

Osherson, D. N., and E. E. Smith. 1981. On the adequacy of prototype theory as a theory of concepts. *Cognition* 9:35–58.

Zadeh, L. A. 1982. A note on prototype theory and fuzzy sets. *Cognition* 12:291–297.

Glossary of Symbols

$\{x, y, ...\}$	Set consisting of elements $x, y, ...$
$\{x \in U: \varphi(x)\}$	Set consisting of elements x in universe U that satisfy property φ
$(x_1, ..., x_n)$	n-tupple consisting of elements $x_1, ..., x_n$
$[a,b]$	Closed interval of real numbers between a and b
$A, B, C, ...$	Sets or fuzzy sets
$A: U \to [0,1]$	A is a standard fuzzy set in universe U (a function from U to $[0,1]$)
$[0,1]^U$	Set of all standard fuzzy sets in universe U
$x \in A$	Element x belongs to set A
$A(x)$	Degree of membership of element x in fuzzy set A
A_α	Level cut (or α-cut) of fuzzy set A
$A \subseteq B$	Set (or fuzzy set) A is included in set (is a subset of) set (or fuzzy set) B
$S(A,B)$	Degree to which fuzzy set A is included in fuzzy set B
$|A|$	Cardinality of set (or fuzzy set) A in a finite universe
$\varnothing$	Empty set
$A \cap B$	Intersection of sets A and B
$A \cup B$	Union of sets A and B

$A \times B$	Cartesian product of sets A and B
L	Set of truth degrees (e.g., $L = [0,1]$)
c	Complement of a fuzzy set
i	Truth function of fuzzy logical conjunction (or intersection of fuzzy sets)
u	Truth function of fuzzy logical disjunction (or union of fuzzy sets)
n	Truth function of fuzzy logical negation
r	Truth function of fuzzy logical implication
h	Averaging operation on fuzzy sets
φ	Logical formula
$\|\varphi\|$	Truth degree of logical formula φ
max	Maximum
min	Minimum
sup	Supremum (or maximum if it exists)
inf	Infimum (or minimum it exists)
(X,Y,I)	Formal context (or formal fuzzy context)
(A,B)	Formal concept (or formal fuzzy concept)
$\mathbf{B}(X,Y,I)$	Concept lattice (or fuzzy concept lattice)
$^\uparrow$ and $^\downarrow$	Concept-forming operators
$\mathbf{R}$	The set of real numbers

Contributors

Radim Belohlavek   Department of Computer Science, Palacky University, Olomouc, CZ-77900, Czech Republic, radim.belohlavek@acm.org.

James A. Hampton   Department of Psychology, City University, Northhampton Square, London EC1V OHB, United Kingdom, Hampton@city.ac.uk.

Rogier A. Kievit   Department of Psychology, University of Amsterdam, 1018 WB Amsterdam, The Netherlands, r.kievit@uva.nl.

George J. Klir   Thomas J. Watson School of Engineering and Applied Science, State University of New York, Binghamton, NY 13902-6000, USA, gklir@binghamton.edu.

Edouard Machery   Department of History and Philosophy of Science, University of Pittsburgh, Pittsburgh, PA 15260, USA, machery@pitt.edu.

Eleanor H. Rosch   Department of Psychology, University of California-Berkeley, Berkeley, CA 94720-1650, USA, rosch@berkeley.edu.

Jay Verkuilen   Ph.D. Program in Educational Psychology, Graduate Center of the City University of New York, NY 10016-4309, jverkuilen@gc.cuny.edu.

Annemarie Zand Scholten   Department of Psychology, University of Amsterdam, 1018 WB Amsterdam, The Netherlands, a.zandscholten@uva.nl.

Index